CONTENTS

I

INTRODUCTION

The conference on First-Language Acquisition was held at Endicott House in Dedham, Massachusetts on October 27-29, 1961. This was the fourth conference in a series planned by the Committee on Intellective Processes Research of the Social Science Research Council. Linguistic development is a very old research topic, but there have been changes in the conception of the problem and in the methods used to study it; these provided the occasion for the conference. Quite recently, investigators in several parts of the United States have begun research on the acquisition of language-as-it-is-described-by-linguistic-science. This new work is concerned, as the earlier work usually was not, with phonemes, derivational affixes, inflections, syntactic classes, immediate constituents, and grammatical transformations. The new work utilizes field methods from linguistics, experimental methods from psychology, naturalistic observation, and the study of deviant cases. There had been no opportunity for the people doing this work to talk with one another and with scientists who could give them expert counsel. The conference provided the opportunity.

While there were, at the conference, a child psychiatrist, an anthropologist, and a sociologist, most of the participants were psychologists or linguists. Ten years before the Dedham conference, in 1951, the Social Science Research Council first arranged for a confrontation of psychology and linguistics. From the early meetings the lively field of psycholinguistics developed. A decade ago, American structural linguistics presented a more united front than did American psychology; there was a substantial consensus among linguists on many important points. It was, therefore, possible for the psychologist studying verbal behavior to think of linguistics as a body of established knowledge which would provide a foundation for their own work. This is what one discipline always dreams of getting from another. We have all winced to hear a literary critic or political scientist or physicist preface some absurdity with : "Modern psychology tells us . . ." But modern psychology in 1951, like modern psychology in 1961, did not speak with a single voice, which may be one reason why, in the past decade, there have been more psychologists who tried to learn linguistics than linguists who tried to learn psychology.

The consensus in American linguistics has thinned out since 1951. The publication in 1957 of Chomsky's *Syntactic Structures* introduced a generative and tranformational approach to grammar that has proved to have revolutionary implications for all branches of linguistic science and for some psycholinguistic problems. The transformationalists were represented at our conference by Noam Chomsky, Morris Halle, and Robert Lees. While there were no linguists present who were in active opposition to the tranformational approach, there were three who are not closely identified with it—Dell Hymes, Lawrence Jones, and Wick Miller.

Since fundamental matters are now controversial in linguistics, psychologists cannot look to this discipline for a single received truth. It became clear at the Dedham conference that a psychologist who wants to use linguistics intelligently has no choice but to become a full participant in the concerns of that discipline. No baptism short of total immersion is efficacious. Perhaps this is always the case when one attempts to utilize a second discipline.

A great deal of the interest and tension of this conference emanated from the communication between the psychologists working in studies of child speech and the linguists who are in the process of developing new theories of the structure of language. The psychologists found that in different parts of the country, using methods that were similar, they were achieving strikingly similar results with regard to child speech. The linguists representing the transformational approach to grammar felt that, while the psychologists were deriving interesting results, there was a clear directive for future work in this area. They argued that little further could be gleaned at this time from naturalistic studies of the recorded speech of the child and asked for a more experimental inquiry into the child's competence; this inquiry ought to include the study of the child's comprehension of grammar.

The conference papers were prepared in advance and sent to all those planning to be present. Several participants (Lenneberg, Brown and Fraser) chose to contribute two papers. For each major paper a formal discussant was assigned. Each of the sessions at Dedham was devoted to one of the major papers, but, since the papers had been read in advance, it was possible to begin with the remarks of the discussant and, from these, to proceed directly to the general discussion. The final meeting was initiated with formal discussions, by Dr. Deese and Dr. Moore, of the conference as a whole. The order in which the major papers are presented in this monograph corresponds to the original order of consideration at the conference. Each major paper is immediately followed by the formal discussion and the open discussion it inspired.

In the months following the conference, the authors of the major papers revised them for publication. Among the formal discussants, Dr. Hymes and Dr. Kagan had written down their remarks in full, and they revised these as they chose following the conference. For those discussants who spoke from notes rather than from a complete manuscript, the editors prepared first drafts from the tape recordings. These drafts were revised, or at least reread, by the discussants. The general open discussion had all been taped, and except for trivia and repetitions it was all transcribed. However, it is not all published here.

There is ordinarily very little continuity between "contributions" in a conference discussion. Reading a transcript, one wonders whether any speaker ever had the attention of the group. Most "listeners" must have been attending to inner voices that were composing their next contributions. Continuity, at the Dedham conference, was sustained over more changes of speaker than usual. This may have been because the topic was relatively specific, or because the participants were interested in one another's views and had often practiced the expression of their own. Still the total transcript made very uneconomical communication. Consequently the editors reduced the open discussion for each session to a set of enumerated major points. The phrasing stays close to the original whenever the original was clear, but where it was not the editors have departed from it. The changes are so great that statements cannot be attributed to particular persons. The participants agreed at Dedham to this procedure.

There are great advantages in this editorial procedure. Because the editors retained much of the original, the gracelessness of the prose ought not to be charged to them. A list of major points does not arouse the same expectation of continuity as does a verbatim interchange. Because statements are not credited to particular persons, it seemed unnecessary to ask the participants to read and revise the general discussion.

The editorial treatment of the open discussion has some shortcomings. There is no way for an idea to move from the original transcript to the published reductions except through the filter of the editorial mind. That filter is certainly coarse and probably distorting. In addition, the reduction of the discussion to a list of ideas deprives the original of its dramatic tension. We thought of preserving a little of this by crediting speeches, not to named persons, but to "irate linguist" or "defensive psychologist" or "would-be mediator." One might even slant things a bit: "A linguist, confessing his error, said . . ." A simple list, we decided, would be more judicious.

There is, finally, some problem of preparation for a reader of this monograph. The papers do often use linguistic concepts, and it is not possible to explain all of these. Happily there is a really excellent *Introduction to Descriptive Linguistics* by Henry Gleason which, in its 1961 edition, teaches everything a reader might need to know.

The members of the conference were: Ursula Bellugi, Massachusetts Institute of Technology; Roger Brown, Massachusetts Institute of Technology; Margaret Bullowa, Massachusetts Mental Health Center; Noam Chomsky, Massachusetts Institute of Technology; James Deese, Johns Hopkins University; Susan Ervin, University of California; Colin Fraser, Massachusetts Institute of Technology; Jean Berko Gleason, Cambridge, Massachusetts; Morris Halle, Massachusetts Institute of Technology;

Dell Hymes, University of California;   James Jenkins, University of Minnesota; Lawrence Jones, Boston College; Jerome Kagan, Harvard University; William Kessen, Yale University; Robert Lees, University of Illinois; Eric Lenneberg, Harvard University; William Livant, University of Michigan; Wick Miller, University of California; Omar Khayyam Moore, Yale University; Lloyd Morrisett, Carnegie Corporation of New York; Paul Mussen, University of California; David Palermo, University of Minnesota; Frank Palmer, Social Science Research Council; A. Kimball Romney, Stanford University; and Hans-Lukas Teuber, Massachusetts Institute of Technology.

II

THE DEVELOPMENT OF GRAMMAR IN CHILD LANGUAGE [1]

WICK MILLER *and* SUSAN ERVIN

University of California

Before describing the development of children's grammar, it is necessary to specify some of the properties of natural languages as used by adults. This is the model presented to the child and the eventual outcome of his development.

It is possible to analyze in all languages two types of constructs (or linguistic units): phonemes and morphemes. There are at least two corresponding systems which can be called the phonological and grammatical levels.[2] While this paper is concerned only with the grammatical level, certain properties of the phonological level will be briefly considered by way of contrast.

The phonetic substance, the raw material of language, can be analyzed into a finite set of mutually exclusive classes. The distinctive features by which the classes are contrasted are few in number. Each phonological system may be described in terms of different privileges of occurrence of the features or the sets of features called phonemes. Phonemes are grouped together into larger units in limited arrangements, and the groupings can be completely described by distributional statements. Thus it is possible to predict *all* possible phonemic shapes.[3] From the standpoint of the learner, the phonemic rules are given. Even nonsense words or coinages normally follow these rules. Imitation of sequences already heard is the normal mode of acquisition and use, and continues with the expansion of vocabulary.

---

[1] The project described in the paper is supported by a grant from the Department of Health, Education, and Welfare (M-3813) to the Institute of Human Development, University of California, Berkeley. Facilities have also been provided by the Center for Human Learning under support of the National Science Foundation.

[2] The term "level" has been used in a variety of ways in the linguistic literature. Our use of the term does not apply to the so-called levels within the syntactic system, or the distinction between morphology and syntax. As we use the term, the two levels correspond to what communication theorists call the channel and the message.

[3] Whorf (1940) has given a succinct statement for phonemic sequences in English monosyllables.

If we turn to the grammatical level, we see many differences. Morphemes, like phonemes, can be grouped into a number of classes, but the nature of the classes is different. The classes can be divided into two groups, which following Fries (1952) we can call lexical and function classes. Lexical classes are large and open and the number of classes is small. English lexical classes include nouns, verbs, and adjectives. A lexical class can normally be divided into subclasses, e.g., English mass nouns, count nouns, proper nouns. In contrast, function classes are small and closed and the number of classes is larger. English function classes include prepositions, conjunctions, interrogatives, noun determiners, and auxiliaries. It is more often possible to point to a simple referent for members of lexical classes than for members of function classes. The contrast between lexical and function classes is often only a relative one, which may mean that it is not always a useful distinction to make in organizing a grammar.

The grammatical productivity of a language is infinite. A speaker can produce utterances which he has never heard before. Unless the words are nonsense or the sentence semantically aberrant, such utterances will be understood by the hearer. This property of grammars is in contrast to the phonological system. Any novel recombination of phonemes, while it may follow phonological distribution rules, is nonsense until or unless conventional meaning is assigned.

Every language has a major predication type formed by placing together two constructions. The predication is *exocentric*—that is, the resulting construction does not belong to the same class as either of the two constitutent constructions. In most languages at least one of the constituents of the predication is a member of a lexical class or an expansion of a lexical class, e.g., the English subject is composed of a noun or noun phrase. Most nonpredication constructions are *endocentric,* or expansions in which the head of the construction belongs to the same class as the resulting construction. An example is the noun phrase, *the three boys,* which is an expansion of the noun phrase, *three boys.*

The term *discourse agreement* is used to indicate formal relationships that cross sentence boundaries. They are of two kinds: (a) *class restrictions,* and (b) *verb restrictions.* The first occur in answers to questions. A question has a formal structure, which normally restricts the formal structure possible in the response, and also a semantic content or a request for information. The comparison of two questions illustrates this point; on formal grounds we would expect the following answers:

A: *Where is Main Street?   I don't know.   or   Straight ahead.*
B: *Can you tell me where Main Street is?   No.   or   Yes.*

Obviously the responses to question B fail to meet the semantic requirements posed by the question. The two questions differ formally but are semantically equivalent.

In addition to "yes-no" questions, there are "or" questions and inter-rogative word questions. "Or" questions require a choice of an alternative if there is a falling intonation. The short response to interrogative word questions must be a word or phrase belonging to the same class as the inter-rogative word or words.

Verb restrictions involve the maintenance of tense or auxiliary features across sentence boundaries, and can be characterized as long components of a grammatical category. Compare the following set of sentences:

A: *This ice cream is good.   Yes, it is.*
B: *This ice cream tastes good.   Yes, it does.*

The initial sentences of A and B are semantically equivalent, but differ formally and require different responses. Verb restrictions can apply to successive utterances of the same or different speakers, but our attention will be focused on situations in which different speakers are involved, in particular when the second speaker is required to answer a "what—do" question.

In this paper we will distinguish three functional categories in the child's utterances. The first may be called *reference* (Skinner's *tacts*). It involves naming or describing and may be accompanied by pointing. Such behavior is initiated by the child and does not necessarily demand a response from another person. The second may be called *direction* (Skinner's *mands*) and demands verbal or active response from the hearer. Such utterances include commands and questions. It is often impossible to discriminate questions from reference utterances of the child. A third category may be called *responsive discourse* and includes informational responses. This category can be initiated by the interlocutor or the child, but we are primarily con-cerned with this category when initiated by the interlocutor.[4]

A person has two grammatical systems, one for encoding and another for decoding, or an active and passive grammatical system. For the adult, a single grammar can normally account for almost all of both systems. Quite clearly this is not the case with the child. We assume that a child must understand a grammatical pattern before he can produce it. Pre-sumably the decoding and encoding systems at any point in time are not independent. It seems likely that rules could be found for the derivation of one from the other. Such a procedure might be a fruitful way to approach grammatical development. We have little evidence concerning the decoding system at this time.

THE RESEARCH PROJECT

The data mentioned in this paper were obtained in a project consisting of longitudinal testing of 25 children and more intensive text collection

---

[4] Linguists frequently distinguish three functions: referential, directive, and expressive; for a recent account see Hymes (in press), and Jakobson (1960).

from a subgroup of five. Texts for four of the children were collected beginning when the children were about 2. The fifth child, Susan, was added when she was 1.9. Text collection was scheduled to continue for two years. The standardized tests collected from the larger group consisted of three tests: a plural test, a pronoun test, and two forms of a discourse agreement test. The children in the smaller sample were older than the other children in the group.

The texts were at first collected weekly, in sessions of 45 minutes, because of rapid change. As the rate of change decreased and the fluency of the children increased, the frequency of text collection was gradually reduced, until texts were collected at two-month intervals, in two or three sets of closely spaced interviews totaling four or five hours.

The texts were all tape recorded. The transcription was at first phonetic, but later it was made in the normal orthography marked for stress and intonation, with a phonetic transcription only for ambiguous material. The texts also included utterances of the investigator and pertinent contextual information.

The earliest texts were collected in unstructured interviews. As techniques which elicited certain types of utterances were noted, the investigator increasingly structured the interviews. For example, attempts to elicit negatives were made by putting clothes on the wrong doll or puzzle pieces in the wrong place. Doll clothing was used for eliciting possessives. To elicit an interrogative sentence, two dolls were "fed," and the child was told to "ask Joe what he wants to eat." Plurals were produced for nonsense objects made of play-doh. If one of the dolls was left behind, "because he is sick," the child was asked to talk on the toy telephone to find out how "Joe" was, another device for eliciting questions. Telephone conversations with the child tested his reliance on verbal rather than gestural cues. Techniques that were discovered in this way were incorporated where appropriate into tests for the larger group.

The plural test consisted of 17 items. In each case a toy object or picture was shown, its name elicited, and then two were shown. "Here are two what?" Thus the test did not give the children the option of using a syntactical plural signal rather than a morphological one. The items included certain pairs in which nonsense items (wooden constructions) were given names which had the same final consonant as a familiar word (*boy-kigh*, *block-bik*, *bed-pud*, *horse-tass*, *orange-bunge*). Irregulars were *foot*, *man*, and *house*. The singular of the regular and nonsense words was offered by the investigator if it was not offered by the child. In the case of *foot* and *man*, however, the singular was not offered by the investigator. This procedure was followed in order to determine which form, e.g., *foot* or *feet*, was used by the child as the singular. Testing was stopped on items after they had been contrasted for several months.

On the pronoun test, the child was questioned about pictures, the questions being designed to elicit sentences containing possessives and nominative pronouns varying in number and gender. In the test of discourse agreement, questions tested the class of responses, verb restrictions, comprehension of subject-object distinctions ("Who is he feeding?" vs. "Who is feeding him?") and "why" questions. There were two matched forms alternated each month, using the same pictures.

THE FIRST GRAMMATICAL SYSTEM

The children in our project began forming primitive sentences of two or more words before their second birthday.[5] It is clear that the grammar of these sentences is not identical with the adult model. It is often striking that one can provide a translation of children's utterances into adult utterances by the addition of function words and inflectional affixes. It appears that the children select the stressed utterance segments, which usually carry the most information. Brown and Fraser have called this a "telegraphic" version of English.

Since children's language undergoes a constant process of change through imitation of adult models, it makes sense that it should be describable in terms of its relation to the adult model. There are, however, some utterances which cannot be described as telegraphic speech:

At 2.3 Christy and her baby sister each had a balloon. The baby bit her balloon and broke it. Christy first said *Baby bite balloon,* then pointed to the unbroken balloon and said, *Baby other bite balloon no.*

Between 2.1 and 2.4 Lisa had a particular kind of construction which often generated sentences that had no adult analogue, e.g., *all-gone puzzle.*

A conversation between the investigator and Susan at 1.10:

Susan: *Book read. Book read. Book read.*
Inv: *You want me to read book?* OK.
Susan: *Read book.*

The last example shows a correction by imitation in the direction of telegraphic speech. However, the child's original utterance either was an unpatterned error or represented a productive pattern that deviated from the model.

Is there any kind of system or pattern to the child's first sentences? In attempting to answer this question we will examine some of the text material of Susan (1.9 to 2.0) and Christy (2.0 to 2.3).

---

[5] We will use the term "word" rather than "morpheme" except when the distinction is necessary. A word class of the model language, as opposed to a word class of the child's language, is indicated by an abbreviation and a superscript "m," e.g., N^m and Adj^m indicate model language noun and adjective. Age is indicated by year and month, e.g., 2.4 indicates 2 years and 4 months old.

Susan

Susan, according to her parents, started putting words together at 1.8 to form multiword sentences. One-word sentences, however, predominated until 1.9½. Thus, the system to be described represents the very beginning of the development of the grammatical level.

During this period the most common words in Susan's vocabulary were *off* and *on*. A consistent pattern emerges when the preceding words, classified as to part of speech in the model language, are charted, as in Table 1.

TABLE 1

Antecedents of *off* and *on* (Susan 1.9–2.0)

	Noun	Verb	Other	Initial	Total
off	28	8	4	1	41
on	29	7	11	3	50

The figures in the chart represent text occurrences, excluding obvious imitations and chain repetitions.

The words that preceded *off* and *on* showed a large amount of overlap, and can be combined into one list, in Table 2. Words marked with an

TABLE 2

Antecedent Types for *off* and *on* (Susan 1.9–2.0)

back	dress	Liz	shoe	that
bandage	dusting	one*	sit*	them*
blanket	fall	pants	snap*	this*
button	fix	paper	sock	this-one
came	flower	piece*	sweater	(neck) tie
chair	hair	salt	take*	
coat*	hat	scarf	(scotch) tape	
diaper	hold*	shirt	tear	

* These words were found only in sentences of more than two words.

asterisk were found only in sentences of more than two words. Other words have been found in two-word sentences. *This-one* is assumed to have been a unit in Susan's speech.

Most of Susan's sentences with *on* and *off* reflected model sentences with two-word verbs, but a few reflected the prepositional use. Susan used *off* and *on* in a construction which had the shape W + I; W stands for any word(s) and I stands for *off* or *on*. We can call this the particle construction. The W will be defined as the complement, the I as the particle.

Most of the characteristics of the particle construction are illustrated in the following example taken from a text at 1.10:

> Susan: *Hat off, hat off.*
> Inv: *That's more than the hat off. The whole Santa's head* [of a toy Santa Claus] *came off.*
> Susan: *Santa head off.* (Pause.) *Head on. Fix on, fix on.*

Class I words had a verbal force. Most of the examples of imitations were imitations of two-word verbs. She was able to construct sentences of this pattern that had no direct adult analogue, e.g., *fix on*; the adult would normally say something like *fix it* or *put it on*. This example also shows that *off* and *on* were opposites for Susan; this may help explain why these two particles were used so much more than other particles.

The particle complement was usually a N^m or noun phrase of the model language, but V^m was not uncommon: *White sweater off*, said while taking her sweater off; *white sweater on*, a request directed to her mother to put her white sweater on her; *salt on*, pretending to salt food; *scarf off*, said while taking her scarf off. The model language provides analogues in which the noun is the object: *I took my sweater off; put my white sweater on! I put the salt on; I took my scarf off*. There are also analogues in which the noun is the subject, but these seem less likely to have been the model for the child: *my sweater is off; my white sweater should be on; the salt is on; my scarf is off*. The fact that there were no sentences like *Susan off* or *Mommy on*, that is, transitive two-word verb sentences of the model analogue with the verb and object deleted, strengthens the view that the N^m usually represents the object of action. There were exceptions to this pattern, such as *chair off*, said while taking a teddy bear off a chair.

There were 12 sentences in which the complement was a two-word phrase:

> White sweater on.
> Blue sweater on.
> Mommy sweater on.
> Susan sweater on.
> Susan coat on.
> Bonnie coat on.
> This dress off.
> Put that on.
> That came off.
> Miller take off shoe sock.
> Shouldn't take off shoe sock.
> Let's take off shoe sock.

It will be seen that there was evidence for distinguishing two-word classes that reflected N^m and V^m. It was not clear if Adj^m should be grouped with N^m or kept distinct. Therefore the formulas $N^m + N^m$, $N^m + V^m$, or $V^m + N^m$, and perhaps also $Adj^m + N^m$ can be used to form expansions of the particle complement. The phrases that reflected auxiliary + verb, however, cannot be accounted for in this fashion. *Susan sweater on* and *Mommy sweater on* were ambiguous. In the first sentence a possessive relation was intended and a model analogue would be *Susan's sweater is on* or *Susan has her sweater on*. The second sentence was a request directed to her mother and a model analogue would be *Mommy, put my sweater on me*.

A rather neat pattern was found for the core of Susan's particle construction. There were, however, loose ends. In some sentences the particle was medial, and in a few it was initial:

> *Take off me* (requesting help in taking her scarf off).
> *Sock off Liz* (in imitation of *Let's take the shoes and socks off of Liz*).
> *Snap on off* (said while playing with the snap of a doll's dress).
> *Want to hold on Liz.*
> *Liz her hat back on* (indicating she wanted to put Liz's hat on after it fell off).
> *This one blue one on.*
> *Susan blue one sweater on* (this and preceding sentence were used to indicate she wanted to wear her blue sweater).
> *On tight* (putting her doll more securely on her Kiddy Kar so it would not fall off again).
> *Off of me* (requesting help in taking her scarf off).

No recurrent pattern can be found for these sentences.

Other particles of the model language were common, but none were as common as *off* and *on*. *Up* occurred 15 times: three times after N^m, nine times after V^m, two times after other words, and once in initial position. There are a few examples that fit the pattern described for the particle construction: *sleeves up*, requesting the investigator to roll up her sleeves; *red shoe up*, leaning her shoes against the door sill, pointed up. *Up bed*, indicating she wanted the side of the crib raised, would be **bed up* if it followed the pattern of *off* and *on*. Several sentences were probably learned units, thus accounting for the larger number of V^m than N^m before the particle: *tear up; come up; Susan get up*.

The remaining model language particles were common as a whole, but no single particle was very frequent. A large number of the sentences followed the pattern of the particle construction, but there were a larger proportion of exceptions to the general pattern than were found with *off* and *on*. A good many exceptions seemed to reflect the prepositional uses of the words in the model language.

When Susan's linguistic system became more mature and more closely approximated the model, transitive sentences with two-word verbs were common. The elements that developed into the object and particle were represented at this stage. The verbs less frequently, and the subjects almost never were represented.

The words *this, this-one,* and *that* showed certain consistent features. We can designate these three words class II. In initial position they formed the demonstrative construction. *This-one* had the phonological shape /disn/ or /disən/, and appeared to be a unit for Susan. The sequence /-n/ or /-ən/ was distinct from the vocabulary item /wən/ *one.* The demonstrative construction had less semantic consistency than the particle construction. It was usually used to identify an item: *this-one yellow, this book, this-one Joe, that bead.* But it could also be used to indicate location and action or quality (the last two are difficult to separate in Susan's speech): *this on top; this-one on; this-one tear.* The word classes of the model language that followed an initial class II word were also more variable, as shown in Table 3.

TABLE 3

Susan's Demonstrative Constructions (Susan 1.9–2.0)

| First Word | S E C O N D W O R D | | | | |
	N^m	V^m	Adj^m	Class I	Other
this	9	1	1	3	2
this-one	3	3	2	3	4
that	9	1	1	6	6

Class II words were usually in initial position; class I words were usually in medial or final position. However the positional preference is more consistent for class I than for class II.

A third class, labeled class III, may be recognized, consisting of *a* (19 occurrences), *the* (nine occurrences), and *(an)other* (11 occurrences). Excluding some examples of *a* (discussed below), class III preceded a N^m or a noun phrase of the model language, except in: *a red* (in answer to *What kind of an apple is that?*); *is that the blue mine?; have another blue.* In addition *a* was found in a few sentences in medial position before words where *a* was inappropriate: *up bed, (side?) a bed,* requesting that the investigator raise the side of her crib; *this a Bonnie pants; have a pants; this-one a Joe?; I know a that; these a Liz pants; this a back on; this a Joe?; mine, all a mine.* Shortly before Susan said *have a pants,* she had said *here a lemon* in imitation of her mother's sentence *here's a lemon.* Sentences like *here's a lemon* and probably also phrases like *all of* (/ə/) *mine, piece of* (/ə/) *toast* provided the model for Susan's pattern. The *a* seemed to have the function of dividing the sentence into two parts. This function was restricted to a two-month period from 1.9½ to 1.11½.

Eight words have been assigned to three classes. The remaining words in Susan's vocabulary were either less frequent or less consistent and cannot realistically be assigned to classes by the methods used for setting up classes I, II, and III. Are we justified in lumping the remaining vocabulary items into one large undifferentiated class? If we group the remaining words into the word classes of the model language and examine only two-word sentences, we find that a certain pattern emerges. The results are given in Table 4. Sentences that included *I, me, my, mine* were excluded because

TABLE 4

Class Contingencies in Susan's Two-Word Sentences (1.9–2.0)

Second Word	**F**I**R**S**T** I	II	III	**W**O**R**D A	B	C	D	E	*it*	*more*	Total
I	..	10	..	6	45	..	..	1	..	..	62
II	..	..	..	6	1	..	1	..	..	1	9
III	..	..	..	..	..	..	..	..	..	..	..
A	..	3	..	1	26	..	1	..	..	..	31
B	..	10	8	18	26	4	6	1	..	3	76
C	..	3	1	..	4	..	..	2	..	..	10
D	..	1	..	4	5	1	..	7	..	..	18
E	..	4	..	12	10	1	..	..	..	1	28
it	..	..	..	6	..	..	..	..	..	..	6
more	..	..	..	..	..	..	..	..	..	..	..
Total	..	31	9	53	117	6	8	11	..	5	240

NOTE.—Thirty-seven sentences that include the following words have been excluded: *night-night, I, me, my, mine, he, you, her, them, one, two, no, what, now, too, please, bye, like,* and *right* (in *right here*).

these words came in late in the period and were replacing *Susan. What* is also excluded because it represented a late development. A number of other words were excluded either because they were rare and their class membership was difficult to assign, or because they appeared to belong to learned formulas. Prepositions and particles have been lumped into one class.

Class A reflected V^m. There was only one example of A + A (*want talk*). The most common patterns were A + B and B + A. There were only six examples of A + *it*, but these comprise all the examples of *it. It* seemed to function as a suffix for class A words, and perhaps marked a subclass of A, words that reflected transitive verbs in the model. Class B reflected N^m and was common before classes A, B, and I, and after class A. Class C, which reflected Adj^m, was not common. The words reflected a variety of subclasses in the model language. Classes B and C show similar patterns and we cannot be sure they represent two classes in Susan's speech. If N^m and Adj^m words belong to one class in Susan's linguistic system, we would expect to find examples of $\text{Adj}^m + \text{I}$, because the pattern $\text{N}^m + \text{I}$ was so common. Class D represents locative adverbs, and class E prepositions and particles of the model. These two classes cannot be sustained by the evidence presented in the table. The words represented in D and E might be aligned in a different fashion but the evidence is too meager to group these words with confidence. There were not many examples of *more,* but the evidence seems to indicate that the word belongs to class III.

TABLE 5

Demonstrative Sentences for Christy (2.0–2.3)

that	that's	this	thatsa	this a	thata	'sa
blue					blue	
broken			broken			
chicken	chicken					
dolly	dolly					
eye	eye					
elephant			elephant			
go		go				
hat	hat					
Joe	Joe					
pants	pants					
pretty			pretty			
truck	truck		truck	truck		truck
yellow	yellow					
			cup		cup	
airplane	bus	one	car	A	doggy	arm
blocks	milk		coffee		horse	baby
bowl	quack-quack		girl			block
cat			owl			boy
Christy's			pig			ear
Daddy's			plane			lion
dolly's						rabbit
fish						Wick
horsie						
huke*						
kitty						
neck						
pin						
pink						
po*						
Sarah						
turn						
yellow						

* *Po* and *huke* were the names of two nonsense shapes of play-doh.

Christy

A somewhat different pattern is found in Christy's grammatical development. The following paragraphs are based primarily on two-word sentences collected during 12 hours of recorded texts. The most common type of sentence began with *that*. The various initial elements of these sentences along with the following words are listed in Table 5. The lists may be pooled into one in view of the similarity of the lists and gradation of phonetic shapes represented by each category: /dæ, dæ?, dæt, dæ, da, dat, dɔ, as, dæs, dædæ, dæda, dæa, æta, dætsa, dæsa, dæza, zæza, æza, sa, za, sæ, tsa/.

This and *this a* (found before *a, go, one,* and *truck*) and the variants of *that* may be pooled as class I. The items in Table 5 and the items found after *this* (*a*) may be called class A. As a result of this classification, a construction can be identified which we may call the demonstrative construction: I + A↓/↑ (the arrows indicate falling and rising intonation). There were 74 examples of such utterances.

Nineteen sentences began with *the* or *a*. The words which followed were *other*, or class A words. *The* and *a* never terminated a two-word sentence. These words have been designated class II.

The words *in, on, out, away, over,* and *under* appeared in 16 sentences. They both preceded and followed class A and preceded class I. There was one set which followed, but never preceded class A: *away, out;* others which preceded but never followed: *over, under;* and others of dual mem-

TABLE 6

Class Contingencies in Christy's Two-Word Sentences (2.0–2.3)

Second Word	F I R S T W O R D											Total
	I	II	III	A	B	C	D	*where*	*what*	*(an)other*	*it*	
I	..	..	..	..	2	..	1	..	1	1	..	5
II	..	..	..	..	..	..	..	..	..	..	..	...
III	..	..	..	3	5	..	5	..	..	..	..	13
A	74	18	9	41	5	..	3	10	..	8	..	168
B	2	..	..	10	2	..	..	1	..	..	..	15
C	..	..	..	4	2	..	..	..	..	..	..	6
D	..	..	..	..	..	..	..	..	..	..	..	...
where	..	..	..	..	..	..	..	..	..	..	..	...
what	..	..	..	..	..	..	..	..	..	..	..	...
(an) other	..	1	..	..	..	..	..	..	..	..	..	1
it	..	..	..	..	2	..	..	..	..	..	..	2
Total	76	19	9	58	18	..	9	11	1	9	..	210

NOTE.—Nineteen sentences were omitted because they contained words of ambiguous class membership from the standpoint of the two-word sentence corpus: *his, walk, oh, no, else, my, right* (*right here*), *more, don't, two, both.*

TABLE 7

Classes in Christy's Two-Word Sentences (2.0–2.3)

I ...	this, thisa, that, that's, that's a, 'sa, thata
II ...	a, the
III ...	here, there
A ...	arm, baby, bus, cat, Christy's, dolly, dolly's, fish, horsie, truck, pretty, yellow, etc.
B ...	come, doed, flying, go, goes, got, hold, see, sit, sleep, sleeping, turn, want, walking
C ...	away, in, on, out, way
D ...	in, on, over, under

bership: *in, on.* The words which occurred in first position have been designated class D, and those in second position as class C. The decision to split these words into two classes, in spite of the overlap in membership, is based on the presumed later evolution into prepositions and adverbs or two-word verb particles. The accent pattern for sentences containing these items was relatively consistent.[6] In 13 out of the 14 cases where the stress was recorded, it occurred on the second word, e.g., *on cóuch, clothes ón.*

In addition to preceding class I and class A, words in class C preceded *there* and *here*, e.g., *in thére* ↑. *There* and *here* may be designated as class III. The words *where* and *what* occurred only in initial position. *Where* only occurred in sentences with falling pitch.

Class A was by far the largest class, both in terms of frequency and variety. Included are items which are N^m, V^m, and Adj^m. We may subdivide this category on certain distributional grounds. The sentences *see this, hóld it, doed it,* and *óther this* were not paralleled by any instances in which N^m or Adj^m occurred in first position in the same frame, in spite of the fact that N^m was far more frequent than V^m. V^m never followed class II, III, or D. The pattern I + V^m was relatively infrequent compared to A + V^m. V^m is designated class B, and the occurrences are shown in Table 6. If only two-word sentences are considered, the separation of class A and B is based on weaker evidence than the other class criteria, but it is quite likely that the analysis of longer sentences would confirm this division. On Table 5 the overlap was greatest between *that* and *that's.* If the words ending in *a* are viewed as in fact two words (*this a, that's a*), so that the sequences form three-word sentences, it may be seen that there are no cases of V^m in the last four columns, though three appear with *this* and *that.* Such sentences as *you hold this, make apple there,* and *take it off* suggest that the analysis of long sequences will require a separate class of verbs. In all cases except *apple eat* the semantic object followed the

---

[6] An accented word, defined for Christy's speech in the section on Prosody, is indicated by a primary stress mark.

verb. The semantic actor normally preceded, except in *I carry Christy* which had two objects and *where go eye* and *where go toast, huh* which had an inversion regularly following *where.* There was insufficient evidence for further subdivision of class A.

Christy's grammar included an accentual system. The locative construction consisted of A + Á or A + IíI. Sentences based on the possessive or adjectival analogue of the model consisted of Á + A: *baby róom* (in answer to *Where's the baby?*); *báby book* (in answer to *Is that the baby's book?*); *big choochoo*. In a few cases, however, the second item was accented in sentences that had a possessive and adjectival analogue: *baby báll* (in answer to *Is that the baby's ball?*); *baby cár* (in answer to *Whose car is this?*); *a big wádi* (wadi = dog). The first example might reveal imitation of the investigator's stress. The accent pattern was not consistent in the possessive or adjectival construction, in contrast to the locative construction.

Discussion

The partial descriptions for Susan and Christy show that the two language systems were quite different in their details. Some of the differences could be ascribed to the age difference, but others were due to a difference in their language style. There were, however, certain characteristics that applied to the speech of all the children in the project except Harlan, who was beyond this phase of development from the beginning.

A few high frequency words tended to be restricted to a given position in the sentence and tended to define the meaning of the sentence as a whole. The use of these words marked the first step in developing the grammatical system of the model language. These words may be called operators. The classes of operators for Susan and Christy have been labeled with Roman numerals. The difference between operator classes and nonoperator classes is relative rather than absolute. The nonoperator words tend to be grouped into large classes, but the division between the classes is sometimes difficult to make. Part of this difficulty is probably the nature of the data. If a low frequency word does not occur in enough different contexts, class assignments are difficult to make. But part of the difficulty may be the nature of the linguistic system of the child. The instability of class assignment is especially probable in a system based on order and not on additional markers. If a child has only heard a word from adults a few times, his sense of the meaning and the appropriate verbal contexts for that word may be easily changed by new experience. Thus, even though some regularity in order for two classes may exist, vacillation with regard to certain specific items may obscure that regularity. The method of classifying the child's words in part by pure distribution and in part by the word classes of the model language will not adequately account for all of the child's vocabulary, or vacillation of specific items. But the regularity displayed in the tables shows that this method yields information about structure.[7]

Operators are defined as those words having high frequency and few members in a class. These properties are found, in adult speech, in function words. The children's operators tended to be derived from adult function words and to be precursors of the function words which characterized a later phase of their own development. The nonoperators were precursors of lexical words. There was some tendency for the most frequent models of operators to be words which could serve as substitutes for lexical classes and carry stress, i.e., pronouns (demonstratives) rather than pure noun determiners, particles of two-word verbs rather than pure prepositions.

If the child used the operators in constructions that had analogues in adult speech, adults reinforced the child's pattern and enabled him to approximate adult patterns more closely. If the operators or constructions did not reflect patterns in the model language, they dropped out. There was one clear example. From 2.1 to 2.4, Lisa used *byebye, no, all-gone, another,* and *please* as operators. These words were used in a construction which consisted of an accented operator plus N^m: *nó toy,* indicating she did not want a particular toy any longer (contrast *no tóy?,* asking if there were any more toys). Many of the sentences can be related to the model only by reversing the order. Thus *all-gone puzzle* (the puzzles had just been put away) would normally be said by the adult as *The puzzle is all gone,* or some such sentence in which the word order is the reverse of Lisa's. It is always possible to find analogues that preserve the child's order, e.g., *It's all gone, the puzzle is* or *That which is all gone is the puzzle.* These are sentences the child is not likely to hear. This construction became less frequent and eventually disappeared.

Most of our analysis has been limited to two-word sentences, and the distinction between endocentric and exocentric constructions cannot apply. It seems clear, however, that this distinction will be needed to account for longer sentences. Most of the child's early constructions have exocentric models, and are probably to be considered exocentric in the child's system also. In addition, many phrases in longer sentences can probably be treated as expansions of single word classes. A characteristic feature of the children's speech was to take a construction that could be a complete predication for them and treat it as an expansion of one part of another construction. Thus the possessive construction in Christy's speech, Á + A, can be used as the demonstrative complement: *that Chrísty rabbit.* This kind of expansion seems to be typical in the early phases, and endocentric features of the

---

[7] A grammar cannot be derived from the tables. The tables only show that the elements in the child's sentences are systematized. The best explanation for the systematization is that the child has word classes, classes that have at least some properties of word classes in adult speech. The tables do not tell what the classes are, but they do provide clues.

model language were weakly represented in the children's language. There are certain problems to this kind of an analysis, however. In Christy's sentence *that one Joe, that one* can probably be treated as an expansion of the demonstrative, but in *-'s a one two* Christy was counting and *one two* appears to be an expansion of the complement. In *that this shoe, that* may be treated as the demonstrative, *this shoe* as the complement, and the complement also as a demonstrative construction. It is not certain, however, that such analysis can be formally sustained.

It seems surprising that the children's relatively systematic arrangement of classes could be sustained with so few overt markers. One explanation may be the relative semantic consistency of English lexical classes for the words in young children's vocabulary, a fact pointed out by Brown (1958b, p. 247). He found experimentally that lexical items with class markers were systematically identified with certain types of referents (*ibid*, p. 251). Thus it may be that regularities of order are aided by the additional cue that is provided by semantic similarities between items in a class. We have very weak evidence on this point, from Harlan. The word *have* in English serves as a verb, but it does not have a meaning of action. Harlan had considerable difficulty in giving *have* the verb markers he used with other verbs. It might be objected that the difficulty stems from its use as an auxiliary, but this is a specialized use that had not yet (at 3.1) appeared in Harlan's speech. Further, *do,* which was used by Harlan both as an auxiliary and main verb, was marked appropriately when *have* was not. Thus we have examples of past tense markers for many verbs, including *do,* at least six months before the past tense was marked for *have,* although contexts in which the past tense would have been appropriate for this verb did occur before that time. At 2.7, after the regular testing of discourse agreement was begun, it was found that Harlan could answer a question about what someone was doing with an appropriate response. Notice that he did not say *having* in response to this question:

> Inv: *What do you think Paul was doing with the hoe?*
> Harlan: *Have.*
> Inv: *Hm?*
> Harlan: *Have it.*

This is not altogether a clear case, since the semantic peculiarity of *have* is reflected in its lower probability in the *-ing* form in adult usage.

The casual observer is often struck by what appears to be a complete lack of any system in the young child's first speech efforts. The composition of words into sentences appears to be random; any words can be juxtaposed. Our evidence shows this not to be the case. There was a complex system even at the earliest stages, even though it was a much simpler system than the extremely complex adult model. Are we justified in calling the kind of system that a young child has a formal grammar? This depends to a large extent on what a formal grammar is conceived to be.

From the standpoint of a linguist, a grammar can be conceived as a set of rules that will account for the sentences produced by the speaker and will not predict impossible sentences. Vocabulary items have to be assignable to word classes so that new sentences can be generated by operating with the grammar. Normally in natural languages many constructions have stateable and consistent semantic correlates, but it might be debated whether this is a necessary property.

It is obvious from the description of Susan's and Christy's speech that for most generalizations there were exceptions. Some sentences seemed to fall outside the system. Other sentences reversed the patterns that held in all other cases. It is sentences like *off of me; clean in, in clean* (in Susan's speech); and *I carry Christy; that one Joe; that one two* (counting); *where rattle Christy; big shoe red, red shoe big; apple more; more apple* (in Christy's speech) that cause problems. Almost any rule that allows these sequences allows others that seem impossible.

How shall we know what is impossible with a child? With adult informants, one can test a grammatical solution by eliciting paradigmatic material or by asking *Can you say . . .?* This implies that a speaker can distinguish the grammatically impossible from the improbable; Maclay and Sleator (1960) have presented evidence that college rhetoric students could not make the distinction. Yet we do know that adults can correct their own grammatical mistakes. Harlan corrected grammatical errors in his speech. Was this simply recognition that the utterances were improbable?

There seem to be a number of views which could be defended as to whether a formal system existed for Susan and Christy. There were a few generalizations which could be made without exceptions, but these were weak in that they also predicted many sentences that did not appear and were improbable. It might be said that they were formal systems, but that they were undergoing change.

Alternatively, it could be said that the statistical tendencies and preferences were precursors of more stable and clearly defined classes. It might be argued that grammatical systems arise first in the child's exposure to differing probabilities in adult substitutions and sequences, which are reflected in a system of regularities which cannot be expressed by exceptionless rules.

THE GRAMMATICAL SYSTEM WITH WORD CLASS MARKERS

Eventually lexical classes could be identified by markers and order, not simply order as in the earlier stage. Nouns were marked by the plural suffix and noun determiners, verbs by verbal suffixes and auxiliaries. At this time it is convenient to describe the child's grammatical system as a simplified grammar of the model, along with added grammatical rules to account for constructions that have no counterpart in the model language.

Most of the mistakes or deviations from the model can be classified as omissions (*I'll turn water off* for *I'll turn the water off*), overgeneralization of morphophonemic combinations (*foots* for *feet; a owl* for *an owl; breaked* for *broke*), the incorrect use of a function word with a subclass of a lexical class (using *a* with mass nouns and proper nouns), or doubly marked forms (adding the possessive suffix to a possessive pronoun, *mine's*). Except for the first kind, these mistakes point to the fact that classes were marked. The children seldom used a suffix or function word with the wrong lexical class, either at this stage or at the earlier stage when markers were not well developed; the only examples of this kind of mistake were provided by Susan: *I by-ed that* where the adult would say *I went by that*, and *stand up-ed* where the adult would say *stood up*. In the second example it could be argued that the *-ed* was not added to the wrong word class, but rather was added to the verb phrase instead of the verb.

Most of our discussion of this stage of development will be centered on the linguistic system of Harlan, who was at this stage of development at 2.2 when we started working with him (the remaining children in the project entered this stage at 2.6 or shortly thereafter).

At 2.2, verbs in Harlan's system could be marked by the past tense suffix *-ed*, the progressive suffix *-ing*, the positive auxiliaries *can, will, want, going*, and the negative auxiliaries *can't, won't, don't*. The sentence: *I pushed it, I can push it* was typical. The markers were not always used, however:

> Inv: *It popped.*
> Harlan: (To his mother) *My balloon pop.*
> Mother: *You popped it?*
> Harlan: *I pop it.*

Harlan's parents reported that he had the past tense suffix a few weeks before we began working with him. At 2.2 a few strong verbs were correctly used with the past tense: *My Daddy-O went to work; I made a somersault.* These forms varied with the base form:

> Harlan: *I go boom boom* (past tense context).
> Inv: *What'd you do?*
> Harlan: *I went boom.*

Normally strong verbs were unmarked. The *-ed* form of the past tense was not added to such verbs until 2.5: *I breaked that.*

At 2.2 the progressive was simply the suffix *-ing* with no form of the verb *to be: Man talking on the telephone.* Thus the suffix had the same, or a very similar, distribution as the *-ed* suffix. At 2.3, forms with *to be* were used sporadically: *Man's taking out the baloney. To be* was not consistently used until 2.8.

Harlan grouped his auxiliaries into two sets, positive and negative. This resulted from his lack of negative transformations. In addition, he had two auxiliaries that are not in the model language, *want* and *going*. These words are analyzed as auxiliaries because they came directly before the verb without the infinitive marker *to: I want make two bowls; I going make a pig.*

At 2.2 the most common noun markers were *the, a,* and the plural suffix *-s.* The markers were sometimes omitted in contexts where they should have been used: *I want the duck, I want the duck, I want duck.* Other words marked nouns, e.g., *some,* possessive pronouns, numerals, but they were less frequent.

At 2.2 Harlan indicated the negative with a negative auxiliary, *not* or *isn't: I can't see the pig; That not go right; Isn't a boy. Isn't* was used primarily in one-word negations. It was not treated as a negative transformation of *is* as can be seen in: *That piece* (puzzle piece) *go right over there.* (Harlan tried the puzzle piece over there, and found it did not fit.) *Isn't.* Unfortunately our material does not allow us to say when the negative was first treated as a transformation, but the transformation pattern was present by at least 2.8.

At 2.2 *yes-no* questions were marked by the rising intonation. The following example at 2.3 indicates that Harlan understood that some sort of inversion should take place:

> Harlan: *Want d'you policeman?* /wan ǰuw pliysmæn↑/
> Inv: *Hm?*
> Harlan: *Want . . . want d'you policeman?* /want | want ǰuw pliys-mæn↑/

We have noted that *want* was interpreted by Harlan as an auxiliary, and this may have had some influence on the inversion. But it is clear that Harlan did not understand the function of *do.* The interrogative inversion was used sporadically after this time, and became a productive pattern at 2.8:

> Inv: *You ask Liz what she wants, OK?*
> Harlan: *D'you want honey, you do? OK.*

The elliptical transformation appeared quite suddenly at 2.7, and was common and productive at that time:

> Inv: *Where's the deer going?*
> Harlan: *Because he is.*

> Inv: *How old are you?*
> Harlan: *Because I am.*

Inv: *Why can't you do it with me?*
Harlan: *Because I can't.*

Inv: *When do you eat breakfast?*
Harlan: *Because I do.*

Inv: *How did the bird get there?*
Harlan: *Because he did.*

Inv: *You've seen this book before, Harlan.*
Harlan: *I have?*

Emphatic transformations occurred sporadically: *I did turn it off* (2.3); *I did wake up* (2.7).

The above paragraphs show that the verbal transformations involving *do* and other auxiliaries started to come in about 2.3, and became an established feature in Harlan's grammar by 2.8. (Transformations with interrogative words, not treated here, came in a little later; the sentences with interrogative words showed more complicated patterns of development.) The verb restrictions in discourse agreement patterns were fairly well controlled by 2.8.

There seemed to be a correlation between Harlan's grammatical development and the functional categories described in the introduction. After the development of the verbal transformations and the verb restrictions in discourse agreement, the functional category of responsive discourse was utilized. Since functional categories are more difficult to recognize than formal categories, and since most attention has been focused on the formal categories, this correlation may not be correct. It seems likely that language functions are correlated with grammatical development, whether or not the suggested correlation is correct.

The linguistic system of the child is very unstable. After the word classes are overtly marked, the instability is very noticeable, as the above sketch of Harlan's grammatical system shows. The formal patterns are not set, and the child frequently lapses back into older patterns. It takes a long time for the learned patterns to become automatic.

When the child is able to correct his mistakes, it indicates that he considers certain sentences to be ungrammatical. This is excellent proof that the child has a formal grammatical system. Harlan, the only child to exhibit this ability early, started correcting himself at 2.9, soon after the appearance of verbal transformations and the development of verb restriction in discourse agreement.

PROSODIC FEATURES

Children are good mimics of prosodic features, particularly pitch, and they can give the impression of having the pitch-stress system under control.

This may be true from a phonetic, perhaps even phonemic standpoint, but does not necessarily entail the use of the prosodic features in the grammatical system. The rising and falling intonations used to distinguish questions and statements were the only prosodic features consistently found in the linguistic system before the use of class markers. Even this contrast may be later than is generally recognized. The earliest and best record of this contrast is for Susan. In the early records for her at 1.9, many sentences that ended in a level or rising pitch were interpreted as questions. The lack of a falling pitch was often the only indication that the sentence might be a question, and sometimes the context suggested that it was a statement. The adult (parent or investigator) always interpreted the sentence as a question and gave Susan an answer. Susan was over 2 years old before the rising intonation consistently indicated a question. It may be that she learned the intonation by noting which sentences drew a response from the adult.

Prosodic features that had no analogue in the model language were sometimes used in the early period. Christy and Lisa had an accentual system based on pitch and stress. Each sentence had one accented word. The accented word received the last high pitch and/or strong stress. The pitch and stress of the preceding words were variable. Each construction in both children's linguistic system had a particular accent pattern, but the accent pattern was not always adhered to.

All of the children had primary and secondary stress, and a two-level pitch system at the time they developed a linguistic system with marked word classes. The two-level pitch system persisted well beyond this period, probably because two levels are sufficient to indicate most of the grammatical contrasts signaled by the English prosodic system.

INDIVIDUAL DIFFERENCES

We have noted that there were certain features common to the early development of the grammatical level for all the children. Each child had a set of operators, usually derived from function words of the model language, that served as a means of breaking into the model language system. The children did not have the same operators, however. These differences between the children in preferences were clear from the beginning and have persisted in differences in foci of development. It is possible that certain types of patterns or constructions are more compatible than others. Greenberg (1961) has pointed to correlated structures in languages and we might find some patterns in the individual differences between the children at various stages, but our evidence is scant at present.

Lisa had a particularly primitive phonological system. As a result, it was often difficult or impossible to understand her. In addition, final sibilants were absent for a considerable period and she was not able to mark the plural with the suffix -s. Instead she used a syntactic device: one two *shoe* meant *more than one shoe*. She later gave this up in favor of other number combinations. According to her mother, she would pick two numbers to indicate the plural, e.g., *eight four shoe*, and then after a few days she would pick another combination, e.g., *three five shoe*. She finally developed a final /θ/ and was able to say *shoeth*. There may be a relationship between Lisa's syntactic marking of the plural and her earlier use of an operator class which had no adult analogue. In addition, at a later stage of development Lisa seemed to develop some grammatical rules of her own, rules which had no counterpart in the model language.

There are some suggestions in our data that linguistic patterns correlate with some nonlinguistic behavior. Susan's favorite operators were *off* and *on*. Susan was a busy little girl who always taking things off and putting them back on. Christy's favorite operator was *that*, and was used in the demonstrative construction to identify things. When the investigator arrived at Christy's house, she would run into the living room, sit down, and wait to be entertained—wait for the investigator to take toys out of his bag. Most of the children had a favorite toy and a favorite activity. Harlan had no favorite toy, but he had a favorite activity: talking. We found that if we could keep a conversation going he was less apt to throw things. Harlan had the most developed linguistic system of any of the children. He talked early and often. He also made more expressive use of language than the other children: the diminutive baby talk suffix *-y* was productive by 2.5; the expressive pitch pattern /312↑/ was in common use by 2.2.

In the preceding sections we have described a technique in which the child develops the grammatical level by composing, by placing words together to form sentences. A less common technique consists of treating a polymorphemic sequence of the model language as a monomorphemic unit, and then at a later stage of development segmenting the sequence into its proper parts. It is our impression from parental reports that this is more common with second children than with the first born, but still never an important pattern; all of the children in the small group are first born. A third, closely allied technique is the learning, or imitating, of a sentence, understanding the meaning of most of the words and the meaning of the sentence as a whole, but not understanding the grammatical function of the elements. If a number of sentences of a similar pattern are learned, it might be possible for the child to come to recognize the grammatical function of the elements. This technique is rare, or perhaps nonexistent, because the child would probably have to learn by heart a large number of sentences before he happened to learn two that contrasted in the proper fashion. Christy had a number of sentences which appeared to have been memorized, e.g., *where are the shoe?* (2.3). At this time neither *are* nor *is* were productive elements in Christy's speech, and there is no evidence that this or similar sentences were instrumental in her learning the copulative pattern.

DEVELOPMENTAL SEQUENCE

One of the purposes of this study is to describe developmental sequences of linguistic features. While the features studied are those of English, it would be valuable to be able to consider features inherent in any linguistic system. This is difficult to do until more is known about language universals and the prerequisites of language.

The relation between the time of mastery of skills may consist of co-occurrence or of necessary sequence. Sequential orders may arise either because one skill is dependent on the prior acquisition of another, because one is less often practiced, or because they differ in difficulty though are practiced equally. Many of the sequential findings of a normative sort have the third property. They occur because, on the average, it takes a different amount of practice to accomplish one task than another. We would like to separate the logically sequential features. These could be found best in an experimental transfer design, but, wherever in our data there are individual differences in acquisition patterns, some information about sequential dependence can be obtained from studying changes in individual systems rather than group averages.

Viewing the acquisition of phonological contrasts in terms of learning to distinguish features or properties rather than classes, Jakobson (1941) has proposed a developmental order for the phonological system of children. He has suggested that the child successively elaborates a phonological system approaching the adult's by binary division. If he begins with one feature or bundle of features for contrast, he can only have two classes; with two sets of independent features he may have four classes. Within each class he may have sounds which are in many respects phonetically different from the adult model.

Does anything of this sort happen in grammar? We have indicated that grammatical classes and grammatical markers do not have the structural properties of a matrix of features which phonemes have. The classes that are identified in grammatical analysis are not usually marked by features that can then be recombined to define another class. However, at various points in the grammatical system there are differing degrees of generalization possible. Proper, mass, and count nouns are contrasted by their occurrence with noun determiners, a function class that is unique to this system of classes. The learning of the morphophonemic series in the contrast plural/singular has greater generality. It can also serve in marking possessive nouns, and in marking third person singular verbs. An analogous series marks the regular past tense. At the level of grammatical transformations, a very broad transfer of skills is possible. We may seek for correlations between these related series. For example, though the contrasts plural/singular and possessive/nonpossessive may be acquired at different times for reasons which are semantic or based on frequency, if the contrasts of one are mastered, the other should be too. We have so far only one instance—Harlan—of mastery of both by a child in our study. He gave as productive forms *po - poez* for singular/plural at 2.3 and *Joe - Joez* for possession at 2.4½. At the latter date we find *nizz - nizzez* for singular/plural. But we do not find the possessive *Liz - Lizez* until 2.7. *Joe* and *Liz* were the names of dolls which were used to elicit possession for body parts and clothing, so the opportunity for these contrasts was frequent. This slight evidence does not support the expectation that the morphophonemic contrasts would generalize.

If we turn back to the learning of division into word classes when it first appears, we are limited by the fact that we have only two types of information on which to base our judgment as to the productive operation of classes. One is rules of order with different words. The other is semantic consistency of constructions using these words. At the point at which we first analyzed the children's speech, there were already many classes discernible. Thus we cannot say that at the initial stage before word classes were defined by markers that there was evidence of a first division into two primordial classes which then were subdivided.

If the division into lexical classes is marked by affixes and function words later, then we may expect to find some of the divisions appearing only at the later stage. The division into mass, proper, and count nouns is possible at this point.

In addition to sequences that depend on the availability of markers, some depend on the availability of vocabulary. Thus the rules of order that apply to subclasses of adverbs only could appear after these words enter the vocabulary of children and co-occur in the same sentences.

The earliest forms of markers which we found were inconsistently used. They were the possessive suffix, the plural suffix, *the, and* and *-ing* which were used sporadically. If they were consistent as to class, though, even sporadic use could help identify a class. Thus the first use for these markers may be to identify lexical classes, rather than to distinguish subclasses within lexical classes or to identify constructions. *Want* and *going,* which were used by most of the children of the project as auxiliaries, marked verbs. On the whole, where suffixed and nonsuffixed forms existed, the children preferred the nonsuffixed forms rather than free variants. This was probably in part a phonological problem, since the children had less control of the final consonants than of the other parts of the phonological system.

At the point where subclasses begin to be distinguished so that markers are used as a consistent signal, it is possible to make some simple predictions. For cases with a semantic correlate, a child will first begin imitating forms correctly, and after using a certain number of contrasts correctly will generalize the contrast to new forms. Until enough instances are learned, there will presumably be a delay between these two points. Generalization to irregular cases should occur also; the preferred form for the singular of irregular nouns probably depends on the relative frequency of the singular and plural and relative ease of pronunciation of the two. We already know from Berko's work (1958) that the plural of nouns with final fricatives, sibilants, and affricates tends to be late.

We have tested 25 children with systematic tests of familiar words, irregulars, and nonsense words with a technique similar to Berko's. Nearly always the contrast with familiar forms preceded the contrast with nonsense forms. Naturally, the familiar forms chosen give a rough estimate only. We do not know whether it is the variety of types or the frequency of tokens showing contrasts which is crucial in determining the length of time before generalization occurs.

The average gap for *boy* vs. *kigh* was 2.4 months; for *ball* vs. *kigh* was the same; for *block* vs. *bik* the gap was 1.1 months; for *cup* vs. *bik* 1.5 months. The cases were too few to estimate the gaps for the other contrasts. Thus the child who calls one cup by a different term than two cups might do the same with the nonsense toy *bik* in a month and a half. This analysis was not specific as to the phonological nature of the contrast.

Does the "concept" of plurality generalize; i.e., when one contrast occurs do the others occur soon after? There are artifacts in the restriction on age range provided by the time at which we stopped testing for this paper. For all items except those with fricative, affricate, or sibilant finals, the range between the first contrast to appear and the last was quite short—averaging 2½ months including the nonsense items.

Two irregulars were used as tests for overextension: *foot* and *man*. Of the 15 children who produced a contrast, three said *feet - feets* and 11 said *foot - foots* about the same age as other stop plurals were produced. One child had *foot - footis* first. For 18 children, a contrast between *man* and a plural was offered. For all, the plural was at first *mans*. Two children showed irregular development that can be shown as follows:

Sarah

2.4	*bik-biks*	*tass-tassez*	*bunge-bunge*	*man-manz*	*foot-foots*	*box-box*
2.5	*bik-biks*	*tass-tassez*	*bunge-bungez*	*man-manz*	*foot-footez*	*box-boxez*
2.6	....	*tass-tassez*	*bunge-bungez*	*man-manz*	*foot-foots*	*box-boxez*
2.7	*bik-biks*	*tass-tassez*	*bunge-bungez*	*man-man*	*foot-foots*	*box-bockez*
2.9	*bik-biks*	*tass-tass*	*bunge-bunge*	*man-man*	*feet-feets*	*box-box*
2.10	*bik-biks*	*tass-tass*	*bunge-bunge*	*man-man*	*foot-foots*	*box-box*

Harlan

2.8	*bik-biks*	*tass-tassez*	*bunge-bungez*	*man-manz*	*foot-footez*	*box-box*
2.9	*bik-biksez*	*tass-tassez*	*bunge-bungez*	*man-manzez*	*foot-footsez*	*box-boxez*
2.10	*bik-biks*	*tass-tassez*	*bunge-bungez*	*man-manz*	*foot-footsez*	*box-boxez*
2.11	....	*tath-tassez*	*bunge-bungez*	*man-men*	*foot-feet*	*box-boxez*
3.1	*bik-biks*	*tass-tassez*	*bunge-bungez*	*man-manz*	*foot-feet*	*box-boxez*

The vacillation in these series illustrates instability, regression, boredom, or, clearly with Harlan at 2.9, playfulness. Harlan frequently invented games with language.

In sum, the acquisition of the plural contrast followed a simple pattern in most children from noncontrast to acquisition of particular instances of contrast, generalization several months after acquisition of particular instances, and finally, differentiation of irregular forms.

In addition to inflectional suffixes, certain derivational suffixes are used to mark classes. For example, the diminutive or baby talk *-y* was used widely by the children in naming animals—*doggy, horsey*—even when we tried to get them to use the nonsuffixed form for the purpose of testing plurality. However, the suffix was used productively by only one child, Harlan, who produced the following in an argument about a name at 2.5½:

> Inv: *Really. His name is Cootes. Bill Cootes.*
> Harlan: *Billzy the Coooootsy.* (singing)

Transformations were not found in the earliest linguistic systems. The first to appear were simple (nongeneralized) transformations, such as the progressive (*be . . . -ing*), inversion of word order for questions, and the use of auxiliaries with *not*. There were some early interrogative inversions by Christy:

> 2.0   *Where's the arm?*
> 2.1   *Where go toast, huh?*
> 2.4   *Where belong shoe?*
> 2.5   *Where go button, Chrity, huh?*

Soon afterwards the coordinative transformation with *and* appeared. The two-part coordinative transformations (e.g., *both . . . and . . .*) and subordinative transformations have not appeared in our data yet.

Preliminary evidence suggests that discourse agreement features are sequentially ordered. We would expect discourse agreement features involving class restrictions to parallel the sequential development of the classes themselves. Appropriate answers to simple "who/what" questions and "what . . . do" questions came early. Preliminary evidence indicates that the child's adverbs are learned in the order locative, temporal, manner; if true, it might be expected that discourse agreement would proceed in the order where, when, how. In a similar fashion the development of verb restrictions in discourse agreement should follow the development of verb structure.

FORMAL DISCUSSION

NOAM CHOMSKY

Massachusetts Institute of Technology

My initial reaction to this paper was one of surprise that so much success could be attained in dealing with this question. It seems that the attempt to write a grammar for a child raises all of the unsolved problems of constructing a grammar for adult speech, multiplied by some rather large factor. To mention just the most obvious difficulty, since the language is constantly changing rather dramatically, it is impossible to use the one "method" available to linguists who attempt to go beyond surface description, namely, learning the language oneself. Clearly the general problem is at least as difficult, and, in fact, much more difficult than the problem of discovering the grammar of the language of a mature speaker, and this, I think, is a problem of much greater difficulty than is often realized. In fact, the only remarks I would like to make reflect an impression that underlying these descriptions of children's speech, laudible and interesting as they are, there is a somewhat oversimplified conception of the character of grammatical description, not unrelated, perhaps, to a similarly oversimplified view that is typical of much recent work on language in psychology and linguistics.

For one thing, it should be clearly recognized that a grammar is not a description of the performance of the speaker, but rather of his linguistic competence, and that a description of competence and a description of performance are different things. To illustrate, consider a trivial example where one would want to distinguish between a description of competence and a description of performance. Suppose that we were to attempt to give an account of how a child learns to multiply (rather than how he acquires his language). A child who has succeeded in learning this has acquired a certain competence, and he will perform in certain ways that are clearly at variance with this competence. Once he has learned to multiply, the correct description of his competence is a statement, in one or another form, of some of the rules of arithmetic—i.e., a specification of the set of triples (x, y, z) such that z is the product of x and y. On the other hand, a description of the performance of either an adult or a child (or a real computer) would be something quite different. It might, for example, be a specification of a set of quadruples (x, y, z, w) such that w is the probability that, given x and y, the person will compute the product as z. This set of quadruples would incorporate information about memory span, characteristic errors, lapses of attention, etc., information which is relevant to a performance table but not, clearly, to an account of what the person has learned—what is the basic competence that he has acquired. A person might memorize the performance table and perform on various simple-minded tests exactly as the person who knows the rules of arithmetic, but this would not, of course, show that he knows these rules. It seems clear that the description which is of greatest psychological relevance is the account of competence, not that of performance, both in the case of arithmetic and the case of language. The deeper question concerns the kinds of structures the person has succeeded in mastering and internalizing, whether or not he utilizes them, in practice, without interference from the many other factors that play a role in actual behavior. For anyone concerned with intellectual processes, or any question that goes beyond mere data arranging, it is the question of competence that is fundamental. Obviously one can find out about competence only by studying performance, but this study must be carried out in devious and clever ways, if any serious result is to be obtained.

These rather obvious comments apply directly to study of language, child or adult. Thus it is absurd to attempt to construct a grammar that describes observed linguistic behavior directly. The tape recordings of this conference give a totally false picture of the conceptions of linguistic structure of the various speakers. Nor is this in the least bit surprising. The speaker has represented in his brain a grammar that gives an ideal account of the structure of the sentences of his language, but, when actually faced with the task of speaking or "understanding," many other factors act upon his underlying linguistic competence to produce actual performance. He may be confused or have several things in mind, change his plans in midstream, etc. Since this is obviously the condition of most actual linguistic performance, a direct record—an actual corpus—is almost useless, as it stands, for linguistic analysis of any but the most superficial kind.

Similarly, it seems to me that, if anything far-reaching and real is to be discovered about the actual grammar of the child, then rather devious kinds of observations of his performance, his abilities, and his comprehension in many different kinds of circumstance will have to be obtained, so that a variety of evidence may be brought to bear on the attempt to determine what is in fact his underlying linguistic competence at each stage of development. Direct description of the child's actual verbal output is no more likely to provide an account of the real underlying competence in the case of child language than in the case of adult language, ability to multiply, or any other nontrivial rule-governed behavior. Not that one shouldn't start here, perhaps, but surely one shouldn't end here, or take too seriously the results obtained by one or another sort of manipulation of data of texts produced under normal conditions.

It is suggested in this paper—and this is a view shared by many psychologists and linguists—that the relation between competence and performance is somehow a probabilistic one. That is, somehow the higher probabilities in actual output converge towards the actual underlying grammar, or something of the sort. I have never seen a coherent presentation of this position, but, even as a vague idea, it seems to me entirely implausible. In particular, it surely cannot be maintained that the child forms his conception of grammatical structure by just assuming that high probabilities correspond to "rules" and that low probabilities can be disregarded, in some manner. Most of what the child actually produces and hears (and this is true for the adult as well) is of extremely low probability. In fact, in the case of sentence structure, the notion of probability loses all meaning. Except for a ridiculously small number (e.g., conventionalized greetings, etc., which, in fact, often do not even observe grammatical rules), all actual sentences are of a probability so low as to be effectively zero, and the same is true of structures (if, by the "structure" of a sentence, we mean the sequence of categories to which its successive words or morphemes belong). In actual speech, the highest probability must be assigned to broken and interrupted fragments of sentences or to sentences which begin in one way and end in a different, totally incompatible way (surely the tapes of this meeting would be sufficient to demonstrate this). From such evidence it would be absurd to conclude that this represents in any sense the linguistic consciousness of the speakers, as have been noted above. In general, it is a mistake to assume that—past the very earliest stages—much of what the child acquires is acquired by imitation. This could not be true on the level of sentence formation, since most of what the child hears is new and most of what he produces, past the very earliest stages, is new.

In the papers that have been presented here—and again, this is not unrepresentative of psychology and linguistics—there has been talk about grammars for the decoder and grammars for the encoder. Again, there are several undemonstrated (and, to me, quite implausible) assumptions underlying the view that the speaker's behavior should be modeled by one sort of system, and the hearer's by another. I have never seen a precise characterization of a "grammar for the encoder" or a "grammar for the decoder" that was not convertible, by a notational change, into the other. Furthermore, this is not surprising. The grammars that linguists construct are, in fact, quite neutral as between speaker and hearer. The problems of constructing models of performance, for the speaker and hearer, incorporating these grammars, are rather similar. This of course bears again on the question of relation between competence and performance. That is, the grammar that represents the speaker's competence is, of course, involved in both his speaking and interpreting of speech, and there seems no reason to assume that there are two different underlying systems, one involved in speaking, one in "understanding." To gain some insight into this underlying system, studies of the speaker's actual output, as well as of his ability to understand and interpret, are essential. But again, it cannot be too strongly emphasized that the data obtained in such studies can only serve as the grounds for inference about what constitutes the linguistic consciousness that provides the basis for language use.

A few other minor remarks of this sort might be made to indicate areas in which experimental methods that go far beyond mere observation of speech in normal situations will be needed to shed some light on underlying competence. To take just one example, it is often remarked, and, in particular, it is remarked in this paper, that in the case of lexical items (as distinct from "function words," so-called) it is generally possible to assign referential meaning rather easily. Of course, as clearly stated in the paper, this is in part a matter of degree. However, I think that the notion that it is generally a straightforward matter in the case of lexical items is a faulty conclusion derived from concentration on atypical examples. Perhaps in the case of "green," "table," etc., it is not difficult to determine what is the "referential meaning." But consider, on the other hand, such words as "useful," where the meaning is clearly "relational"—the things in the world cannot be divided into those that are useful and those that are not. In fact, the meaning of "useful," like that of a function word, in some respects, must be described in partly relational terms. Or, to take a more complicated example, consider a word like "expect." A brief attempt to prescribe the behaviors or situations that make application of this word appropriate will quickly convince one that this is entirely the wrong approach and that "referential meaning" is simply the wrong concept in this case. I don't think that such examples are at all exotic. It may be that such atypical examples as "table" and "green" are relatively more frequent in the early stages of language learning (though this remains to be shown, just as it remains to be shown that determination of referential meaning in such cases is in some sense "primitive"), and, if true, this may be important. However, this is clearly not going to carry one very far.

Consider now a rather comparable phonetic example. One of the problems to be faced is that of characterizing the child's phonemic system. Phonemes are often defined by linguists as constituting a family of mutually exclusive classes of phones, and this is the definition adopted in this paper. If this were true, there would be, in this case, a fairly simple relation between performance (i.e., a sequence of phones) and the underlying abstract system (i.e., the phonemic representation of this sequence). One might hope that by some simple classification technique one might determine the phonemic system from the phonetic record or the phonemic constitution of an utterance from the sequence of its phones. There is, however, extremely strong evidence (so it seems to me, at least) that phonemes cannot be defined as classes of sounds at all (and certainly not as mutually exclusive classes) and that the relation between a phonemic system and the phonetic record (just as the relation between a phonemic representation of an utterance and its actual sound) is much more remote and complex. I do not want to try to give the evidence here; it is being presented elsewhere in fair detail.

But I would like to reiterate, for what it is worth, my conviction that the evidence is extremely strong.

These two examples are randomly chosen illustrations of a general tendency to oversimplify drastically the facts of linguistic structure and to assume that the determination of competence can be derived from description of a corpus by some sort of sufficiently developed data-processing techniques. My feeling is that this is hopeless and that only experimentation of a fairly indirect and ingenious sort can provide evidence that is at all critical for formulating a true account of the child's grammar (as in the case of investigation of any other real system). Consequently, I would hope that some of the research in this area would be diverted from recording of texts towards attempting to tap the child's underlying abilities to use and comprehend sentences, to detect deviance and compensate for it, to apply rules in new situations, to form highly specific concepts from scattered bits of evidence, and so on. There are, after all, many ways in which such study can be approached. Thus, for example, the child's ability to repeat sentences and nonsentences, phonologically possible sequences and phonologically impossible ones, etc., might provide some evidence as to the underlying system that he is using. There is surely no doubt that the child's achievements in systematizing linguistic data, at every stage, go well beyond what he actually produces in normal speech. Thus it is striking that advances are generally "across the board." A child who does not produce initial s + consonant clusters may begin to produce them all, at approximately the same time, thus distinguishing for the first time between "cool" and "school," etc.—but characteristically will do this in just the right words, indicating that the correct phonemic representation of these words was present to the mind even at the stage where it did not appear in speech. Similarly, some of the data of Brown and Fraser seem to suggest that interrogatives, negatives, and other syntactically related forms appear and are distinguished from declaratives at approximately the same time, for some children. If so, this suggests that what has actually happened is that the hitherto latent system of verbal auxiliaries is now no longer suppressed in actual speech, as previously. Again, this can be investigated directly. Thus a child producing speech in a "telegraphic style" can be shown to have an underlying, fuller conception of sentence structure (unrealized in his speech, but actively involved in comprehension) if misplacement of the elements he does not produce leads to difficulties of comprehension, inability to repeat, etc., while correct placement gives utterances intelligible to him, and so on.

I would, finally, like to say that I don't intend these remarks as criticism of the present work, as it stands. It is clear from what has been presented already that quite a bit can be learned from observation of the spoken record. I make these remarks only to indicate a difficulty which I think is looming rather large and to which some serious attention will have to be given fairly soon.

OPEN DISCUSSION

The group focused on the distinction between receptive control of grammar (comprehension) and productive control (speech). The research work of Miller and Ervin and also that of Brown, Fraser, and Bellugi had concentrated on the analysis of obtained speech, and so the papers of these investigators were concerned almost exclusively with productive control. The linguists judged it to be very important, even for a proper understanding of production, to make a parallel study of comprehension.

1. How is the study of sentence comprehension relevant to an appropriate description of sentence production? One of the linguists had noticed that in the papers reporting data on child speech there was evidence of a rather abrupt shift from speech completely free of auxiliaries (such as *to be, have, can, will*) to speech manifesting the full auxiliary system. Such a shift —if it is in fact relatively complete and abrupt—would suggest that the auxiliary system had been built up internally before being utilized in production. In addition, there is some evidence from common observation that children understand the use of auxiliaries even when they do not produce them. For example, auxiliaries are used by adults to form interrogatives "Will you play now?" "Are you hungry yet?" and children do seem to distinguish questions from declaratives.

Suppose that we distinguish between the "computation" of a sentence and its "print out." Computation may include both the grammatical analysis of sentences fed in, which is a part of comprehension, and also the planning or programming of sentences to be spoken or "printed out." It is also conceivable that the analysis of input and programming of output are accomplished separately. In any case, it may be incorrect to say that a child who produces no auxiliaries does not possess the auxiliary system. He may have the system on the computational-comprehension level. With greater maturity, when it is possible to increase the length or span of the "print out," a rule is added to his programming operation which directs: "Produce the auxiliaries." Alternatively, it might be appropriate to say that, until a certain age, the computational level has included a rule: "Delete the auxiliaries in printing out." This latter rule would then be dropped with increasing age.

2. It was pointed out that the kind of description given above credits the child with much more grammatical competence than he is manifesting in speech, and we ought not to do that without good evidence. One kind of evidence could be obtained from production itself: if both the declarative

TWENTY-SECOND MICHIGAN ANTIQUARIAN BOOK AND PAPER SHOW

Special Attraction: Antique Advertising

SUNDAY, OCTOBER 1, 1995

9:30 a.m. to 5:00 p.m.

New Lansing Center
333 E. Michigan Ave.
Lansing, Michigan

(3 blocks east of Capitol, next to the river - Free parking in ramp across river)

MICHIGAN'S LARGEST !

Over 120 U.S. and Canadian Dealers

ADMISSION $4.00

CHILDREN 12 AND UNDER FREE

For more information call or write:
Curious Book Shop
307 E. Grand River Ave.
East Lansing, MI 48823
(517) 332-0112
FAX (517) 332-1915

- First Editions
- Illustrated Books
- Autographs
- Michigan History
- Children's Books
- Travel
- Magazines
- Science Fiction
- Civil War
- Sheet Music
- Advertising Signs

- Americana
- Prints • Maps
- Postcards
- Art • Photographs
- Literature
- Fine Bindings
- Cookbooks
- Mysteries
- Private Press
- Ephemera
- Advertising Tins

NEXT SHOW
Sunday
March 31, 1996
Same Location

and interrogative uses of auxiliaries emerge together, that argues that the system has existed prior to production. In addition, however, there would have to be evidence of comprehension itself.

It is a familiar generalization from diary studies of child speech that comprehension is always more advanced than production. The same kind of thing is said of second-language learning: the comprehension performance is generally more impressive than the production performance. But the evidence for comprehension in the natural situation of a child at home leaves much to be desired.

Suppose a parent says: "Are you hungry yet?" and a child responds: "Yes." There may have been a rising interrogative intonation on the question, and it may be *that* feature that governs the child's response. He might have reacted in the same way to such other forms as: "You hungry?" or "Hungry?" It is not clear in the ordinary case that he needs to grasp the use of the auxiliary. Parents, even those who keep diaries, do not ordinarily test for the range of variations in a sentence that will produce the same response from a child. A linguist suggested that one might experimentally interchange articles and auxiliaries or simply delete auxiliaries to see whether children were "computing" them internally.

A monograph by Kahane, Kahane, and Saporta (1958) has, from the evidence of diary studies, concluded that children first do not code a distinction they can comprehend, while later on they do so. However, the authors of this monograph have often simply assumed that since an adult would have understood a certain distinction in a given situation a child must also have understood it. A child may use the present tense in cases when an adult would use either the future or past. The authors of the monograph would be inclined to credit him with understanding the difference but not yet coding it. Ervin and Brown and their collaborators would be more inclined to say that he does not have the future or past tenses but only the present. What is badly needed is evidence independent of tense production that the child either does or does not understand the past and future.

3. Chomsky in his discussion had said that comprehension competence seems generally to be in advance of production competence; he pointed out that, while most of us can understand a play by George Bernard Shaw, none of us can write one. A psychologist pointed out that the performance standard shifts in this comparison; if we ask how many of us can understand a Shaw play *as Shaw understood it,* the answer is unknown. The difficulty is that behavioral criteria of comprehension are less clear than criteria of production. We do not even know how to find out whether someone fully understands a Shaw play. Evidence for comprehension has usually been little more than the child's correct pointing to or approach to a named referent or his performance of a verbalized command. This evidence does not demonstrate grammatical comprehension since it is quite likely that the substantive words alone—the noun naming a referent or the verb naming

an action to be performed—would suffice to produce the appropriate reaction.

A linguist noted that, while the psychological investigation of production seems easier than the investigation of comprehension because the utterance output can be recorded, when it comes to formulating the internal process it is comprehension that is the more easily handled. The sentence of another person is the input, and we can suggest that some data-processing device utilizes the information in the comprehending person's grammar to analyze the sentence—yielding as output a structural description of the sentence that is part of understanding. No one knows how this is done, but at least the problem can be phrased. However, if we ask the comparable problem—how the grammar in the brain operates to generate sentences—it is difficult even to pose the problem. What are the inputs that select sentences? They are not often referents, since we seldom name objects or describe the immediate scene. What, for example, is the input for a person who says: "I would like a cup of coffee."?

III

THE ACQUISITION OF SYNTAX[1]

ROGER BROWN *and* COLIN FRASER[2]
Harvard University

What is done in a developmental study of behavior depends upon the investigators' conception of the terminal state, the outcome of the development. Normal adults speaking their native language seem to us to possess a set of rules of word construction and sentence construction which enables them to go beyond the speech they have actually heard and practiced to the creation of lawful novelties. If new monosyllables are created, speakers of English will agree that *stug* is "better English" than *ftug*. Probably this is because they have a shared implicit knowledge of the initial consonant clusters that are acceptable in English. If this new word is to be pluralized, they will agree that *stug/-z/* is better than *stug/-s/*. Probably this is because they have shared knowledge of a rule of regular English inflection. If the new word is first heard in the sentence: "Here is some stug" they will agree that a second sentence: "The stug is there" is more likely to be grammatical than a second sentence: "A stug is there." Probably this is because they have shared knowledge of the syntactic rules for the employment of mass nouns.

The construction rules of which speakers have implicit knowledge are, in their explicit form, the grammar of a language. As these rules have been written down in traditional grammars, they constitute a collection of largely unrelated statements about such matters as the parts-of-speech, paradigms of conjugation and declension, the marking of gender, and the agreement of adjectives and nouns. Chomsky (1957) has shown that it may be possible to systematize traditional grammar into a mechanism for the generation of all the sentences of a language that are grammatical and none that are ungrammatical. Grammar becomes a theory for a range of phenomena—the sentences of a language—and also a program for generating sentences—a program that might be followed by an electronic device (Yngve, 1961).

[1] The work described in this paper was supported by the National Science Foundation by a grant administered through the Center for Communication Sciences, Massachusetts Institute of Technology. From *Verbal behavior and learning: problems and processes,* edited by N. Cofer and B. S. Musgrave. Copyright, 1963. McGraw-Hill Book Company. Used by permission.

[2] Now at the University of Exeter, Exeter, England.

It is the development in children of this kind of sentence-generating grammar that we are trying to study.

The child growing up hears, from his family, his friends, and the television, a large sample of the sentences of a language, and we think that he induces from the regularities in this sample an implicit grammar. First-language learning, so conceived, reminds us of two other operations with language: that of the linguist in the field and that of the adult learning a second language. The descriptive linguist trying to work out the structure of an unfamiliar tongue begins by collecting a large set of utterances—his "corpus." From regularities in the corpus and from inquiries of a native informant, he induces rules that predict beyond what he has observed. One check on the adequacy of his rules is their ability correctly to anticipate new utterances. Another check is the ability of the rules to duplicate the distinctions made by a native informant who has been asked to judge of each of a collection of utterances whether it is or is not a well-formed sentence. It may be that the linguistic procedures for discovering syntax in distributional facts are a good model for the child's learning of his native language—with the difference that the linguist works deliberately and aims at explicit formulation whereas the child works unwittingly and arrives at implicit formulations. The child's syntax is made explicit for him in "grammar" school, but we suggest that he operates with syntax long before he is of school age.

In learning a second or foreign language, it does not seem to be possible to memorize a list of sentences that is long enough to provide the right one when you need it. Somehow the situation is never exactly right for any of the sayings one has rehearsed. To be effective in a second language, it is necessary to be able to "construct" sentences, and there are two techniques for giving the student this ability. The traditional method is explicit instruction in the rules of grammar. With these rules and a stock of words, one puts together the sentence to suit the occasion. A difficulty is that deliberate construction is a slow business, and the boat will have sunk before you can properly call for help. Some modern instruction treats the second-language learner like a child and has him practice again and again the same set of sentences. The sentences may be delivered to an entire group by film strip, or the student may pace himself with one of the Richards and Gibson pocketbooks. Eventually the student finds himself the creator of a new sentence—one not practiced but somehow implied by what has been practiced. Second-language learning by sentence rehearsal relies on this step into automatic construction, though nothing much seems to be known about how to contrive sets of examples that will facilitate its occurrence.

It has seemed to us, then, that first-language learning must have much in common with second-language learning and also with scientific techniques for the discovery of linguistic structure. The shared characteristic that is the ground of the analogy is the necessity in all three cases of inducing general construction rules from sets of sentences. Of course the analogy suppresses those features of first-language learning that are not to be found in the other two processes, and it has taken considerable pressure from reality to bring them to our attention.

This paper is divided into three sections. The first reviews some studies with invented linguistic materials which show that children do indeed have rules of word construction and of sentence construction. The second discusses techniques by which an investigator might induce a child's generative grammar from a large collection of the child's utterances and the, possibly parallel, techniques by which the child could have induced that grammar from a large set of parental utterances. Most of the discussion in this section makes use of materials from a record of four hours of speech from one child of 25½ months. The third section discusses some substantive results from the records of 13 children between 2 and 3 years of age; these are the results that forced us to recognize that there are differences between children and either linguistic scientists or adult students of a second language.

Evidence That Children Have Construction Rules

In the natural situation of the child with his family the best evidence that he possesses construction rules is the occurrence of systematic errors. So long as a child speaks correctly, it is possible that he says only what he has heard. In general we cannot know what the total input has been and so cannot eliminate the possibility of an exact model for each sentence that is put out. However, when a small boy says "I digged in the yard" or "I saw some sheeps" or "Johnny hurt hisself," it is unlikely that he is imitating. Furthermore, his mistake is not a random one. We can see how he might have made it by overgeneralizing certain existent regularities. Many verbs ending in voiced consonants form the simple past with /-d/ and many nouns ending in voiceless consonants form the plural with /-s/. The set of forms *me, my, myself* and *you, your, yourself* strongly suggests *he, his, hisself*. As it happens, actual English usage breaks with these simple regularities and prefers *dug, sheep,* and *himself*. By smoothing the language into a simpler system than it is, the child reveals his tendency to induce rules. Guillaume made this point in 1927 and illustrated it with a rich collection of French children's systematic errors.

A Study of Morphological Rules

Although Smith (1933) attempted to do a study of the development of the rules of inflection by simply waiting for the emission of erroneous forms, it is more economical to invent nonsense syllables and try to elicit inflections. This is what Berko did for English in her doctoral research (1958).

This is a wug.

Now there is another one.

There are two of them.

There are two _____.

FIGURE 1—Illustration of Berko's method for eliciting inflections.

A child is shown the small animal of Figure 1 and told: "This is a wug. Now there are two of them. There are two ———." The experimenter holds her voice up to signal the child that he is to complete the sentence; he will usually supply *wug*/-z/. For a different animal the word is *bik* and the correct plural *bik*/s/. For a third animal it is *niss* and the plural *niss*/-əz/. Printed English uses the letter "s" for all of these endings, but, as the phonemic notation shows and as attention to your own pronunciation will reveal, the endings are distinct. The rule in English is: A word ending in a voiceless consonant forms its plural with the voiceless sibilant /-s/ as in *cats, cakes,* and *lips;* a word ending in either a vowel or a voiced consonant forms its plural with the voiced sibilant /-z/ as in *dogs, crows,* and *ribs;* a word ending in the singular with either /s/ or /z/ forms its plural with /-z/ plus an interpolated neutral vowel as in *classes* and *poses.* We all follow these rules and know at once that a new word like *bazooka* will have, as its plural, *bazooka*/-z/, even though most speakers of English will never know the rule in explicit form.

Berko invented a set of materials that provides a complete inventory of the English inflectional system: the plural and possessive endings on nouns;

the simple past, the 3rd person present indicative, and the progressive on verbs; the comparative and superlative on adjectives. She presented these materials as a picture-book game to children of preschool, first-, second-, and third-grade age levels and worked out the development of the rules with age.

The productivity of the regular inflections for children seems to be greater than it is for adults. Both kinds of subjects were shown a picture of a man swinging something about his head and told: "This is a man who knows how to gling. He glings every day. Today he glings. Yesterday he ———." Adults hang suspended between *gling, glang, glung,* and even *glought* but children promptly say *glinged.* Berko also tested to see whether children who generalize the regular inflection would correctly imitate irregular forms or would assimilate them to the rules. She showed a picture and said, for instance, "Here is a goose and here are two geese. There are two ———." Most of her subjects said *gooses* and performed similarly with other irregular forms. These observations suggest that rules of great generality may survive and override a number of counter instances.

Knowledge of the paradigms of inflection could take a child beyond his corpus to the correct construction of new forms. It will not be necessary to hear each new noun in its plural and possessive forms; these can be anticipated from the regular paradigm and, except for an occasional *sheep* and *alumni,* the anticipation will be correct. The rules of inflection are rules of morphology, i.e., rules of word construction rather than rules of syntax or sentence construction. In English, though not in Russian and many other languages, inflection is a rather trivial grammatical system and knowledge of inflection cannot take a child very far beyond his corpus. There is much greater power in syntax.

A Study of Syntactic Rules

The fundamental notion in linguistic syntax is that the words of any natural language can be grouped into classes which are defined by the fact that the members of a class have similar "privileges of occurrence" in sentences. Certain very large and rough syntactic classes are traditionally called the parts-of-speech. In English, count nouns like *house, barn, table,* and *fence* are words that can be plugged into such sentence contexts as: "See the ———"; "I own a ———"; "The ——— is new"; "This ——— is mine." If a child has learned to organize words into such classes, to enter them on mental lists of syntactic equivalents, he will have a very powerful means of getting beyond his corpus.

Hearing *car* as a new word in the sentence: "See the *car*" a child could use this context as a basis for listing *car* with count nouns and so be prepared to hear and say such additional sentences as: "I own a *car*"; "The *car* is new"; "This *car* is mine." And a multitude of others. Of course the particular sentence uttered on a given occasion would depend on semantic and motivational factors, but the population of sentences from which the particular could be drawn would be established by the syntactic kinship linking *car* with *house, barn, table,* and *fence.*

What evidence do we have that a child acquires, with increasing experience of his native language, implicit rules of syntax? Brown and Berko (1960) invented a game for children that utilizes nonsense syllables but not, as in the inflection game, for the purpose of eliciting endings. For one problem the child was asked: "Do you know what a *wug* is?" He was then shown a picture of a little girl and told: "This is a little girl thinking about a *wug.* Can you make up what that might mean?" The picture was included only to engage the child's attention—it did not portray the referent of the new word but only someone thinking about it. The new word, *wug,* had been introduced in two sentences. In both cases it was preceded by the indefinite article; it functioned once as a noun complement and once as the object of a preposition. The positions of *wug* in these two contexts serve to identify it as a singular count noun. An adult speaker of English would have expected such additional sentences as: "Wugs are good" and "That wug is new" to be grammatical. Brown and Berko were interested in seeing whether young children would answer the question: "Can you make up what that might mean?" with a flow of sentences employing *wug* as a count noun.

In the complete study 12 nonsense syllables were used and they were placed in sentences identifying them as belonging to one of six parts-of-speech. Where *wug* was to be identified as a transitive verb, the investigator said: "This is a little girl who wants to wug something." As an intransitive verb the same sentence was used with the omission of *something.* With *wug* as a mass noun the little girl would be "thinking about some wug." *Wug* became an adjective by having the girl think of "something wuggy" and an adverb by having her think of "doing something wuggily."

Children in the first, second, and third grades all went on to make up sentences using their new words, but they did not always use them correctly. They did better as they got older and better at all ages with the count noun, adjective, transitive and intransitive verbs than with the mass nouns and adverbs. For the purposes of the present argument[3] the important result is that children showed an ability, increasing with age, to construct grammatically correct sentences using new words.

---

[3] The same children were given a word-association test employing familiar English words belonging to the same six parts-of-speech involved in the nonsense syllable task. The principal finding was that the frequency of paradigmatic word associations (i.e., a response word that belongs to the same part-of-speech as the stimulus word: *house-barn; run-walk; milk-water*) was related, across the various parts-of-speech and age groups, to the tendency to make correct syntactic use of the nonsense syllables. This result was taken to mean that paradigmatic word associations reflect the developing organization of vocabulary into syntactic classes.

The eliciting of speech with standard invented materials brings some very desirable control to the study of grammar acquisition. It left us, however, with the suspicion that we had only been chipping at the problem. The things we thought of doing were largely suggested by fragmentary facts about adult grammar and guesses as to what children would have to learn. If we were to collect a large number of utterances from an individual child, would it be possible to subject this collection to the kind of distributional analysis that a linguist applies to an unfamiliar language and thereby to discover the child's total generative grammar? Could one write grammar programs for children at different ages and describe language development as a sequence of progressively complicating programs?

INDUCING A GRAMMAR FROM A CORPUS

Before collecting any data, we studied English grammar in its more traditional forms (Jespersen, 1938; Smart, 1957) and also in the recent works of Francis (1958), Hockett (1958), Chomsky (1957), and Lees (1960). The traditional works supply most of the substantive knowledge about word classes—knowledge which has been reinterpreted and systematized in recent works. The substance is often more effectively taught by the earlier grammars since this is knowledge that contemporary theorists often take for granted. The generative grammar using constituent analysis and transformation rules has been worked out for a part of English, but there is not yet a complete grammar of this kind for any language.

Rules of grammar are cultural norms; like other norms they are descriptive of certain regularities of behavior within a community, and they also are prescriptive in recommending this behavior to new members of the community. In general, the student of culture can discover norms either by observing behavior and inducing regularities or by asking participants in the culture (informants) to tell him what kinds of behavior are "right" (proper, correct) and what kinds are "wrong" (improper, incorrect). For example, if we were interested in the rules of etiquette of the American middle class we might ask informants what a seated gentleman should do when a lady enters a room and what a hatted gentleman should do when a lady enters an elevator. In addition, we might observe the behavior of seated and hatted gentlemen in the two situations. When the cultural rules to be discovered are linguistic, the possible approaches are the same: direct inquiry of informants as to what it is proper to say and what it is not proper to say; direct study of what is, in fact, said. Students of grammar have varied in the degree to which they have relied on one procedure rather than another.

The partial generative grammars for adult speech that have thus far been written have been written to meet the test of the grammar writer's own delicate sense of what is and what is not a well-formed sentence in his native language. This is a special case of the technique of direct inquiry of a native informant concerning right and wrong behavior; in the present case the investigator is his own informant. Of course the linguist working out a generative grammar believes his personal judgments of the "grammaticality" of utterances represent a community consensus. The evidence so far reported for judgments made by informants who are not linguists (Hill, 1961; Maclay and Sleator, 1960) suggests that there is some consensus on grammaticality in English but that the consensus is not perfect.

While we have adopted the generative model for grammar, we have not been able to use the method of the linguists who have written generative grammars. Clearly we ought not to rely on our own sense of grammaticality in writing the grammars of very young children. In addition, however, we have not found a way to make direct inquiries of native informants between 24 and 36 months of age as to what they regard as well-formed sentences. For older children, judgments of grammaticality may possibly be elicited in terms of what it is "right" and "wrong" to say. For the younger children, we have so far worked entirely from obtained behavior: a sample or corpus of what has actually been said.

It is by no means certain that the direct study of obtained speech is an alternative and equivalent approach to the eliciting of judgments of grammaticality. Chomsky (1957) certainly does not suggest that the notion of the "well-formed" or "possible" sentence can be operationally translated into the "obtained" sentence. Common observation shows that adult speakers of English often produce verbal sequences that are not well-formed sentences. In the case of such another set of norms as the rules of etiquette, behavioral practice might depart rather radically from ideal recommendations. The truth is that the relation between grammatical norms and verbal behavior is quite unexplored both theoretically and empirically. Without waiting for clarification of this relation for adult speakers, we have proceeded to explore the possibility of writing rules for the actual verbal behavior of children. Chomsky (1957) has argued that there are no really adequate mechanical procedures for discovering an adequate grammar, and our experience causes us to agree with him. Still there are some helpful tips, and Harris (1951) is the best source of these. In addition to reading about grammars, we practiced working them out from a speech corpus long before we collected data of our own. As practice materials we used the records collected by Barker and Wright (1954) for their Midwest studies. If anyone has a taste for word games, the grammar discovery game is an engrossing one, and, not surprisingly, it yields more understanding than can be obtained from the reading of theoretical works.

We decided to begin work in the age range from 24 to 36 months. The younger age is the approximate time at which most children begin producing two-word utterances (McCarthy, 1954). Some preliminary work showed us that by 3 years many children had about as complex a grammar as we were able to describe. We located 13 children in this age range whose parents were willing to have us spend a large part of one day at their homes recording the child's speech. For the first seven cases our procedures varied from one to another, but for the last six they have been reasonably uniform.

The families were of the professional, college-educated class, and it is likely that the linguistic behavior of these children was "advanced" in terms of age norms for the American population. Only two of the 13 children were acquainted with one another and so, with the exception of these two, the speech of any one child in the sample could not have been directly affecting the speech of any other. Many of the families had first arrived in Boston just seven months earlier, and the speech of these parents had been learned in several different parts of the country.

We hoped to get as much speech as possible in as little time as possible and to have examples of the full variety of sentence types the child could produce. There were those who warned that the child would be shy and speechless in our presence; this was not the case. Mothers told their children that visitors were coming and, in general, we were eagerly welcomed, shown a parade of toys and games, and talked to rather steadily. It became clear that the child expected a guest to put in some time as a playmate, and so the recording was a two-man job with one of us taking data and the other prepared to play cowboy, horsie, blocks, coloring, trains, and the mule in "Kick the mule." Several of the early records were made by Fraser alone, but for the last six cases both of us were always there. We found that by about noon we needed a rest and so went away for lunch, returning about two; the child took his nap in the interval. About half of each record was made before lunch and about half after lunch.

Much of the time the child was occupied with his normal routine of play, talking with his mother, washing, and eating. So long as these activities involved a reasonable amount of speech, we took no active part beyond delivering signals of attention and approval. When the operant level was very low, we sometimes tried to raise it. In the first days we did the sort of verbal prompting that is anyone's first notion of a technique for eliciting speech from children. You ask what something is called and this brings out vocabulary items—which are not useful for a study of grammar. Or you ask a "yes-no" question such as: "Is that your horsie?" to which the answer is either "yes" or "no." We eventually learned that it is easier to "inspire" speech by doing something interesting than to elicit it with questions. If the adult "playmate" starts a game that is simple, repetitious, and destructive, the child will usually join him and start talking. A universal favorite is to build (painstakingly) an unsteady tower of blocks and register chagrin when the child sends it crashing down. A simple game involving implicit rules—such as the green blocks belong to me and the red ones to you—

creates a situation in which negative sentences can be elicited. If the adult playmate breaks the established rule and moves one of the child's blocks, he is usually told that he is *not* to do that.

How were the child's utterances recorded? After trying several different things, we found that it was not restrictive to ask the mother to limit activities to one floor of the house and a small number of adjoining rooms. Then with two Wollensak tape recorders and long extension cords we were able, in the last six cases, to get almost everything on tape. The machines were handled by the "playmate," and the other member of the team made a continuous transcript of the child's utterances. This on-the-spot transcript was later checked against the tape and corrected into a final best version. Going over the tape takes about four hours to each hour of recording time.

What is the level of detail in the transcription? It is neither phonetic nor phonemic but only morphemic. It is, in short, as if we were to write down in conventional English spelling what an adult seemed to be saying in an interview. Of course the intelligibility of speech in the youngest children was not very good. We found it helpful to do no writing for the first half hour and to have the mother interpret for us everything her child said in that period. In this time we learned to allow for the child's phonetic peculiarities and sometimes found an initial near-complete unintelligibility giving way to about 75 per cent intelligibilty. At grammatically crucial points our general rule was to credit the child with the regular adult contrast if he made any sort of appropriate phonetic distinction. For instance, the emergence of the modal auxiliary *will* in a sentence like *I will get my book* is not at first marked with a well articulated /wil/ but probably only with a shift of the vowel formants in the *I* toward a back vowel like /u/. If we could hear a difference between this *I* and the way *I* sounded in *I got my book*, the child was credited with *will*. For the last six cases we were ultimately able to transcribe fully an average of 78 per cent of the total utterances on the tapes; this is a degree of success quite similar to that reported in previous studies (McCarthy, 1954). Where we were uncertain about the accuracy of transcription, the material was placed in brackets. Utterances were also marked with the following symbols: I for a functional imperative; ? for an interrogative; M for an utterance that mimics an immediately preceding utterance from another person; R for an utterance that is a response to a question.

One difficulty we had anticipated did not materialize—only one. We had thought that division of the flow of speech into utterances might be an uncertain business. In fact, however, the usual criteria of either a prolonged pause or a shift of speakers worked very well. There were few instances of uncertain utterance division.

For the last six cases we aimed at and obtained a minimum of 500 different utterances from each child. Since the utterance rate of the younger children is lower than that of the older children, we spent more time with the younger ones.

Methods for Discovering a Provisional Grammar

The process of grammar discovery has two facets. It is, most immediately, the technique of the investigator who is trying to describe the grammatical apparatus of a particular child. The investigator induces from obtained utterances a probable generative mechanism. Since, however, the child is also presumed to have built this internal mechanism by processing obtained utterances, it follows that the investigator's procedure may be a good model of the child's learning. Of course the child has not induced his grammar from his own sentences but rather from the somewhat more varied and complex sentences heard from adult speakers. A comparison of the recorded speech of mother-to-child with the speech of child-to-mother shows that the grammars induced by children from adult speech are not identical with the adult grammars that produced the sentences. The investigator of a child's speech, on the other hand, hopes to find the very grammar that produced the original utterances. Even so the similarity in the tasks of investigator and child is very great—to get from sentences to a grammar—and so while acting as investigators we shall want to consider whether the child may have carried out operations similar to our own.

For the kind of grammar we are trying to write the fundamental problem is to discover the syntactic classes.[4] Members of a common class are supposed to have similar privileges of occurrence, and these privileges are supposed to be different from one class to another. In addition to syntactic classes our grammars will involve rules of combination describing the ways in which members of the various classes may be put in sequence. Generally the rules of combination will get simpler as the syntactic classes get larger and fewer. If *a* and *an* in English were words having identical privileges of occurrence, our grammar would be simpler than it is. As it stands, however, the two forms must be separated, and a rule of combination written that requires *an* before count nouns with an initial vowel and *a* before count nouns with an initial consonant.

As a basic technique for the discovery of syntactic classes we might undertake to record for each different word in the corpus all of the utterance contexts in which that word occurs; in short we might make a concordance. The contexts of each word could then be compared with the contexts of each

---

[4] The generative grammar, as Chomsky (1957) has described it, is more than a set of sequence rules for syntactic classes; it also provides several levels of appropriate constituent analysis. We have so far not accomplished this result for the speech of children because we have not been able to invent appropriate behavioral tests of the child's sense of constituent structure. The requirement that a grammar make appropriate structural analyses does of course help greatly in the evaluation of adult grammars, and it is desirable to meet this requirement wherever it is possible to do so.

TABLE I

Total Contexts of Four Words in the Record of Adam

Total Contexts of "Mum"

Here it is, Mum.	(The) pan, Mum.	Apple, Mum.
Here, Mum.	I want apple, Mum.	Again, Mum?
Here (the) coffee pot broken, Mum.	I want blanket, Mum.	Out, Mum?
	I want blanket now, Mum.	Salad, Mum?
More sugar, Mum.		See, Mum?*
There it is, Mum.	I want juice, Mum.	Coffee, Mum?
What's that, Mum.	Mum, I want some, Mum.	Turn, Mum?
Mum, (where is the cards)?	Popeye, Mum?	No, you see, Mum?
Mum, (where's the rags)?	I wanta do, Mum.	No help, Mum.
	I wanta help, Mum.	Won't help, Mum.
Want coffee, Mum.*	I found, Mum.	Coffee, Mum.
Want apple, Mum.	I do, Mum.	Hi, Mum.*
Want blanket, Mum.	I don't, Mum.	O.K., Mum.
Want more juice, Mum.	I get it, Mum.	Here, Mum.
I want blanket, Mum.	(Gonna) dump, Mum.	Over here, Mum.
I want (it), Mum.	Fall down, Mum.	Enough, Mum.
I want paper away, Mum.	Fall, Mum.	Silver spoons, Mum.
	An apple, Mum.	

Total Contexts of "Dad"

See paper, Dad.	See, Dad?*	Work, Dad?
Want coffee, Dad.*	Dad, want coffee?	Hi, Dad.*
I want cream, Dad.	Some more, Dad?	

Total Contexts of "Here"

Here (a car).	Here more bricks.	Here (we go).
Here all gone.	Here more blocks.	See the bolt here, see?
Here (block).	Here more firetruck.	That block here.
Here brick.	Here more toys.	That one here.
Here chairs.	Here more. truck.†	That one right here.
Here coffee is.	Here Mum.†	I put bucket here.
Here comes Daddy.	Here Mummy.	Come here.
Here flowers.	Here my bricks.	Do here.
Here goes.†	Here not a house.	Leave that block here.
Here is.†	Here stars.	Put it here.
Here it goes.†	Here (the) coffee pot broken, Mum.	Here not a house.
Here it is.†		Right here.†
Here it is, Mum.†	Here the card.	Over here.
Here's it here.	Here the cards.	Over here, Mum.
Here light.	Here the cheese.	Now here.
Here (mail) more paper.	Here (the) flowers.	
Here more.	Here the paper.	

Total Contexts of "There"

There goes.†	There more block.	I wanta put (it) right there . . . (under) the couch.
There (he) goes.	There more truck.	
There is.†	There more nails.	Me see (in there).
There it goes.†	There Mum.†	Blanket in there.
There it is.†	There my house.	In there.
There it is, Mum.†	There my nails.	Right there.†
There kitty.	There Noah.	

* Identifies contexts common to "Mum" and "Dad."
† Identifies contexts common to "Here" and "There."

other word and tentative syntactic classes set up so as to put together words
having many contexts in common and so as to separate words having few or
no contexts in common.

To illustrate the method of shared contexts, we have taken from the
record of Adam[5] (28½ months) the word: *here, there Mum,* and *Dad.* In
adult English *here* and *there* are locative adverbials while *Mum* and *Dad*
are animate nouns. Will the pattern of shared contexts taken from Adam's
record suggest the assignment of *here* and *there* to one class and *Mum* and
Dad to a different class? In Table 1 all of the utterances containing these
four words are listed and the shared contexts indicated. The upper limit to
the number of contexts that two words can share in a given record is set by
the number of contexts obtained for the less frequent of the two. *Here*
occurs in 48 different contexts and *there* in 19. It would be possible for the
two words to share 19 different contexts; in fact they share eight or 42 per
cent of the possible contexts. *Mum* occurs in 49 different contexts and *Dad*
in eight; they share 38 per cent of the possible contexts. *Here* shares no
contexts with *Mum* and none with *Dad,* and the same is true for *there.* The
pattern of shared contexts suggests the class break that operates in adult
English.

If one has read about the notion of syntactic equivalence but never
actually lined up the contexts for sets of words, it is startling to find such
small numbers of identical contexts; especially startling since *here-there* and
Mum-Dad must be as near to perfect syntactic equivalence as any pairs of
words in the language and, in addition, the short sentences and small
vocabulary of a child maximize the probability of repetition. Is a 38 per cent
overlap enough for us to assume that the members of a pair are interchangeable? It may be.

We have taken the word *here* alone and set down all its different contexts in the first half of Adam's record and also all of its different contexts
in the second half of the record (Table 2). A context that has already appeared in the first half is listed again on its first appearance in the second
half. *Here* in the first half is the same word as *here* in the second half, and
so we know that these two *heres* are syntactic equivalents. In the first half
the word occurs in 33 different contexts; in the second half in 19. There are
four shared contexts or 21 per cent of the possible—a lower value than the
value obtained for *here-there* and *Mum-Dad.*

Perhaps it would be possible to set an exact percentage-of-shared-contexts
criterion for the assignment of two words to the same class, the criterion to
be empirically determined from percentages of shared contexts of identical
words at various levels of absolute and relative frequency in two time
periods. Clearly, the obtained percentages will be very unstable for small
numbers of occurrences. For less frequent words only a mammoth speech
sample would serve and the whole thing becomes a job for a machine. The

---

[5] The names used in this report for identifying child subjects are not the actual names
of the children who were studied.

TABLE 2

Contexts of "Here" in the First and Second Halves of the Record of Adam

First Half

Here all gone.	Here more.*	Here the cheese.
Here (block).	Here more bricks.	Here the paper.
Here brick.	Here more firetruck.	That block here.
Here chairs.	Here more toys.	That one here.
Here coffee is.	Here more truck.	That one right here.
Here comes Daddy.	Here Mum.	Come here.
Here is.*	Here my bricks.	Leave that block here.
Here it goes.*	Here not a house.	(Put it) here.
Here it is, Mum.	Here (the) coffee pot	Here not a house.
Here light.	broken, Mum.	Over here.*
Here (mail) more paper.	Here the card.	
Right here.	Here the cards.	

Second Half

Here (a car)	Here's it here.	In here?
Here flowers.	Here more.*	(Over here)?
Here goes.	Here more blocks.	Over here, Mum.
Here is.*	Here Mummy.	Over here.*
Here it goes.*	Here stars.	Now here.
Here it is.	Here (the) flowers.	
Here (we go).	See the bolt here, see.	

* Identifies contexts common to first and second halves of record.

basic problem of setting a criterion for that machine to use or of writing the program for working out a criterion may also be a problem in the child's learning of syntax.

Once the classes have been established by some shared-contexts criterion, some contexts will turn out to be more "criterial" or distinctive for a given class than will others. After *the* in English one can have count nouns in the singular, count nouns in the plural, and mass nouns (which are used in the singular only). After *a* one can have only count nouns in the singular, and so this context is, for singular count nouns, the more criterial of the two. The introduction of new words to a child in highly criterial "tracer" contexts (like "Hi ———" for personal names) should be the best guarantee of subsequent correct usage.

A corpus of 500 utterances is not large enough to take us very far with a mechanical shared-contexts procedure. However, a generally adequate mechanical procedure for the discovery of grammars has not been worked out in any case. Grammar writing is for the present like theory writing in science, an undertaking for which there are some guides, clues, and models but not a set of guaranteed procedures. Let us therefore take one record, the utterances of Eve (25½ months) and, allowing ourselves a very free use of inductive reasoning, see what we can make of it.

It is a useful first step to restrict ourselves to the simplest utterances in the record, those of just two words, and, among these, the utterances in which the initial word occurs at least twice. In Table 3 the recurrent initial

TABLE 3

Two-Word Utterances with Recurrent Initial Words from Eve

Second Word	A	Daddy	Mummy	's	See	That	The	There	Two
bear		+	+						
bird				+		+	+	+	
block	+								
boat						+		+	
Bobby									+
book	+	+				+	+	+	
bowl						+			
boy					+	+		+	
broken						+			
candle	+								
car						+			
carriage							+		
chair								+	+
cricket	+								
cookie						+			
cow						+			
Daddy				+		+		+	
dimple			+						
dirty						+			
do			+						
dog	+								
doggie						+			
doll								+	
dollie								+	
Dru								+	
eye					+				
fall	+								
fuzzy						+			
Gale									+
girl							+		
go			+					+	
goes								+	
going						+			
honey		+							
horsie						+	+		
is								+	
kitty	+					+	+	+	
man								+	
meatball	+								
men									+
mike							+		
Mummy					+	+		+	
nurse	+								
pea								+	

(Table continued on next page)

TABLE 3 (*continued*)

Two-Word Utterances with Recurrent Initial Words from Eve

Second Word	I N I T I A L W o R D s								
	A	Daddy	Mummy	's	See	That	The	There	Two
peas							+		
Peter						+			
picture			+						
pillow	+								
potty								+	
pretty						+			
puff		+				+			
puppy							+		
radio					+			+	
Rayma							+		
reel	+						+	+	+
rocker					+	+			
rug							+		
sun						+			
that					+				
'tis								+	
whistle							+		
wire						+			

NOTE.—"+" indicates that utterances of this type occurred.

words are listed at the heads of columns, and each row represents a second word that occurs in at least one utterance after one of the recurrent first words. The second word is given a + in a column if it occurs after the word that heads the column, and so a filled square represents an obtained two-word utterance defined by the column and row headings.

Table 3 is simply a technique for making a first inquiry into shared contexts, an inquiry limited to the most frequently repeated and so most informative contexts. By comparing the filled slots for any two rows, one can determine the number of shared contexts for two second words. By comparing the filled slots for any two columns one can determine the number of shared contexts for two initial words.

Table 3 is itself a descriptive grammar for an obtained set of two-word sentences. The table is a description that is only very slightly more economical than actual listing of the sentences; the single slight economy is accomplished by writing the recurrent first words just once instead of repeating them on each appearance. The descriptive grammar of Table 3 can easily be turned into a generative grammar. Table 4 presents the generative version. It reads: "In order to form an utterance: select first one of the initial words; select, secondly, one from the class of words that are permitted to follow the initial you have chosen." A machine that can go through this program would produce all-and-only the obtained set of utterances.

TABLE 4

A Grammar Describing All and Only the 89 Utterances Obtained

$$
\text{Utterance} \rightarrow
\left\{
\begin{array}{lcl}
A & + & C_1 \\
Daddy & + & C_2 \\
Mummy & + & C_3 \\
\text{'}s & + & C_4 \\
See & + & C_5 \\
That & + & C_6 \\
The & + & C_7 \\
There & + & C_8 \\
Two & + & C_9
\end{array}
\right\}
$$

$C_1 \rightarrow$ *block, book, candle, cricket, dog, fall, kitty, meatball, nurse, pillow, reel*

$C_2 \rightarrow$ *bear, book, honey*

$C_3 \rightarrow$ *bear, dimple, do, go, puff*

$C_4 \rightarrow$ *bird, Daddy, picture*

$C_5 \rightarrow$ *boy, eye, Mummy, radio, rocker, that*

$C_6 \rightarrow$ *bird, boat, book, bowl, boy, broken, car, cookie, cow, Daddy, dirty, doggie, fuzzy, going, horsie, kitty, Mummy, Peter, pretty, puff, Rayma, rocker, sun, wire*

$C_7 \rightarrow$ *bird, book, girl, horsie, kitty, mike, peas, puppy, reel, rug, whistle*

$C_8 \rightarrow$ *bird, boat, book, boy, carriage, chair, Daddy, doll, dollie, Dru, go, goes, is, kitty, man, Mummy, pea, potty, radio, reel, 'tis*

$C_9 \rightarrow$ *Bobby, chair, Gale, men, reel*

NOTE.—{ } means a choice of one of the contained sequences.

Table 3 constitutes a list of different utterances: each is listed just once. In the original record the utterances varied in their frequency of repetition. One could write a generative grammar that would do a better job of mimicking the original record by setting probabilities at the various choice-points: the route "That-broken," for instance, ought to be taken more often than the route "That-Rayma." A printed record turned out by this machine would be indistinguishable from actual obtained records, indistinguishable as a list of sentences but perfectly distinguishable in the life situation for the reason that the machine described takes no account of semantics. It is quite capable of greeting the appearance of Daddy with "That doggie" or "That cookie." We have a grammar machine, not a machine that is a complete model for human sentence production.

Now we want to go beyond the obtained sentences to the syntactic classes they suggest. Is there any ground for considering all of the initial words to be members of a single class? Consider first the possibility of a shared-contexts criterion, of the type discussed, with reference to *here-there* and *Mum-Dad*.

The previous discussion was greatly simplified by restricting the problem to single pairs of words. However, the number of candidates for membership in a common syntactic class is generally greater than two, and that is the case with the initial words of Table 3. Each single word that is a candidate for inclusion can be compared for shared-contexts with each other word in the presumptive class. The criteria for class identification must then prescribe minimal levels of overlap for the full set. This is a complicated problem for which many different solutions can be imagined.

In the present case the words *that* and *there* are the most frequent in the set. They share seven second word (*bird, boat, book, Daddy, kitty,* and *Mummy*) which is 33 per cent of the number of contexts that could be shared. Of the other words in the set *'s, see, the, a, Mummy,* and *Daddy* all share at least one context with both *that* and *there*, while *two* shares with *there* but not *that*. One might use the syntactically close pair *that* and *there* as touchstones and count as members any words that share at least one context with either critical word. That rule would put all of the initial words into the same syntactic class (class 1).

What evidence is there that the entries in the rows of Table 3 constitute a second syntactic class? The words *bird, book, kitty,* and *reel* are most frequent. Since the contexts are the words of class 1, and so are few, these frequent words have a high degree of mutual overlap. Using the four as touchstones, most of the words entered in rows could be entered in class 2 on the criterion of having at least one context in common with one of the touchstones. A few, such as *dimple* and *do,* would be left out. Most of the words in class 2 are count nouns, and if we had a larger corpus, we should probably find that *dimple* belongs here for Eve while *do* does not. Our criterion is probably not good enough to separate out just the few words that do not fit.

The members of a syntactic class are credited with identical privileges of occurrence. In Table 3, the initial words are far from having identical patterns of actual occurrence, and the second words are also far from this pattern. If the actual occurrences were identical in either set, then the assignment to a common class might be confidently made, but the assignment would not take us beyond what we have obtained. If we do go beyond what has been obtained in our description of privileges of occurrence, then, of course, we will not have "proved" our description. This is the familiar problem of the impossibility of proving a generalization that goes beyond what has been examined—the very sort of generalization that is most valuable and which the human mind is most bent on making. We are, in the setting up of syntactic classes, trying to move from a partial similarity of actual occurrence to an identity of potential occurrence. This is the process of induction—uncertain but powerful.

To hold that the members of each of our present classes have identical privileges of occurrence is to hold that all the empty positions in Table 3

may properly be filled—they are utterances we should expect to hear from
Eve. The generative grammar changes to the form of Table 5. This grammar will turn out more sentences than Table 4, and it ought to be very
much easier to remember since the sequential contingencies are greatly
simplified.

TABLE 5

A Grammar that Results from Filling In the Blanks in Table 3

Utterance $\rightarrow$ $C_1 + C_2$

$C_1 \rightarrow$ *A, Daddy, Mummy, 's, See, That, The, There, Two*

$C_2 \rightarrow$ *bear, bird, block, boat, Bobby, book, bowl, boy, broken, candle, car, carriage,*
        chair, cricket, cookie, cow, Daddy, dimple, dirty, do, dog, doggie, doll, dollie,
        Dru, eye, fall, fuzzy, Gale, girl, go, goes, going, honey, horsie, is, kitty, man,
        meatball, men, mike, Mummy, nurse, pea, peas, Peter, picture, pillow, potty,
        pretty, puff, puppy, radio, Rayma, reel, rocker, rug, sun, that, 'tis, whistle, wire

NOTE.—This grammar predicts the 89 utterances obtained plus 469 others.

The utterances of Table 4 and Table 5, since they are two-word utterances, can very well be thought of as a set of paired associates. It is usually
the case in paired-associate learning that initial words and second words
occur always and only in their pair relation. In the present case some initial
words and some second words occur in a variety of combinations. If these
utterances were to be made up as experimental materials, what task could
we set the subject? If he were simply asked to respond to each initial word
with some one of the acceptable second words, then he could meet the
requirements by learning single associates. Suppose, however, he is required
to do what the grammar does—respond to each initial word with all acceptable second words. There could be two sets of materials: one made up on
the model of Table 4 with only the obtained secondaries occurring and one
on the model of Table 5 with any member of class 2 likely to occur after
any initial word. I think we can foresee that for the first set of materials
it would take a long time to learn the exact set of words that can go after
each initial word. With the second set it should not take very long to learn
the principle that any second word can follow any initial word, but it would
take some time to memorize all of the second words. But after how many
pairs, of what kinds, will subjects move to the generalization of Table 5?
We think it would be interesting to try paired-associate learning of this kind.

Refinements on the provisional grammar. Turning to utterances of three
or more words, we find evidence to indicate that not all of the members of
class 1 have identical privileges. Consider first the words *the* and *a*.
Table 7a presents a set of utterances in which *the* or *a* occurs after members
of class 1 and before members of class 2. However, *the* and *a* do not occur

after all members of class 1; they do not occur after *the, a, Mummy,* or *Daddy.* There are no utterances like "The the doggie" or "The a horsie." These facts suggest that *the* and *a* should be withdrawn from class 1 and set up as a new class 3. The grammar would then be rewritten as in Table 6a.

TABLE 6

Grammars Suggested by Three-Word Utterances

a. Eve's Grammar with the Articles Separated Out

$$\text{Utterance} \rightarrow (C_1) + (C_3) + C_2$$

$C_1 \rightarrow$ *Daddy, Mummy, 's, See, That, There, Two*
$C_2 \rightarrow$ *bear, bird, block, boat,* etc.
$C_3 \rightarrow$ *a, the*

b. Eve's Grammar Allowing for Possessives

$$\text{Utterance} \rightarrow (C_1) + (C_3) + C_2$$

$C_1 \rightarrow$ *'s, See, That, There, Two*
$C_2 \rightarrow$ *bear, bird, block, boat,* etc.
$C_3 \rightarrow$ *a, the,* plus human terms

NOTE.—( ) means that selection of the enclosed is optional.

The optional markings in Table 6a indicate that a class can be completely bypassed. It is necessary to make class 3 optional so as to get sentences like "That bird" and "There boat." Making class 1 optional makes it possible to obtain "The boat," "A book," and the like. If neither optional class is bypassed we get such utterances as "That the cup" and "See the reel." If both optional classes are bypassed, we get such one-word utterances as "Dolly," "Book," "Reel," and utterances of this kind were very numerous in Eve's record. We cannot get from this grammar such utterances as "The the horsie," "The that bird," "A see that" and other radically un-English sequences.

The grammar of Table 6a does turn out some kinds of utterance for which Eve's record provides no models. It is possible, for instance, to obtain "Two the bear" or "Two a bird." Eve produced nothing like these, and for adults they are definitely ungrammatical. It is quite likely that *two* should go with *the* and *a* in class 3 so as to yield: "That two bear" and "See the bird." However, Eve's record gives us no utterances like these, and indeed no three-word utterances including *two,* and so we may as well leave *two* in class 1. We have identified a point at which more evidence is needed in order to choose between formulations.

There is another sort of utterance that the grammar of Table 6a will produce for which Eve's record provides no model: "Mummy the bird" or "Daddy a book." These sentences do not use *Mummy* and *Daddy* in the vocative; the vocative would involve a distinctive juncture (pause) and intonation which is suggested in print by a comma (e.g., "Mummy, the

TABLE 7

Three-Word Utterances that Refine the Original Grammar

a. Utterances with *the* or *a* in Middle Position

's a man	See the horsie	That the bowl
's a house	See the radio	That the cup
's a Daddy	See the reel	That a horsie
There the kitty	See a boat	

b. Utterances with Human Terms in Middle Position

See Evie car	That Daddy car	That Evie dish
See baby eyebrow	That Daddy honey	That Evie pillow
That Mummy book	That man car	That Evie spoon
That Mummy paper	That baby bed	There Evie car
That Mummy hair	That Evie book	There man coat
That Mummy spoon		

bird"). An adult might form the vocative version as a kind of ellipsis of "Mummy, see the bird," but he would not form the nonvocative utterance that the grammar of Table 6a produces.

Thus far, *Mummy* and *Daddy* are in the same limbo as *two;* there is reason for withdrawing them from class 1, but we do not yet know where to put them. Eve's record provides no three-word utterances with *two*, but it does provide such utterances with *Mummy* and *Daddy* and these are listed as Table 7b. We find *Mummy* and *Daddy* in middle position between *that* (a class 1 word) and the class 2 words: *book, hair, paper, spoon, car,* and *honey*. Furthermore, we find in this same position the words: *Evie, man,* and *baby*. All of these middle-position words are names of human beings, and so we may hypothesize that such terms constitute a syntactic class.

The difficulty now is that the middle position between class 1 and class 2 already belongs to class 3 which is composed of *the* and *a*. This means that there are three clear options: (a) to include the human terms with *the* and *a* in class 3; (b) to set up the human terms as a separate class 4 and put this class in the selection sequence ahead of class 3; (c) to put the independent class 4 in sequence after class 3. Here now are examples of utterances that are predicted by the three versions of the grammar: (a) "That Mummy book"; (b) "That Mummy the book"; (c) "That the

Mummy book." Our interim decision is fairly clear. Since the record provides instances of (a) but not of either (b) or (c), we will put the human terms in class 3 with *the* and *a* as indicated in Table 6b. However, if a larger corpus were drawn, we would have to be on the alert to correct this decision.

It may be worthwhile to consider the very complicated rules required for adult English at an analogous grammatical point. Utterances like "Mummy book" and "Man car" and "Evie dish" are, we know from the situational contexts, Eve's version of the possessive; she omits the inflection. In forming possessives with human terms, the adult speaker will use an article before such generic human terms as *man* ("the man's car"), and so these terms cannot be classified as alternatives to *the* and *a*. With personal names like *Evie* the adult will form possessives but, with personal names, articles are never used, and so we will say "Evie's dish" but neither "The Evie's dish" nor "Evie's the dish." This means that personal names cannot be classified as alternatives to either the articles or the generic human terms. A final exasperating fillip is provided by the fact that some morphemes, like *Mummy* and *Daddy*, can serve either as personal names ("Mother's purse") or as generic terms ("the mother's role") and so would have to be listed in two syntactic classes.

Even the simple grammar we have now produced for Eve involves double syntactic listing for some forms—the human terms. They must be in class 3 because of such utterances as "That Mummy book," but they must also remain in class 2 because of such utterances as "That Mummy." The combinational formula predicts "That Mummy Mummy" (Grandmummy?) which is reasonably probable but also "That Evie Evie" which would not

TABLE 8

Utterances with Recurrent Second Members

Initial Word	S E C O N D		W O R D	
Baby				tired
Bird*	all gone			
Carriage*		broken		
Chair*		broken	fall down	
Doggy*				tired
Dollie*		broken	fall down	
Eyebrow	all gone			
Kitty*	all gone		fall down	
Microphone	all gone			
Mummy*				tired
Reel*	all gone			
Rocker*		broken		
Something		broken		

* A word already identified as a member of C_2.

be produced by an adult. As to whether Eve would say it, we cannot tell from the present materials.

Expansion of Eve's grammar. Recurrence of a context is always what is needed for the identification of a syntactic class. We started with recurrence of initial members, but recurrence at the end of an utterance can be equally useful. In Eve's record there is a set of terminal recurrences (*all gone, broken, fall down, tired*) which appears in Table 8. The first thing to note is that most of the initial members of these utterances have already been identified as members of class 2. Their appearance here with overlapping privileges of occurrence before *all gone, broken, fall down*, and *tired* is a valuable confirmation of the preliminary analysis.

Since the initial terms are already regarded as one class, we are inclined to assume that they have identical privileges of occurrence which means that empty cells could be filled. This makes a new class 4 of *all gone, broken, fall down*, and *tired*, and we now have a second type of sentence. The full grammar (Table 9a) involves two major routes corresponding to the two kinds of sentences.

There is a slight addition to be made to the grammar of Table 9a. The addition is suggested by three sentences: "The chair broken"; "The baby tired"; and "The book fall down." The initial word *the* has already been placed in class 3, and so it is a good guess that any word from class 3 can appear in first position in this new sentence type, and Table 9b presents this version. Class 3 must be entered as optional in the grammar since most of the obtained sentences omit it. It is not certain that our analysis of the limited materials in Table 8 is correct. The word *tired*, for example, does not actually overlap in the obtained distribution with any of the other second members. Our analysis, relying on the prior identification of the first members as class 2, assumes that the overlap would occur if more sentences were gathered. However, it should be noted that *tired* occurs only after names of animate beings—*baby, doggy, Mummy*—whereas the other second members are not restricted in this way. This is a fragment of evidence pointing to the eventual separation of animate nouns from the general syntactic class of nominal expressions. This separation is a necessity for adult grammar; certain verbs can only take animate nouns as objects. We can say: "It surprised John" or "It surprised the dog" but not: "It surprised the chair." In our discussion of the possessive we considered the possibility of separating out a class of generic human terms. The distributional facts of adult English will show that this class has to be broadened into animate nouns (we can have "the dog's house" as well as "the man's car") and is the same class hinted at by the restrictions on *tired*. However, Eve's utterances are so few that we cannot be sure these restrictions would be maintained.

The reciprocal of *tired* in Table 8 is *broken*, for *broken* only occurs after inanimate nouns—*carriage, chair, dolly, rocker, something*. In adult English *broken* would be restricted in this way, but we cannot be sure that it will continue so for Eve. *All gone* is interesting because Eve uses this form where an adult speaker would not—after count nouns. We would not say "The microphone is all gone" or "A kitty is all gone." For us *all gone* goes after plural count nouns ("The microphones are all gone") or mass nouns ("The sand is all gone"). Eve does not give us any plural count nouns in this record and does not make a syntactic distinction between mass and count nouns, and she uses *all gone* without any discoverable restrictions.

TABLE 9

Grammars Suggested by the Terminal Recurrence of Table 8

---

a. Eve's Grammar with Two Basic Sentence-Types

$$\text{Utterance} \rightarrow \left\{ \begin{array}{c} (C_1) + (C_3) + C_2 \\ C_2 + C_4 \end{array} \right\}$$

$C_1 \rightarrow$ *'s, See, That, There, Two*
$C_2 \rightarrow$ *bear, bird, block, boat,* etc.
$C_3 \rightarrow$ *a, the,* plus human terms
$C_4 \rightarrow$ *all gone, broken, fall down, tired*

b. Eve's Grammar with Articles Added to the New Sentence-Type

$$\text{Utterance} \rightarrow \left\{ \begin{array}{c} (C_1) + (C_3) + C_2 \\ (C_3) + (C_2) + C_4 \end{array} \right\}$$

$C_1 \rightarrow$ *'s, See, That, There, Two*
$C_2 \rightarrow$ *bear, bird, block, boat,* etc.
$C_3 \rightarrow$ *a, the,* plus human terms
$C_4 \rightarrow$ *all gone, broken, fall down, tired*

NOTE.— { } means a choice of one of the contained sequences.

The grammar of Table 9b does not represent the distributional distinctions among the class 4 members for the reason that we have so very little evidence on this point. Still, as we shall see in the next section, there are reasons for preferring to represent the distinctions rather than to assume identical privileges. If we were forced to freeze the grammar on the present evidence, it would probably be better to write the more differentiated version.

The sentences we have been discussing all begin with a class 2 word (*bird, book,* etc.) with a prior class 3 (*the, a,* etc.) being optional. There are many other sentences answering this description in Eve's record, but they do not have the recurrence of second members that made the sentences in Table 8 useful. These additional sentences are all unique and they vary in length: "Daddy fix it"; "Eve listen to tick-tock"; "The reel go round and round"; etc. The best thing to do with these sentences, at present, is to make a cut after the class 2 words (*Daddy, Eve, reel*) and call all of the remainder second members. These second members are, from the point of view of adult English, complex predicates. With our present inadequate materials we can only add them to *all gone, broken, fall down,* and *tired* as additional members of class 4. There is not enough material for a finer breakdown. The fact that some of these complex predicates contain class 2 words and some do not hints at an eventual distinction between transitive and intransitive verbs.

TABLE 10

Utterances of Previously Identified Types with Interrogative Intonation Added

---

Utterances that Have Occurred in Declarative Form*

's Daddy,	Book?
That daddy?	Doggie?

Utterances that Have Been Predicted in Declarative Form but Have Not Occurred

Daddy fix this?	See baby eyebrow?
Daddy work?	See baby horsie?
's a Daddy?	See cow?
's cow?	That block?
's Mummy?	That Evie spoon?
	Daddy?

---

* Utterances that have occurred without rising interrogative intonation.

There remains a collection of utterances belonging to types already identified but modified by the addition of a rising interrogative intonation (?), and these appear in Table 10. Since instances of both kinds of utterances allowed by our grammar occur with the interrogative intonation, it seems reasonable to suppose that any sentence allowed by that grammar can be so modified. The result is the revised formula of Table 11 which at one swoop doubles the number of sentences the grammar can generate. Table 11 is the complete version of our provisional grammar.

There are several things worth noting about the grammar of Table 11. It will produce most of the 500 utterances actually obtained from Eve and will produce many thousands beyond the obtained. The only classes that are not optional in the grammar are the reference-making words of class 2 (*bear, bird,* etc.) and class 3 (*all gone, broken,* etc.). These are, by our observation, the forms that are used as single-word "mands" and "tacts" (Skinner, 1957) for some time before the two-word utterance begins.

The generative grammar written out as a formula suggests a distinction between lexical meanings and structural or syntactic meanings. The class

TABLE II

Complete Provisional Grammar for Eve

$$\text{Utterance} \rightarrow \left\{ \begin{array}{l} (C_1) + (C_3) + C_2 \\ (C_3) + (C_2) + C_4 \end{array} \right\} \ (?)$$

$C_1 \rightarrow$'s, See, That, There, Two

$C_2 \rightarrow$ bear, bird, block, boat, etc.

$C_3 \rightarrow$ a, the, plus human terms

$C_4 \rightarrow$ all gone, broken, fall down, tired, fix it, listen to tick-tock, etc.

listings are the lexicon, and an utterance involves a shift of lexical meaning whenever there is a change in the selection within a class (e.g., from "That bird" to "That bear"). Structural meanings may perhaps be defined as those that shift whenever there is a change in the selections within the formula. Thus if we shift from the first major sentence route to the second, there seems to be a shift from demonstrative naming ("There bird" or "See boat") to predication ("Bird all gone" or "Bear fall down"). If we shift from not selecting ? to selecting it, we shift from a declaration to an interrogation. It is more difficult to say what the changes of meaning could be that go with selecting or not selecting the various optional classes.

Testing the Adequacy of a Grammar

In our discussion of techniques for the discovery of a grammar we have repeatedly pointed to the existence of equally reasonable alternative decisions. The arbitrariness of choice could be somewhat reduced by taking a larger corpus. However, we are sure that the best-founded grammar will not be uniquely determined but will only be a good provisional try. The same thing is surely true for the rules a child induces from adult speech; they will be hypotheses about the form of future speech events. Is there any way to check such hypotheses?

Very roughly the test of a grammar must be the same as the test of any theory of empirical events—the ability to make correct predictions. In the present case this means the ability to anticipate sentences that have not entered into the construction of the grammar. One might, for example, have tested our grammar for Eve by taking a second large collection of utterances on the following day or days and seeing how many of those that occur were predicted.

Three different kinds of successful prediction may be distinguished. There is, in the first place, occurrence of an utterance that has already occurred in the corpus from which the grammar was induced. This sort of occurrence does not help to validate the grammar as a set of generalizations that go beyond the data; the occurrence of a familiar sentence could have been predicted from a simple list of sentences in the original corpus. There is, in the second place, the occurrence of an utterance not included in the original corpus but allowed for by the generalized rules. For example, Eve's record did not include the sentence "There horsie" though it did include "That horsie" and "The horsie." By adopting the general rule that any class 2 word can follow any class 1 word, the utterance "There horsie" is predicted. If it occurs, that fact would increase our confidence in the generalization.

Suppose that, in a second corpus collected from Eve, we obtained the utterance "That lion." The word *lion* did not occur in the original corpus, and so the utterance was not predicted. It is not to be expected that a speech sample of only 500 utterances would exhaust a lexicon, and it would be unreasonable to permit incompleteness of lexicon to discredit a grammar. It would be better to say that an utterance does not come within the province of a grammar unless all of its words are included in the lexicon of the grammar—the lexicon being the lists of forms belonging to each syntactic class. Therefore, the sentence "That lion" counts neither for nor against the grammar. However, the occurrence of this sentence enables us to add *lion* to the class 2 list since the criterion for inclusion is occurrence after a class 1 word and *that* is such a word. Subsequent utterances such as "There lion" and "The lion" could be counted as evidence for the grammar since they are predicted once *lion* has been added to the lexicon.

We cannot think of any way to set a definite criterion as to the number of sentences, out of a collection of obtained sentences, that must be predicted for a grammar to be judged acceptable. It is clear, however, that the number of successful predictions can be increased by simply writing the grammar in the most general terms possible. We found, you recall, that the forms *all gone, broken, fall down,* and *tired* all occurred after class 2 words (Table 8). Looking more closely at Table 8, we found that the word *broken* occurred only after the names of inanimate things and *tired* only after the names of animate things. This fraction of the grammar could have been written in either of the two forms presented in Table 12. The less general form predicts 39 utterances, and the more general predicts these 39 plus 13 others. The more general will make all of the successful predictions made by the less general and has the possibility of making some that the less general cannot make. The way to write a "successful" grammar, if "success" is simply measured by the prediction of obtained events, is to write a grammar that predicts every conceivable sequence of obtained forms.

The job of a grammar, however, is to predict sentences that are possible while *not predicting sentences that are impossible.* This second part of the job gives an additional criterion of evaluation that will prevent us from always preferring the most general grammar. That grammar is to be preferred which predicts what occurs while predicting as little as possible that

TABLE 12

Alternative Forms for a Fragment of Eve's Grammar

a. The More General Form

Utterance $\rightarrow$ $C_2 + C_4$

$C_2 \rightarrow$ *baby, bird, carriage, chair, doggie, dollie, eyebrow, kitty, microphone, Mummy, reel, rocker, something*

$C_4 \rightarrow$ *all gone, broken, fall down, tired*

b. The More Restrictive Form

$$\text{Utterance} \rightarrow \left\{ \begin{array}{ll} C_2 & + C_5 \\ C_{2\,an.} & + \textit{tired} \\ C_{2\,inan.} & + \textit{broken} \end{array} \right\}$$

$C_2 \rightarrow$ *baby, bird, carriage, chair, doggie, dollie, eyebrow, kitty, microphone, Mummy, reel, rocker, something*

$C_{2\,an.} \rightarrow$ *baby, bird, doggie, dollie, kitty, mummy*

$C_{2\,inan.} \rightarrow$ *carriage, chair, eyebrow, microphone, reel, rocker, something*

$C_5 \rightarrow$ *all gone, fall down*

does not occur. Therefore, the less general grammar will be better than the more general if it is equally successful in predicting what happens. A grammar should stay as close to the obtained materials as is consistent with generalizing beyond the obtained materials so as to predict future events. Only by invoking both criteria can we hope to obtain distinct grammars representing a developmental sequence. Our next step in this research program will be an empirical and logical study of techniques for evaluating grammars in terms of their predictive powers. (See Brown, Fraser, and Bellugi.)

In sum, the most that we are now able to conceive by way of grammar-evaluating techniques is a set of rough criteria for preferring one version to another. This problem of evaluation probably exists in implicit form for the child learning to speak. How does he judge the adequacy of his inductions? He can see how well they anticipate what others say. He can construct new utterances and see whether others appear to find them acceptable and comprehensible. He can ask direct metalinguistic questions: "Mother, can one say 'The carriage is tired'?"

CHILD GRAMMAR AS A REDUCTION OF ADULT GRAMMAR

The provisional grammar we have written for Eve is not a grammar of adult English. Most of the utterances it generates are not, for us, grammatical sentences. We cannot accept "That horsie" or "Kitty all gone" or "There Mummy hair" or "Two chair." Words that seem to be syntactically equivalent for Eve are not so for us. For example, the words *see* and *that* are members of class 1 for Eve and equivalent in that they can precede class 2 words such as *doggie, dollie,* etc. For the adult who might say "That is a doggie" and "I see a doggie," *that* and *see* are syntactically unlike. For Eve the word *two* is roughly equivalent to *the* and *a,* but that is because she does not pluralize count nouns. It is clear that Eve does not speak adult English, and so we cannot use an adult English grammar to describe her speech. It would be quite misleading to list Eve's *that* as a demonstrative pronoun and her *see* as a transitive verb though that is a correct classification of these words in adult English.

Since the speech of the younger children in our set of 13 is clearly not English, it is necessary to "discover" the grammar that is implied by their utterances. We have not in this first try collected large enough corpuses to write convincing grammars. However, for the younger children it does look as if we might manage with about 1500 different utterances to get a good provisional grammar. The prospect of "discovering" grammars for the older children is not nearly so good. Since the older children have larger vocabularies and longer utterances, there is less of the recurrence that is the basis of a structural analysis. The anthropological linguist who wants to describe adult usage in an unfamiliar language is likely to try something like 1,000 hours of speech, and there are times when we fear that not very much less than this would suffice for children of about 3 years.

The speech of the children in our collection who are nearly 3 years old is mostly English. They produce acceptable simple sentences. Furthermore, these simple sentences correspond very well with the set of English sentences for which a satisfactory generative grammar has been written by Chomsky (1957) and Lees (1960). For these records, then, it does not seem necessary to "discover" the grammar; it is quite reasonable to analyze them in terms of the syntactic categories of the adult grammar. We have done this job, classifying utterances under headings: copular sentences, transitive verb sentences, intransitive verb sentences, sentences with modal auxiliaries, sentences with progressives, sentences with preliminary verbs, imperatives, negatives, Wh-interrogatives, Yes-No interrogatives, and unclassifiable fragments.

When this analysis in terms of an adult grammar had been done for the most advanced records, we realized that it could, with some additional assumptions, be extended to the records of all the other children. For the striking fact about the utterances of the younger children, when they are approached from the vantage point of adult grammar, is that they are almost all classifiable as grammatical sentences from which certain morphemes have been omitted. You may have noticed that while Eve's sentences are not grammatically "complete" they are somehow intelligible as abbreviated or telegraphic versions of familiar constructions. "Mummy hair" and "Daddy car" seem only to omit the possessive inflection. Both "Chair broken" and "That horsie" become acceptable copular sentences if we leave the word-order intact and fill in *is* and *a* or *the*. We have, therefore, analyzed all of the records in terms of English simple sentences by assigning each utterance to the sentence-type it most closely approximates.

We have not yet hit on any good techniques for summarizing our compendious data, but one illustrative table (Table 13) will make a few im-

TABLE 13

Estimates of Mean Utterance Length and Reports on Selected Grammatical Forms for 13 Children

Name of Child	Age in Months	Mean Number Morphemes*	Be in Progressive	Modal Auxiliaries will or can
Andy	26	2.0	no	no
Betty	31½	2.1	no	no
Charlie	22	2.2	no	no
Adam	28½	2.5	no	no
Eve	25½	2.6	no	no
Fanny	31½	3.2	yes	no
Grace	27	3.5	yes	yes
Helen	30	3.6	yes	yes
Ian	31½	3.8	yes	yes
June	35½	4.5	yes	yes
Kathy	30½	4.8	yes	yes
Larry	35½	4.8	yes	yes
Jimmy	32	4.9	yes	yes

* Mean count from 100 consecutive utterances.

portant points. For each child we made an estimate of the mean length of utterances by counting morphemes from 100 consecutive utterances occurring in midmorning. From this count we thought it wise to omit the single-word rejoinders and exclamations: *No, Ok, Yeah,* and *Oh* since these are sometimes emitted many times in succession by speakers of any age, and if the small utterance sample happened to include such a repeating circuit the estimate would be very unrepresentative. The estimates appear in Table 13, and the children's names appear in an order of increasing average utterance length. This order is related to the chronological age order but not identical with it. An age-related increase in the mean length of utterances is, of course, one of the best established facts in the study of child speech (McCarthy, 1954). There is, however, no reason to expect perfect correspondence with age. We conceive of developmental sequence as a Guttman scale with performances following an invariant order but not

TABLE 14

Imitations of Spoken Sentences

Model Sentence	Eve, 25½	Adam, 28½	Helen, 30	Ian, 31½	Jimmy, 32	June, 35½
1. I showed you the book.	I show book.	(I show) book.	C	I show you the book.	C	Show you the book.
2. I am very very tall.	(My) tall.	I (very) tall.	I very tall.	I'm very tall.	Very tall.	I very tall.
3. It goes in a big box.	Big box.	Big box.	In big box.	It goes in the box.	C	C
4. Read the book.	Read book.	Read book.	——	Read (a) book.	Read a book.	C
5. I am drawing a dog.	Drawing dog.	I draw dog.	I drawing dog.	Dog.	C	C
6. I will read the book.	Read book.	I will read book.	I read the book.	I read the book.	C	C
7. I can see a cow.	See cow.	I want see cow.	C	Cow.	C	C
8. I will not do that again.	Do again.	I will that again.	I do that.	I again.	C	C
9. I do not want an apple.	I do apple.	I do a apple.	——	I do not want apple.	I don't want a apple.	I don't want apple.
10. Do I like to read books?	To read book?	I read books?	I read books?	I read book?	C	C
11. Is it a car?	't car?	Is it car?	Car?	That a car?	Is it car?	C
12. Where does it go?	Where go?	Go?	Does it go?	Where do it go?	C	C
13. Where shall I go?	Go?	——	——	C	C	C

NOTE.—C means imitation correct. —— indicates that no intelligible imitation was obtained. ( ) indicates that the transcription was uncertain.

pegged to particular ages. The sequence can be covered at varying rates of speed; the rate would be a function of intelligence and learning opportunities.

When the analyzed records are ordered by mean utterance length, it becomes apparent that children all "reduce" English sentences in similar fashion. If the utterances of one child are, on the average, shorter than the utterances of another child, then, of course, the first child will be omitting some morphemes that the second child is producing. However, utterances could be shortened by omitting any morphemes at all; there are many ways to abbreviate sentences, and it is perfectly conceivable that individual children would hit on different ways. They do not do so. We have checked all the records for progressive constructions (e.g., "I am going to town"). Without exception, children whose mean utterance length is below 3.2 form this construction by omitting the forms of the verb *to be* (e.g., "I going"). We have checked sentences in which the verb would, for an adult, ordinarily require such a modal auxiliary as *will* or *can* (e.g., "I will park the car"). Children whose mean utterance length is below 3.5 invariably form these sentences by omitting modals ("I park the car" or "I go outside" or "I make a tower"). In general, it appears that children whose speech is not yet English are using grammars which are systematic derivatives of adult grammar and that the particular features of the derivative grammar are predictable from the mean length of utterance.

The abbreviation effect can be more directly studied in the utterances a child produces when he is asked to repeat back a sentence said by an adult. For the last six cases we presented 13 simple sentences of various

TABLE 15

Summary of Results with Sentence Imitations

Name and Age of Child	Number of Morphemes Imitated Correctly in Each of Three Serial Positions			Mean Length of Imitations (in morphemes)
	Initial	Middle	Final	
Eve, 25½	4	5	12	2.2
Adam, 28½	9	3	12	3.1
Helen, 30	6	8	9	3.7
Ian, 31½	9	7	12	3.5
Jimmy, 32	12	11	13	5.0
June, 35½	12	13	13	4.9
Per cent correctly imitated	70%	64%	96%	
Mean length of model sentences ..				5.2

NOTE.—The difference between initial and final positions is significant by sign test (two-tailed) with $p = .032$; the difference between middle and final positions is significant with $p = .062$; the difference between initial and middle positions is not significant.

grammatical types and ask the subject to "Say what I say." Half of the sentences were presented at the end of the morning session and half at the end of the afternoon session. For each child a different random order was presented. The sentences were spoken slowly and carefully and always by the same investigator. The child had the microphone directly in front of him, and so good recordings were made. Table 14 presents the first efforts of each child, and Tables 15 and 16 a summary of the main results.

TABLE 16

Percentages Correctly Imitated of Morphemes in Various Syntactic Classes

Syntactic Class	Correctly Imitated
Classes Having Few Members in English	
Inflections	44%
Pronouns	72
Articles	39
Modal auxiliaries	56
Copular verbs (*to be*)	33
Classes Having Many Members in English	
Nouns	100
Adjectives	92
Main verbs	85

NOTE.—Using tests for differences between two percentages, the percentage correct in each of the classes with many members is significantly greater than the percentage correct in any of the classes with few members ($p < .001$, 2-tailed test).

With increasing age, children produce more imitations that are morphemically identical with the original. With increasing age, the imitative utterances produced include larger numbers of morphemes—approaching the numbers in the model sentences. The morphemes produced are invariably in their original order. Omissions do not appear to be random or idiosyncratic. On the contrary, it looks as if, across children and across sentences, there is a consistent tendency to retain one kind of morpheme and drop another kind. The two sorts of morphemes contrast on several correlated dimensions. The morphemes most likely to be retained are: morphemes that occur in final position in the sentence; morphemes that are reference-making forms; morphemes that belong mainly to the large and expandable noun, verb, and adjective parts-of-speech;[6] morphemes that are relatively unpredictable from the context; and morphemes that receive the heavier stresses in ordinary English pronunciation. The morphemes least likely to

------

[6] Aborn and Rubenstein (1956) have published evidence that, in six-word sentences, nouns are most frequent in final sentence position whereas function words tend to be most frequent in the fourth and fifth positions. This tie between position and part-of-speech is found also, and not by our intention, in the sentences we provided for imitation.

be retained are: morphemes that occur in intermediate positions in the sentence; morphemes that are not reference-making forms; morphemes that belong to such small-sized grammatical categories as the articles, modal auxiliaries, and inflections; morphemes that are relatively predictable from context and so carry little information; and morphemes that receive the weaker stresses in ordinary English pronunciation. This does indeed seem to be telegraphic English. There is substantial support for our findings in the results with sentence repetition for 100 children at ages 2 and 3 obtained by Gesell and his associates (1940) and also in work of Stutsman (1926).

Let us suppose that very young children speak a rather uniform telegraphic English. How do they come by it? It is conceivable that they hear it from adults, that they are imitating a "baby talk" which is an adult invention. We have on our tapes a large quantity of speech from mother to child, and, while this material has not yet been transcribed or analyzed, it is quite clear that Eve's mother and the mothers of the other children do not usually use telegraphic English. The very young children are exposed to a much more complicated grammar than they use and the older children to a somewhat more complicated grammar than they use.

While it seems safe to say that children do not learn their telegraphic English from adults, it is probably also safe to say that the average adult can do a good job of producing telegraphic English if he is asked to talk like a baby. We have even heard a 3-year-old drop his more mature grammar in speaking to a 2-year-old and produce a very good version of the 2-year-old's speech. It is an old observation of linguists that the "baby talk" version of a language is very uniform from one adult to another. We can see good reasons why this should be so. If there is something about the operation of the child mind that causes each child to "reduce" English in a similar form, then adults everywhere could learn the same sort of baby talk from their own children. It is even possible, of course, that baby talk in all languages shows certain stable features, e.g., omission of low-information, predictable forms. If, in addition, baby talk is a systematic transformation of adult simple sentences accomplished by the omission of certain kinds of words, then an adult should be able to throw some simple mental switch that activates the baby grammar.

A basic factor causing the child's reduction of adult sentences is surely an upper limit on some kind of immediate memory span for the situation in which the child is imitating and a similar limit of programming span for the situation in which the child is constructing sentences. A comparison of the mean lengths of utterances produced as imitations (presented in Table 15) with the mean lengths of spontaneously produced utterances from the same children (presented in Table 13) shows that the paired values are very close and that neither is consistently higher. An increasing span for random digits is so reliably related to increasing age as to be a part of the Stanford-Binet test (e.g., a span of two digits at 30 months, three at 36, four at 54 months are the norms). Munn summarizes the results of many studies by saying: "That the memory span of children increases with age has been shown for all kinds of material investigated" (1954, p. 413). We know from Blankenship's review of memory span work (1938) and from Miller's discussion of "the magical number seven" (1956) that it is not yet possible to reduce the various measures of span to a common unit (bits) and thereby reconcile variations in the data. But there does seem to be ample indication that one-or-more memory spans show a steady increase in early childhood. It is this limitation of span in children for which the work of the descriptive linguist provided no parallel, and our obsession with linguistic technique long diverted us from recognizing the systematically derivative nature of child speech.

Span limitation is probably the factor compelling children to reduce adult sentences, but it does not, of course, account for the systematic tendency to drop one sort of morpheme and retain another sort. Because the two sorts of morphemes differ in numerous correlated respects, there are many conceivable explanations for the child's selective performance, and this will be so until the variables are experimentally separated. Here are a few of the many ways in which the story can now be put together. Perhaps the human mind operates on an unlearned "recency" principle, and English sentences (maybe also sentences in other languages) are nicely adapted to this principle in that the least predictable, most informative words fall usually into the final position. Perhaps, on the other hand, the "recency" effect in human serial learning is an acquired tendency to pay particular attention to material in final position, a tendency acquired from the fact that sentences are so constructed as to place in that position words carrying a lot of information. Perhaps it is differential stress that selects what the child will reproduce and sentences are nicely adapted to this predilection in that the heavier stresses fall on the less predictable forms. Or perhaps it is some combination of these ideas.

Conclusion

This paper began with an argument that the correct English sentences produced by a child are not good evidence that he possesses construction rules for the reason that we can never be sure that a correct sentence is not directly copied from a model. It seemed to us that systematic errors and manipulation of invented words were better evidence, as a child is not likely to have had exact models for these. In the second section of the paper we discussed techniques for inducing construction rules or a generative grammar from the child's natural speech. Since this speech, for Eve at least, is not good English, it can be argued that she had no models for it and so it is legitimate to infer rules from such data. In the third section, however, we have seen that child speech can be rather well characterized as a systematic reduction of adult speech, and so, after all, there were models for Eve's sentences. She could have learned most of them by selective imitation if not by imitation per se.

Eventually children must do more than imitate and memorize if only because there is not enough time for them to learn as particular verbal responses all the sentences they will be able as adults to produce and evaluate as to grammaticality. (For a detailed statement of this argument, see Bruner, 1957, p. 156; or Miller, Galanter, and Pribram, 1960, pp. 146-147.) In addition to the logical argument that children must learn construction rules in view of their terminal linguistic achievement, there is much empirical evidence that children older than Eve do, in fact, learn construction rules. Some of this evidence is available to every parent in a child's systematic errors (*sheeps, I bringed,* etc.), and some of it has been collected in a controlled fashion by Berko (1958) and by Brown and Berko (1960).

While children must and do eventually induce construction rules, it is not necessary that they do so from the very earliest age at which words are combined. Eve, after all, is not yet prepared to produce an infinite set of sentences, nor, so far as we know, is she able to distinguish all grammatical sequences from ungrammatical sequences. It is possible that for the earliest linguistic accomplishments one sort of learning theory will serve—a theory developed largely from the study of animal behavior—while for later accomplishments a completely different theory will be necessary—a theory permitting the inductive formation of syntactic classes that generalize far beyond obtained information. However, it is also possible that the induction of rules goes on from the very first. Eve, for example, produces such utterances as "Two chair" and "Kitty all gone" which could conceivably ·be either direct or selective imitations, but might very easily be constructions resulting from overgeneralized rules for the use of *two* and *all gone.* For a single example, we will show how Eve might be forming construction rules at the same time that she is practicing selective imitation without this construction process being clearly revealed in the present data.

Selective reduction might cause Eve to imitate "That is a doggie" as "That doggie"; "That is a horsie" as "That horsie"; and "See the doggie" as "See doggie." At this point induction could operate and she might, because the context "That ———" is shared by "doggie" and "horsie," assume that the other context "See ———" can be shared and so form the utterance "See horsie." It is quite possible that the child reduces first, then forms inductive generalizations, and makes new utterances on the model of his reductions.

It will often happen if the above suggestion is correct that a child will find forms syntactically equivalent that are not so for the adult. Suppose Eve heard the sentence "I see the man" and reduced it to "See man." The original demonstrates the nonequivalence of *see* and *that* since *see* occurs after a pronoun, and, in addition, the original version does not justify adding *man* to the list started with *doggie* and *horsie*. The reduced sentence, on the other hand, leaves *see* equivalent to *that* and suggests that *man* belongs with *doggie* and *horsie*. If a child induces a grammar from its own reduced sentences, it should generally lose the distributional detail provided by such morphemes as *an, the, will, do*, and */-z/*. The result would be syntactic classes not identical with those of adult speech, few in number and large in size. In addition there would be loss of numerous semantic distinctions, e.g., the difference between "See the man" and "I see the man." It is important to note, however, that the gross sense of a sentence will usually be retained; e.g., in "See man" as in "I see the man" it is clear that *man* is the object of seeing. The crude sense of the sentence is generally recoverable from the child's reduction for the reason that one profound dimension of English grammar is perfectly preserved in telegraphese, and that dimension is word order.

For the present, then, we are working with the hypothesis that child speech is a systematic reduction of adult speech largely accomplished by omitting function words that carry little information. From this corpus of reduced sentences we suggest that the child induces general rules which govern the construction of new utterances. As a child becomes capable (through maturation and the consolidation of frequently occurring sequences) of registering more of the detail of adult speech, his original rules will have to be revised and supplemented. As the generative grammar grows more complicated and more like the adult grammar, the child's speech will become capable of expressing a greater variety of meanings.

EXPLORATIONS IN GRAMMAR EVALUATION [1]

ROGER BROWN, COLIN FRASER,[2]
and URSULA BELLUGI
Harvard University

In the 1961 edition of Gleason's *An Introduction to Descriptive Linguistics* the following paragraph appears:

The difference between a description of a corpus and of a language is partly a matter of scope. A corpus consists of a few thousand sentences. A language might be considered as consisting of a very large number of sentences—all those, either already spoken or not yet used, which would be ac-

[1] The work described in this paper was supported by the National Science Foundation by a grant administered through the Center for Communication Sciences, Massachusetts Institute of Technology.
[2] Now at the University of Exeter, Exeter, England.

cepted by native speakers as "belonging" to that language. Even the largest corpus can be only an infinitesimal portion of the language (pp. 196-197).[3]

In the summer of 1961 we collected 26 hours of speech in one week from a 24-month-old boy whom we are calling Abel. In 26 hours Abel produced 2,081 different utterances. These utterances are a corpus and Abel is a native speaker. The problem is to find Abel's *language*.

Here are fragments of two additional paragraphs from Gleason:

> A second corpus of roughly comparable scope should also exemplify a similarly high percentage of the pertinent constructional patterns. This being the case, the greater part of the grammatical features of either corpus should be shared by the other.
>
> This gives a test for a grammar. It is only necessary to elicit another sample, independent of the first. If the grammar fits the new corpus equally well, it is highly probable that it is correct (p. 201).

A grammar is a set of generalizations induced from given data but going beyond the given data. Consequently a grammar makes predictions. From things already said, a grammar predicts things likely to be said and things not likely to be said. For the linguist working with adults an important test of the grammar written from one corpus is its ability to anticipate the sentences of a new corpus. This test is also available to the student of child speech.

The prediction test has never been made precise. The linguist in the field does not write down alternative grammars, generate predictions, and keep track of outcomes. He works at a single grammar, revising it so as to accommodate new data, but never subjecting it to an explicit, comparative, quantitative evaluation. Is such an evaluation possible? We are able to imagine some relevant calculations, and, being empirical mathematicians who do not know what numbers will do until they do it, we decided to work through some exercises with Abel's utterances.

The transcribed utterances were divided into two sets: one consisted of the utterances produced in 15 hours (the 15-hour corpus) and the other of utterances produced in 11 hours (the 11-hour corpus). The division was made in such a way as to guarantee that the two sets were similar to one another in the proportions of speech taken from each day and from each time of day. It was our plan to study first the 15-hour corpus and, from this study, to write grammatically rules whose predictions would be tested against the utterances obtained in the 11-hour corpus.

We began with a restricted grammar written from a subset of the utterances in the 15-hour corpus. The subset consisted of all two-word utter-

---

[3] This statement does not represent Gleason's final opinion but is for him, as for us, the starting point of an extended argument. In chapter 13 of *An Introduction to Descriptive Linguistics* (1961) the reader will find Gleason's full discussion of the relation between language and grammars.

ances created from a list of 79 words which were selected because they occurred frequently and in a variety of contexts. The restricted grammar was
written from and designed to generate all of the two-word utterances using
the given lexicon of 79 words in the 15-hour corpus, and it was tested by
its ability to anticipate such utterances in the 11-hour corpus. The subset of
utterances was chosen so as to reveal with maximal clarity certain problems
that arise in the evaluation of any grammars written from the speech of
very young children.

TABLE 1

The Sample Lexicon

a	blanket	cookie	George	need	shovel	this
Abel	block	cup	get	nice	sock	throw
all	boat	Da	glass	no	some	two
another	book	Daddy	hat	on	soup	up
away	box	down	here	one	sweep	want
Baby	bubble-drink	draw	in	orange	swim	water
ball	bye-bye	eat	jump	paper	table	where
bathtub	cake	eye	man	pencil	telephone	
bed	car	find	milk	penny	tiger	
bell	chair	firetruck	Mommie	pillow	that	
big	clean	for	more	ring	the	
bike	coffee	fork	my	see	there	

The lexicon of 79 words appears as Table 1. On the distributional evidence (see Brown and Fraser) of the 15-hour corpus the 79 words were
placed in 13 syntactic classes. There were five residual words which had
little in common with the members of any syntactic class or with one
another, and these must be dealt with individually. Adult speakers of English use a terminal sibilant inflection to pluralize regular count nouns and
to mark the third-person present indicative of regular verbs. Abel sometimes
used such an inflection, but he would add it to mass nouns as well as to
count nouns and to any verb in any person. We provided for these possibilities by allowing a terminal [s] to occur with any member of four syntactic
classes: count nouns, mass nouns, transitive verbs, intransitive verbs. This
rule has the effect of entering each noun and verb into a lexicon twice and
so brings the total number of words to 128. The classified lexicon appears
as Table 2.

In order to determine how Abel combined the lexical items to form
two-word utterances, we constructed the matrix of Table 3 in which the
13 classes and 5 residual words are listed on each axis. The abscissa is the
word in initial position, and the ordinate the word in second position. An
"X" means that one or more combinations of the type indicated occurred

TABLE 2

The Lexicon Distributed among Word Classes

Word Class	Lexicon
Definite articles (Art_d)	*my, the, two*
Indefinite articles (Art_i)	*a, another*
Descriptive adjectives (Adj)	*big, nice*
Count nouns (N_c)	*ball, bathtub, bed, bell, bike, blanket, block, boat, book, box, cake, car, chair, cookie, cup, eye, fire-truck, fork, glass, hat, jump, man, orange, pencil, penny, pillow, ring, shovel, sock, table, telephone, tiger* (Plus *-s*)
Mass nouns (N_m)	*bubble-drink, coffee, milk, paper, soup, water* (Plus *-s*)
Proper nouns (N_p)	*Abel, George, Baby, Mommie, Daddy, Da*
Intransitive verbs (V_{in})	*sweep, swim* (Plus *-s*)
Transitive verbs (V_t)	*clean, draw, eat, find, get, need, see, throw, want* (Plus *-s*)
Locatives (Loc)	*here, there*
Demonstrative pronouns (Pro_d) ...	*this, that*
Prepositions 1 (Pr_1)	*away, down, up*
Prepositions 2 (Pr_2)	*in, on*
Qualifiers	*all, more, some*
Others	*where, for, bye-bye, no, one*

(e.g., $Art_d + N_c$), and a blank that no combinations of the type indicated occurred (e.g., $N_c + Art_d$).

From this matrix it is possible to write a rule for each class and each residual word describing the classes and words that have followed it and those that have preceded it. These rules may be considered a two-word grammar which produces all of the 371 two-word combinations of the designated lexicon. In addition, of course, the grammar generalizes the distributional facts of the 371 utterances since it permits the formation of all utterances of a given type if at least one utterance of that type has actually occurred.

It was then possible to determine the total number of combinations predicted by the rules. For example: there are three definite articles (*my, the,* and *two*). The first rule says that each of these can occur with any count noun (32 in the singular and 32 in the plural, or 64). Multiplying 3 × 64 yields 192 possible combinations of the type: $Art_d + N_c$. The three definite articles can also occur with all of the six mass nouns in either the singular or plural, and the result is 3 × 12, or 36 additional sentences. Finally, the

TABLE 3

The Matrix of Two-Word Combinations

Word	Art$_d$	Art$_1$	Adj	N$_c$	N$_m$	N$_p$	V$_{in}$	V$_t$	Loc	Pro$_d$	Pr$_1$	Pr$_2$	Qual	*Where*	*For*	*By-bye*	*No*	*One*
Art$_d$										X								
Art$_1$																		
Adj				X	X													
N$_c$	X	X	X	X	X	X	X	X	X	X	X	X	X			X	X	X
N$_m$	X		X	X	X		X	X	X		X	X	X			X	X	X
N$_p$	X		X	X			X	X	X	X	X	X	X	X	X	X	X	
V$_{in}$		X	X	X	X			X	X			X						
V$_t$		X	X	X	X		X	X	X			X						
Loc				X	X						X	X						
Pro$_d$											X							
Pr$_1$			X	X	X			X				X				X	X	
Pr$_2$				X			X											
Qual			X	X	X	X	X	X	X	X	X					X	X	
Where									X									
For																		
Bye-bye																		
No																X		
One		X		X	X													

NOTE.—"X" indicates that utterances of this type occurred.

grammar says that the three articles can occur with the six proper nouns, which is 18 more. The total number of utterances predicted by the first rule is then: 192 + 36 + 18, or 246. Proceeding in this fashion through all the rules, we found that the grammar as a whole generates 13,154 different utterances.

We looked next at the utterances of the 11-hour corpus selecting out all of the two-word combinations made up from the original lexicon. There are 90 exact repetitions of utterances from the original 371; 105 utterances predicted by the grammar but not in the original set; eight not predicted by the grammar. Clearly this grammar predicts most of the events of the second set that fall within its purview. Is it then a good grammar? Is it a better description of Abel's behavior than some other possible description?

We decided first to compare the grammar with a maximally general and simple prediction, a prediction of all possible combinations of two forms drawn from the lexicon. The total number of possible combinations is 16,384, and this figure includes 3,230 combinations not predicted by the grammar. For the obtained utterances of the second set the total-combinations rule predicts all 203 whereas the grammar predicts 203 — 8, or 195.

As a third comparison we decided to consider the obtained 371 utterances of the first set as predictors of the second set. What happens if we simply say that Abel does with two-word combinations in one corpus what he does with such combinations in the other corpus. In the second set there are 90 exact repetitions of utterances in the first set, and these are the only utterances predicted; the remaining 113 are not predicted. The numbers for the various kinds of combinations appear in Table 4.

TABLE 4

Two-Word Combinations in the 15-Hour Corpus and in the 11-Hour Corpus

15-Hour Corpus	
Number of forms in lexicon	128
Obtained combinations	371
Combinations grammar predicts	13,154
All possible combinations	16,384
Possible combinations not predicted by grammar	3,230
11-Hour Corpus	
Number of forms in lexicon	128
Obtained combinations	203
Exact repetitions	90
Predicted by grammar but not repetitions	105
Not predicted by grammar but obtained	8

Clearly it is to the credit of a grammar if occurring utterances are predicted, and to its discredit if occurring utterances are not predicted. On first thought, then, we might express the value of a grammar as the ratio of occurrences predicted to occurrences not predicted. The three ratios for the grammar, the total-combinations rule, and the original list rule appear in Table 5 under the heading "Ratio A."

The total-combinations rule has the largest ratio, of course, since it predicts everything conceivable. The grammar is next best, and the first set of utterances is least good. This index alone must therefore be insufficient since it would always lead us to prefer the same description—all possible combinations of items. This first ratio (A) offers a translation of one requirement of a grammar—production of all grammatical sentences—which is rendered as prediction of all obtained utterances. However there is a second requirement of a grammar—production of no ungrammatical sentences. We will try rendering this second requirement as: prediction of no utterances that do not occur.

Clearly it is to the credit of a grammar if utterances not occurring are not predicted. But what is the number of utterances not occurring and not

Table 5

Possible Grammar-Evaluating Ratios

Ratio A—Prediction of All Grammatical Sentences

Value$_A$ of grammar		= Occurrences predicted / Occurrences, not predicted		
Grammar	=	195 /	8	=	24.38
All possible combinations	=	203 /	0	=	∞
First set of utterances	=	90 /	113	=	.80

Ratio B—Prediction of No Ungrammatical Sentences

Value$_B$ of grammar		= Nonoccurrences, not predicted / Nonoccurrences, predicted		
Grammar	=	3,222 / 12,959		=	.25
·All possible combinations	=	0 / 16,181		=	0
First set of utterances	=	15,900 / 281		=	56.58

predicted? We decided to interpret this notion as utterances conceivable in terms of the designated lexicon and the limitation on length, but yet not predicted by the grammar and not occurring in the sample. In the present case there are 3,230 such conceivable utterances (predicted by the rule of total combinations) which were not predicted by the grammar. Of these 3,230, only eight were obtained, and so 3,230 — 8, or 3,222, is the number of utterances not predicted and not occurring. Because these utterances are to the credit of the grammar, we entered them as the numerator of ratio B.

Utterances not occurring but predicted are to the discredit of a grammar. The present grammar predicted a total of 13,154 combinations, and, of these, 195 occurred. This leaves 13,154 — 195, or 12,959 combinations that were predicted but failed to occur. Because this number tells against the grammar, it is entered as the denominator of the new ratio.

A ratio of this second kind was also calculated for the total-combinations rule. For this rule there are no nonoccurrences not predicted since all conceivable combinations are predicted. There are very many nonoccurrences that are predicted (16,181). The numerator, which expresses the fact that nonoccurrences cannot be to the credit of this rule, causes the ratio for the total-combinations rule to have a value of zero. The total-combinations rule which does a perfect job of producing all grammatical (obtained) sentences is no good at all when it comes to not producing ungrammatical sentences.

Consider now the same ratio B for the list of utterances from the first set. There are very many combinations which do not occur and are not predicted (15,900), and a relatively small number of predictions that fail (281). The first set of utterances which is not very good at producing all grammatical sentences is the best of the three at not predicting ungrammatical sentences. Note that if the ratios were calculated for the total corpus the value of ratio B for the list would be infinity, since there would be no non-occurrences predicted.

Ratios A and B operationalize the two requirements of a generative grammar, and the summary of Table 6 shows how the three descriptions stand with respect to both requirements. A grammar is good in the degree that it is able to generate all the utterances that occur without generating any that do not occur. The rule of total combinations perfectly satisfies the former requirement but completely fails to satisfy the latter. The first set of utterances perfectly satisfies the second requirement but completely fails to satisfy the first requirement. Only the grammar can, in some degree, meet both requirements, and that is a reason for preferring the grammar to either the rule of total combinations or the first set of utterances as a description of what Abel knows. However, from the 15-hour corpus one could write a large number of grammars alternative to the one presented here but equally well adapted to the data of that corpus. Let us see why this is so.

TABLE 6

Values of the Three Descriptions for the Two Ratios

Description	Ratio A	Ratio B
Grammar	24.38	.25
Total combinations	∞	0
First set of utterances	.80	56.58
		(∞ for total corpus)

Consider the grammatical rule: $N_c + N_c$. This rule permits any count noun to go with any count noun, and since there are 64 count nouns in the lexicon (including both singular and plural forms) the rule generates 64 $\times$ 64, or 4,096 combinations. The rule is a generalization of a small number of such actual occurrences as: "baby boat," "book bed," and "chair Mommie." What rules other than the rule $N_c + N_c$ will cover these occurrences? At one extreme there is the rule that simply summarizes the obtained utterances: Nouns-occurring-in-first-position (No_1) + Nouns-occurring-in-second-position (No_2). This rule exactly describes utterances of a certain type in the 15-hour corpus, but it does not generalize at all and so will fail to anticipate the utterances of the 11-hour corpus. What generalized rules other than $N_c + N_c$ might be written?

In principle one could write general rules in terms of any categories into which No_1 and No_2 can be placed. Suppose that all the No_1 happened to begin with the letter "p" and all of the No_2 with the letter "q." One could generalize the facts as: $N_p + N_q$. This degree of distributional consistency with regard to a grammatically irrelevant attribute is not likely to exist in any real corpus. However, there would always be some degree of consistency in terms of initial letters or final letters or length-of-word that could be generalized into a predictive rule.

In writing rules for Abel, we only consider word categories that had a grammatical function in adult English and count nouns are one such category. However there are other noun categories. The majority of the combinations $No_1 + No_2$ are made up of an initial noun naming some animate being (N_{an}) and a subsequent noun naming something inanimate (N_{inan}). It seems likely that these combinations are "telegraphic" versions of a possessive construction. In adult English it is necessary, for syntactic reasons, to distinguish N_{an} from other sorts of nouns. Suppose then that we were to drop the $N_c + N_c$ rule from Abel's grammar and replace it with the rule: $N_{an} + N_{inan}$.

Since N_{an} are much less numerous in Abel's lexicon than are N_c, the new rule would greatly reduce the number of predicted combinations. Since most of these predicted combinations did not occur in the 11-hour corpus, the denominator of ratio B would go down and the value of ratio B would go up. However, the new rule fails to generate a few of the utterances in the 15-hour corpus that are generated by the old rule. For example, "book bed" and "chair Mommie" are covered by $N_c + N_c$ but not by $N_{an} + N_{inan}$. In the 11-hour corpus, too, a few utterances occur which the old rule covered but which the new rule does not cover. These then become "occurrences, not predicted," and they must be added into the denominator of ratio A. The result is that this ratio goes down. In the above example, then, one cannot simultaneously maximize both ratios. The cost of making the grammar less general is to make it less adequate to the facts.

It is not logically necessary that a less general rule be less adequate to the facts. If all of the members of No_1 in both corpuses had been animate nouns and if all the members of No_2 had been inanimate nouns, then the rule $N_c + N_c$ and the rule $N_{an} + N_{inan}$ would have been equally adequate though unequally general. In such circumstances the choice is clear—the less general formulation is to be preferred. However these circumstances are rare with Abel's utterances. The usual case is that improving the value of the grammar in terms of one criterion entails a certain cost in terms of the other criterion.

We have explored these problems of evaluation for grammars written from all of Abel's utterances as well as for grammars written from only the subset of two-word utterances. When all the utterances of the 15-hour corpus are considered, the size of the lexicon increases and the range in utterance length is from one to four words. With these increases the number of possible combinations runs into billions. It is possible to write a grammar that will cover all of the obtained utterances and yet will fall far short of generating this set of possible combinations. But the least general grammar that is adequate to all the utterances generates many millions of possibilities.

If we insist on generating all utterances, on using only categories that are relevant to grammar, and on preferring the least general set of rules that will meet these conditions, the choice of a grammar becomes reasonably determinate. Perhaps this is what we should do. It would mean crediting Abel with a machinery for generating millions of utterances. He may have such machinery. However, it is not obvious that one should insist on covering every obtained utterance when the cost of doing so is to predict astronomically large numbers of utterances that have not been obtained.

Here is a final quotation from Gleason (1961). "The occurrence of a sentence in a carefully elicited corpus is prima-facie evidence that the sentence does 'belong' to the language, but nothing more. Informants do make mistakes. Occasionally very bad sentences will occur" (p. 197). The linguist in the field commonly exempts his grammar from the obligation to cover certain ones of the utterances that have actually been obtained. If we allow ourselves to exclude utterances from Abel's 15-hour corpus, we can write less general grammars. But by what criteria does one select the utterances to be excluded?

An utterance produced by a child may be either a construction or a repetition. Only constructions should be consulted in formulating grammatical rules since these rules are intended to model the construction process. However, Brown and Fraser have argued that in the normal case of the child at home one cannot usually determine whether an utterance is a construction or a repetition. The basic difficulty is that one never knows exactly what a child has heard, and so any utterance, except certain errors, might be a repetition. If we had a rule for distinguishing constructions from repetitions in spontaneous speech, we would exclude repetitions from the corpus but the rule is hard to find.

Some of Abel's utterances immediately followed adult utterances which they closely resembled. Such seeming imitations are almost certainly repetitions rather than constructions, and we have excluded them in writing grammars. However a repetition need not immediately follow its model. When an utterance does not resemble anything that has immediately preceded it in the speech of others, how can one tell whether it is a construction or a well-practiced repetition of some earlier model?

Suppose we have a set of two-word utterances such that all the members have one word in common and the remaining words, which are not identical across the utterances, are drawn from the same part-of-speech. Abel produced many such sets. One of them is: "Big blocks," "Big boat," "Big car," "Big cookie," "Big fish," "Big man," "Big pockets." It seems likely that at least some of these two-word utterances have been constructed. It seems likely because the set establishes a very simple and definite pattern (*Big* + Noun) which makes new constructions very easy. We do not find it difficult to believe that Abel has abstracted this pattern and can commute nouns in the open position.

Abel also produced the two-word utterance: "Coffee cup." There were no other utterances of the type: *Coffee* + Noun, and none of the type: Noun + *cup*. There were, however, utterances of the type: Noun + Noun. It is possible that Abel constructed "Coffee cup" on that abstract model, but we feel that it is more likely that he has learned "Coffee cup" as a prefabricated whole, a repetition of a common adult utterance.

Some utterances, then, can be assigned to a recurrent type such that the type is partially defined by a particular word or words. Other words can only be assigned to recurrent types which are defined entirely in terms of word classes. We have a hunch (it is no more) that utterances which fall into the narrower, more concrete patterns are more likely to be constructed than utterances which can only be placed in abstract patterns. This hunch ultimately concerns what we think it reasonable to suppose that a 24-month-old child has learned to do.

Using the narrow sort of recurrence as a ground for excluding material from the 15-hour corpus, we have found it possible to write grammars that generate these more regular utterances of the corpus and only predict some thousands of utterances beyond those obtained. Such grammars, of course, fail to generate the many less regular utterances.

Some of us believe that the grammars which exclude the more intractable utterances come nearer to describing Abel's actual constructional competence than do the grammars that generate everything. However the exclusion criterion was fixed by pure hunch. A case can be made that it is just the odd utterance, the one that does not fall into any narrow recurrent type, that is most likely to have been constructed. The grammar-evaluation problem has not been solved.

Perhaps our problem has begun to seem rather "scholastic"—in the medieval sense. Is it sensible to worry about whether a child who has produced 2,000 utterances has a rule system for producing 50,000 utterances or 50,000,000 utterances? This problem seems particularly "scholastic" when you consider that the rule system would be likely to change before the child had time to turn out more than a fractional part of the supposed possibilities. However, you will grant that it can be reasonable and even practically important to determine whether a child knows how to add numbers. Suppose that the child cannot tell us anything about the addition process—and most children cannot. All he can do is operate with numbers. How would we decide whether or not he knew how to add?

The operation of addition predicts an infinite set of occurrences and an infinite set of nonoccurrences. If a child knows how to add, he will be prepared to say: "2 plus 2 are 4"; "12 plus 83,120 are 83,132"; "750 plus 91 are 841"; etc., and not to say: "2 plus 5 are 6"; "15 plus 19 are 22"; etc. We never hear a child say more than a triflingly small number of the acceptable utterances; yet we do not hesitate, on the basis of such evidence, to credit him with knowledge of addition. Furthermore most children will occasionally make a mistake; they will occasionally produce an incorrect sum. When that happens we do not feel that we must adjust our conception of the rules in the child's head so as to generate the unpredicted occurrence. We confidently exclude the difficult case from the corpus and decide that he knows how to add but sometimes makes computational errors. How do we come to be so confident here and so uncertain in the case of grammar?

The addition rule predicts more precisely than does a grammar. Given the numbers to be summed it generates the particular outcome. The chances of doing that if you have not got the correct rule are small, and that may be why we feel confident that the rule is right. A grammar, given the words to be made into a sentence, would in some extremely simple cases predict a particular outcome. Usually, however, the grammar would only generate a set of possible outcomes. For the particular sentence one must go beyond grammar to meaning and the motivation of a speaker. One difference between addition and grammar, then, seems to be in the precision of prediction.

There are rules other than the grammatical which only generate possibilities, rules that do not generate particular outcomes. Consider the rules for bidding in contract bridge. These rules do not tell us what a particular player will bid on a particular occasion, but they do permit one set of bids and proscribe another set. The class of permitted bids narrows with the accumulation of prior bids; if someone has bid "three diamonds," it is no longer acceptable to bid "two diamonds." However there is always more than one acceptable response.

Of course there are guides to intelligent bidding which do prescribe particular bids. In the case of language the particular sentence can only be prescribed by considering semantics and motivation in addition to grammar. The particular bid in bridge can only be prescribed by considering the hand the player holds as well as the rules of the game. The rules of bidding in themselves do not require that a bid be sensible, only that it be drawn from the population of lawful bids.

Suppose a player had not told us the rules of bidding, and most players could not easily do so. The player can only play, and we must judge whether he possesses the rules we have in mind. Even though these rules do not predict the particular bid, if the player repeatedly drew his bids from the class of possibilities, we would come to believe that he possessed the rules. I think we would not be convinced quite so quickly as in the case of addition, but it would not take very many games to persuade us that the player had the rules. If he then made a mistake, perhaps bidding "two diamonds" when it is not permitted to do so, we would not revise our conception of his knowledge so as to incorporate this deviant case. We would instead decide that he knew the rules of proper bidding but had lost track of the prior bids. How so?

There is a critical difference between the adding child or the bridgeplayer and the sentence-producing child. The child who has mistakenly said "2 plus 5 are 6" will sometimes correct himself or will accept our correction and agree that 2 plus 5 are 7. The bridgeplayer, if he is told that someone has already bid "three diamonds," will apologize for his "two diamonds" and offer instead an acceptable bid. We can be confident that these actions must be excluded from the corpus because they elicit a characteristic reaction from the person producing them. They are judged to be incorrect and so are separated out from the other sums or bids. The rule system identifies certain behavior as unlawful and the subject also identifies it as unlawful. It is very improbable that this would happen if our formulation of his rules were mistaken. It is chiefly because of this coincidence between the boundaries defined by the rules and the boundaries marked out by the subject that we can be so confident in attributing to him knowledge of bridge or of addition.

The linguist working with an adult informant gets reactions to utterances as well as the utterances themselves. The informant will sometimes stop and strike out an utterance following it with a corrected version. The linguist can test his hypotheses about the grammatical system by constructing possibly acceptable sentences and asking for judgments of grammaticality. The linguist is able to get judgments of the acceptability of behavior, and this is the kind of data that is so decisive for the adding child and the bridgeplayer. Can such data be obtained from very young children?

With Abel we were not successful in eliciting judgments of grammaticality. Of course there was no point in asking him whether an utterance was "grammatical" or "well-formed." We experimented with some possible childhood equivalents. The first step was to formulate tentative grammatical rules, and the next to construct some utterances that ought to have been acceptable if the rules were correct and other utterances that ought not to have been acceptable. For Abel "The cake" should have been grammatical and "Cake the" ungrammatical. How to ask? The experimenter said: "Some of the things I will say are silly and some are not. You tell me when I say something silly." Abel would not. If Abel had a sense of grammaticality, we were unable to find the word that would engage it. When do children begin to make judgments of grammaticality? We plan to find out.

How stands the problem of evaluating grammars written for the speech of children? There are two basic criteria: the grammar should generate as many as possible of the utterances that will be produced while generating as few as possible of the utterances that will not be produced. It is ordinarily the case that changing the grammar so as to better its performance with respect to one criterion entails a cost in that the change worsens the performance of the grammar with respect to the other criterion. It is not ordinarily possible to optimize performance on both criteria at the same time. There is no good rationale for pursuing one criterion to the neglect of the other. We might aim at achieving some minimal excellence in terms of both criteria but the setting of the acceptable levels would be quite arbitrary. It would be as if we tried to decide how many addition problems a child must solve correctly and how few incorrectly if he is to be credited with a knowledge of addition. A decision would be arbitrary and unsatisfactory.

The way out of this dilemma in the case of addition and also in the case of the linguist writing a grammar for adult speech is to obtain *reactions* as well as *actions*, reactions which judge the acceptability of actions. With one 24-month-old boy we could not obtain such reactions. Perhaps they can be obtained from older children. Children who are first combining words may not have a sense of grammaticality, and it may never be possible to settle on the best general description of their speech output.

Judgments of grammaticality and nongrammaticality are data for a grammar to fit; data in addition to occurrence and nonoccurrence. These additional data greatly reduce the number of conceivable grammars and so increase our confidence in any one that fits. It may be possible to obtain from children other kinds of data that will help to select among grammars, possibly data on the perception or comprehension of speech or data on imitation.

The psychologist working on computer simulation of cognitive pocesses has the same problem we have. If he simulates some single simple problem-solving performance, he cannot feel very sure that his simulation is similar to the information-processing of the human being because there will be a large number of alternative equally-adequate simulations. If the simulator increases the range of data he can generate, the number of alternative simulations will decrease and confidence in any one that works will increase. Of course with a greater range of data it is more difficult to create satisfactory generative rules. For the grammars of children, we have been setting ourselves too easy a task. We have not required very much of these grammars, and so they have not been very difficult to invent. But, also, there have been too many alternatives and no clear ground for choosing among them.

FORMAL DISCUSSION

Robert Lees
University of Illinois

The Miller and Ervin and the Brown, Fraser, and Bellugi papers may have been planned with the idea that, if one moved back into the very earliest stages of language, then the language would be so primitive that it would be a relatively easy task to say just what it is like. But it turns out perhaps to be exactly the opposite. When we move back to the very earliest stages of language acquisition, we may get data that are very difficult to analyze. I would like to suggest, therefore, that a better procedure might have been to start with older children where at least at first glance the language seems to be very much like adult speech. In fact it is not, if you listen carefully. The advantage would be that perhaps one could get better hypotheses about what kinds of productions are occurring if one moves backward from adult speech through older children towards younger ones. It may be that the few differences that are found will turn out to be formulatable in relatively simple terms. And thus one would have better hypotheses about what is happening in the stage where all you get are sentences with two words in them.

When one is working with a corpus of material and attempting to find a grammar which might underlie it, it is not safe to assume that every utterance in the corpus has been constructed by the child according to bona fide rules. In adult speech we find a tremendous amount of variation in the faithfulness with which an individual will confine himself to the grammatical rules which in fact he thinks he is using. It is reasonable to assume that we find the same variation in child speech. When a child has a sentence with a noun in the first position and an adverb in the second position, and another the other way around, it is not obvious that the two sentences aren't really for him the same sentence. This may be simply a stylistic variant. It may be very difficult to tell, but you have to assume that children in this respect are like adults.

Another difficulty in these papers is the limited notion of grammatical description that was used. One is looking for some kind of articulated structure in a corpus of data, but the notion of structure which is used is a relatively primitive one, and so are the data relatively primitive, so it is not too surprising that one finds very little. For example, if the notion of grammatical description of a sentence is confined to the notion of a set of classes of words and a set of positions in which these classes can occur, naturally there is not very much one can say. One is almost naturally led, as a matter of fact, to the kind of classical American descriptive technique of giving a morpheme order chart, which doesn't say very much about sentences which may in fact be quite different. There may be underlying regularities that one cannot see immediately if one confines one's attention only to the position of classes of words. In the case of earliest language it is difficult to demonstrate. With older children who have language very much like that used by adults, we are already familiar with cases that show that, if all one tried to describe is a set of positions and a set of classes of words that go in them, there are underlying regularities which could not be expressed.

There was some concern with the use of auxiliaries in these papers, because this is one of the systems of normal English that seem to be dropped out in the earliest stages and then acquired during the time of development that is of interest. Notice that a very simple description can be given of how the auxiliaries are used, providing one is willing to depart from the description of sentences as sequences of position classes. Of course the auxiliaries do not go in the same places for all different types of sentences which are really much the same if you look at them from the point of view of an underlying structure. Where one can easily treat "Can John come?" as a simple permutation of "John can come," one cannot treat "Does John come?" as a simple permutation of "John comes." Actually the sentences are related in exactly the same fashion. In order to do this, however, one has to have an analysis of sentences that uses something more sophisticated than simply order positions of classes of words. The same thing would apply to child language.

With regard to the lack of auxiliaries in early language of the child, the authors would like to say that perhaps what is happening here is that the child has a limited memory span or attends only to phonetically prominent words, and thus somehow or other manages to drop the auxiliaries out of the adult sentence and produce the child's telegraphic sentence. Yet there are some data which do not accord with this, given in Table 14 in the Brown and Fraser paper, where the child was asked to give back a full-fledged rendition of the experimenter's adult sentence. I was very much struck by the fact that, when asked to repeat "I do not want an apple," every single child from the youngest to the oldest manages to reproduce *do*. Yet in this sentence *do* is a low-stressed, low-information-carrying, utterly predictable auxiliary word. In the sentence before that, "I will not do that again," the morpheme *do* appears as the main verb. In this case it is fully stressed, it is not predictable, and it is a content word. Two children missed *do*, but the rest of them seemed to get it. I am not used to talking in terms of percentages, and I would like to know what happened on that particular occasion. Maybe it is true that if one looks over a thousand utterances it turns out that very few of them are exactly like the results of these two; maybe these are exceptions in some random sense. But I think it is a rather strange view of human behavior to assume that the children said *do* randomly, as though you have a kind of random output that every now and then does give a *do*. That seems very dubious, and one gets the impression that that is not what happened here. In other words it is not that the children miss all the auxiliaries in adult sentences and drop them out for some relatively simple reason. Apparently a child of the age when the auxiliary system is not fully functional still somehow does manage to use auxiliaries. Clearly, the child at this age may be understanding the use of auxiliaries very well, but not using them very well.

One of the suggestions made was that perhaps what accounts for the particular kind of reduction that one observes from adult language to the telegraphic style of the early language learner is sentence position.

There was an argument given that maybe it is primarily the last part of the sentence which people concentrate on, remember well, and learn to reproduce quickly. Perhaps the last part of the sentence then comes to be the emphatic part, the part which is strongly-stressed, and so on. In fact, this is true of simple sentences in English. The last word of the sentence does tend to be the object of the verb or a semantically very prominent adverbial, or some such thing, and has primary stress on it.

The trouble with this notion is that it does not work for other languages. In Turkish, for example, generally speaking the last morpheme to occur will be a very unemphatic and a very unstressed verbal auxiliary, or what corresponds to a verbal auxiliary in English. Next to the last will generally be a more strongly-stressed verb, and the object of the verb will come before that. In general, the most emphatic position in the sentence is the position immediately before the verb. The third position from the end is the position of contrastive emphasis in Turkish. This must be occurring in parents' speech, and children must be hearing the emphasis on the word third from the end of the sentence. This really does not accord very well with the view that it is the last thing in the sentence which counts. So there are a lot of ins and outs to the question of what properties of a sentence one looks at to account for why the child reduces from the adult to the telegraphic in a particular way. I think the suggestion that things are dropped out (if that is the correct way to describe this) only when they are weak-stressed or low-information-carrying, and so on, is very plausible, but whether it is true or not is hard to say. But surely it cannot be something like: "Look at the end of the sentence and forget the beginning." Again, if one looks at the data in Table 14, which are by far the most interesting data to me, one sees that on many occasions this is not at all what happens. The first part of the sentence is almost invariably remembered when it is the pronoun "I," for example.

The authors, in regard to this, introduce the notion of *memory span*. Whether or not one can apply this idea to sentences is a big question, because in the case of digits, where the measurements are usually made, it seems fairly clear what the elements are that are being memorized. In the case of sentences, what are the elements? There is an implication that the elements ought best to be considered words, but in view of the fact that there is already at the very early stages some manipulation of an auxiliary system, it is likely for the purposes of a syntactic description of sentences to be not words but probably morphemes. One can also describe a sentence correctly as consisting of a very large number of individual phonemes. For phonemes, then, the span is large, but for morphemes it is small.

Now suppose one did want to confine oneself simply to the problem of finding a reasonable grammar which underlies a certain corpus of utterances. We can assume that the corpus is very large, in order to get out of the problem of not finding very much in a small set of two-word utterances. One point that one has to pay attention to is the following: if all one demands of a description is that it simply generate the utterances of the corpus, it is quite possible—especially for early language—that there will be such a huge number of alternative grammars available to do that job that one will never be able to make reasonable choices. When one examines linguistic behavior in adults and tries to give a reasonable theory of what they are doing, one has to demand more of a description than simply an enumeration of utterances. One would like, in order to explain linguistic behavior, that the enumeration produce a set of structural descriptions of the utterances, not simply the utterances themselves.

This requires one to specify very exactly what will count as a structural description. In fact, one wants to demand even more than that. The problem immediately arises, since people produce all sorts of grammatical and ungrammatical things: What, in fact, are the utterances that one is trying to explain? It would seem reasonable, as Chomsky has suggested, to demand of a theory of linguistic behavior in its formal aspects that the theory yield an assignment of a degree of grammaticalness to every sequence of letters in some basic underlying alphabet, say a phonetic alphabet. In other words, one wants a description of sentences such that all of the so-called partly-grammatical utterances can be described as deviations from a central set. One would like to have a theory that yields an assignment of degree of grammaticalness to all sequences. If you demand that a linguistic theory provide a set of grammatical descriptions for all sequences, and also permit the assignment of degrees of grammaticalness or degrees of departure from a central set, then—since so many more requirements are being made of the theory—it is possible to pick from a wide variety of different descriptions only that one or very small number of grammatical descriptions which can satisfy these requirements. In cases of a very simple corpus, or a corpus of utterances which are very simple, the problem is really acute. As the authors indicate, they seem to be wrestling with the idea of how one can possibly decide which is the real description of the many different descriptions one could give of a small corpus of utterances. The point I am trying to emphasize is that perhaps too little has been demanded of what is called the grammar. If one demands more, then one gets more specificity. One can then choose more accurately which grammar must underlie the linguistic behavior.

In the case of adult linguistic behavior, for example, one would like to be able to explain why an adult has the feeling that one sentence is related to another. This is going to be difficult in the case of infants, because of course one cannot question them directly. Again, maybe one can devise ingenious experiments to show that the child in fact treats two apparently dissimilar sentences really as versions of the same underlying sentence.

The last comment I should like to make refers primarily to the second paper in where there was an attempt to examine the question: Given some data and a bunch of alternative explanations, how does one choose the right one? I am not sure whether or not there is a confusion in the authors' minds about the notion of evaluation procedure, but the term was used. There was at least a suggestion that the development of some kind of device such as they were seeking in this paper was derived from the ideas of Chomsky in *Syntactic Structures* (1957). Chomsky pointed out that one reasonable minimal and perhaps also maximal requirement that one could make on a linguistic theory is that it afford what he called an evaluation procedure. The attempts made in this paper were called evaluation procedures, but I would like to point out that what the authors are doing here is very different from what was intended by the notion of evaluation procedure in *Syntactic Structures*. Presumably Chomsky meant that one might reasonably expect to find a grammatical theory or a theory of linguistic behavior which would not only afford a recursive enumeration of structural descriptions of all sentences in the language. One might expect also that, given any two such descriptions which are equivalent over the same data, there might then be an algorithm (meaning a mechanical automatic procedure) to decide which of the two is the more general. Notice that the important thing is that the two things being compared are already known to be descriptions of the same data. They are equivalent grammars, in a sense. One wants to know which of the two grammars that account for the same data is the more general or the simpler. All the authors are at pains to discover in the case of this second paper is some sort of a procedure, presumably a mechanical procedure if possible, which would give the best grammar in a kind of minimal sense, given a certain corpus of utterances supposed to be a sample of the language. Given two such grammars, then, which is the better one; but by "better," the authors apparently mean which one is converging on the data faster, or better. This is the general question that scientists are always asking. The so-called evaluation procedure was a much more restricted sort of task: Given two theories which are already known to be equivalent over the data, which is the more general? It is not clear that one could develop, at least easily, an evaluation procedure of the type attempted in this paper. The coefficients of fit that the authors try, they give up themselves because they don't seem to be reasonable measures of how well the grammar is doing.

I would suggest, then, in keeping with the remarks I made before, that perhaps one has simply demanded too little of the grammar and one has too few data to try to explain. All you have is a corpus of utterances which is supposed to be a sample of a very large corpus of utterances, and one is asking simply for an enumeration of that set. In the case of trying to find a reasonable English grammar, it is very hard to think of many different alternatives, given all the data one wants to experiment with. If one would throw in as data many other observations on what children do linguistically, and, if in addition one desires of the explanatory theory much more than simply an enumeration of the utterances, then perhaps the problem of how to choose a grammar will be solved.

OPEN DISCUSSION

1. A linguist described the methods that he uses in arriving at a satisfactory formulation of a grammar. In the case of adult English, the linguist writes rules because they correctly formulate his convictions about a certain set of utterances. The linguist's beliefs about the sentences of a language enable him to separate sentences from nonsentences, to know which things are related, and to distinguish degrees of grammaticality, etc.

It was pointed out again that a grammar for adult speech is intended to do more than separate out sentences from nonsentences. Ideally it would distinguish degrees of grammaticality and would provide a description of every sort of utterance produced. Many utterances are not actually sentences but are—presumably lawful—deviations from sentences.

There are many respects in which actual performance can deviate from the rules of the grammar, giving one different degrees of grammaticality. One way of deviating is by breaking constituent boundaries, as in the sentence "John read and Bill saw the play." Another way of deviating is by increasing category size, as in the saying, "Misery loves company." This is not a properly formed English sentence, since the verb *to love* is classified as an animate verb, which means a verb that must have an animate noun as subject. Parenthetically, this grammatical category can be given a name that suggests a semantic factor ("animate") because the syntactic regularities have a correlated regularity of reference: the nouns that serve as subjects of verbs like *love* and *breathe* and *wish* are names of living things. *Misery* is not an animate noun and so cannot properly serve as the subject of *love*. To combine *misery* and *love* in this way is to violate the regularities that lead the grammarian to form the particular subclass of nouns and verbs called "animate nouns" and "animate verbs." The speaker who says "Misery loves company" operates as if these subclassifications did not exist. This is a very minor departure from grammaticality. It is the sort of thing that is usually involved in creating metaphors, and English speakers readily understand the meaning of such an utterance.

Little is known as yet about the ability of ordinary adult speakers of English to judge degrees of grammaticality. With very young children no one has yet figured out how to elicit the simple dichotomous judgment of grammatical/not-grammatical. Clearly we are very far from knowing how to elicit from young children judgments of degrees of grammaticality.

Since the child has a rudimentary grammar, with only a small amount of subclassification, there is very little possibility for stratification of degrees of grammaticality. Because the grammar which we are ascribing to the child has structure only in the minimal sense of proscribing certain conceivable combinations, there cannot be many deviations from such structure. A small number of levels of deviation will lead one to include all possible combinations of words. In the case of adult English, this is not true—there are a variety of changes which can be made even along a single dimension, which result in utterances with different degrees of grammaticality.

2. A psychologist pointed out that the imitation results reported by Brown and Fraser bring to mind certain findings on the free recall of verbal material by adults. In free recall when there is no structure in the original material, it is generally the case that the strongest responses are emitted first and most reliably. These will usually be items near the end of the sequence. When there is structure in the material, free recall generally starts at the beginning of the sequence, and it is the items near the beginning that are most reliably produced. In the imitations of sentences produced by very young children, whatever words are produced are always produced in the original order, from the beginning toward the end. This suggests an appreciation of structure. On the other hand, the words most reliably produced are those near the end, which suggests that recent items have the greatest strength. By constructing sentences having varied properties in terms of stress and information placement. it should be possible to investigate experimentally the determinants of the child's imitations.

3. One of the psychologists working in child speech described his impression of the nature of this speech. The child between 2 and 3 years of age seems to be using English phrase structure grammar, with a few constructions not appearing and with some word-classes overgeneralized. Certain constructions, such as the inflection for plurality, when they appear at all, are generally used correctly. However, it is not the case that the child speech advances abruptly from the total absence of such inflections to the invariably correct use of them, which is what one might expect if they are learned as rules. Rather, the inflection is first used in some small percentage of the cases where it is required, and this percentage shows a gradual increase with age. This aspect of development looks more like a gradual increase of habit strength than like the acquisition of a rule.

Finally, it seems to be true that many of the nonsentences produced by young children are not even constituents of sentences, as they would usually be in the case of adult speech. A linguist found this observation very provocative. In writing adult grammars, the principal reason for assuming that sentences have a phrase structure is the way that sentences behave under transformations. The psychologists studying child speech have seen no necessity for crediting the child with transformations, and now it appears that there is also little evidence of constituents or phrase structure at the very early stages. The psychologists have written their descriptions entirely in terms of word categories and rules of sequence. It should be interesting to see whether behavioral evidence of phrase structure develops around the same time as the appearance in child speech of the transformations which require phrase structure analysis for their correct operation.

4. A linguist reported his impression that children who are producing very simple two- and three-word combinations are nevertheless understanding sentences of quite complex grammar. The question is, of course, does a child really understand the grammar of the sentence, or does he simply react with crude appropriateness to one or two salient words. If a parent at home says, "Would you like some ice cream?" the child may walk to the refrigerator that contains the ice cream. However, he might have done the same thing if the parent had said, "I do not want any ice cream" or, "We will not have ice cream for dinner" or "There is no ice cream in the refrigerator" or, even, "Cream ice like you would" or, "Colorless green ice cream sleeps furiously." In the natural situation at home, one does not produce the variations in a sentence that might indicate what the child has actually understood. It should be possible to vary sentences experimentally and discover what range of constructions is equivalent for the child.

IV

THE DEVELOPMENT FROM VOCAL TO VERBAL
BEHAVIOR IN CHILDREN

Margaret Bullowa, Lawrence Gaylord Jones,
and Thomas G. Bever[1]
Massachusetts Mental Health Center and *Harvard University*

This paper consists of a description of the research design for the study
of language development which we have adopted. Vocal development of
presumably normal babies is followed from birth by nonparticipant observation. The observations are made in the babies' own homes. The behavioral
context in which each of the babies' recorded vocalizations takes place is
specified. Detailed study of each child's development by independent observers makes it possible to relate vocal development to other aspects of the
child's development in terms of maturational and environmental influences.

This study has been initiated because of concern with the verbal aspects
of communication in the pathology and psychotherapy of schizophrenia.
The link between normal speech development and the communication difficulties of schizophrenics is supported by the widely held impression that
many of the phenomena of schizophrenia may be understood in terms of
regression to less mature stages of development (Freud, 1914). It is also
possible that deviations occur in the early speech development of people
who later become schizophrenic. Knowledge of the details of the normal
course of speech development is essential to detecting any such abnormalities
in maturation. Since most schizophrenics give the general impression of
speaking with normal articulation, possible deviation would have to be
explored at the microlinguistic level. Schizophrenic language has long been
known to have peculiarities in the ways in which words are used. More
recently, note has been taken of peculiarities in tone of voice and other
paralinguistic features connected with the expression of affect. The elucida-
tion of these aspects of the pathology of schizophrenia cannot take place
until the normal process is clearly defined and understood. It was the need
for this information, not currently available in sufficient detail, which led
to the initiation of these investigations.

---

[1] Principal Investigator, Linguist, and Acoustic Assistant. Study titled as above at Massachusetts Mental Health Center and Harvard University, Department of Psychiatry, supported by NIMH Research Grant, M-4300.

The *aims* of this investigation may be summarized as follows:

1. To study in the vocal productions of children the natural stages of development of two separable characteristics: (a) patterns observable in the paralinguistic features such as tone of voice, loudness, and rhythms, and (b) patterns observable in the phonemic features, the sound units out of which words are built. Both of these developing vocal patterns are to be related to speech patterns in the child's environment.

2. To determine whether a definite order of development can be demonstrated in the emergence of the child's ability to babble, use and recognize the phonemic contrasts of vocalization, i.e., to test the hypothesis concerning the step by step acquisition of speech sounds in children as set forth by Grégoire (1937) and elaborated by Jakobson (1941).

3. To study the mutual influence of the mother's and the child's speech patterns in the course of the child's development from vocalization to verbalization, with attention to the speech patterns of other members of the family and other environmental sounds.

4. To determine whether there is any consistent relationship between the child's development from vocal to verbal behavior patterns and the development of other behavior patterns.

METHOD

Subjects

The infants are selected before birth from an already well-studied population, the "Maternal-Infant Health Program" at the Boston Lying-In Hospital. This is a cooperating unit of the "Collaborative Study on Cerebral Palsy" under the National Institute for Nervous Diseases and Blindness. The use of this source provides normative data and protects us from unwittingly drawing conclusions from study of an unusual child. In order to obtain linguistically comparable data, the selection of subjects is controlled for certain characteristics. We have chosen to study first-born babies in families in which English has been the exclusive language used for three generations. We seek parents who are free from major physical and mental pathology. We prefer nonintellectual families to avoid undue concern with language development.

Developmental Observation

In order to be able to relate vocal development to maturational rather than chronological age, an independent team of observers assesses the progress of each child beginning at birth. The first examination is made immediately after delivery and includes specific tests of neurological adequacy and of sensory response to visual, auditory, tactile, and kinesthetic stimuli. These investigators hope to document individual differences in neonatal equipment. Two additional examinations are made during the lying-in peri-

od. The child is seen by this observation team in his own home at one week
and three weeks after leaving the hospital and at four-week intervals thereafter throughout the study. Each observation is documented with about
four minutes (100 feet) of black and white 16 mm film taken at 18 frames
per second to show typical behavior and responses to tests. The findings
are worked up independently by the child development observers, a psychi-
atrically trained pediatrician, and a senior child psychologist.[2]

This team is attempting to evaluate the impact of environmental influences on the innate equipment of each infant as it is reflected in all observable areas of his development. A prospective view of each child's personality
and general development might lead to a better understanding of his use
of speech as a specific response to his inner needs and his communication
with his environment.

Vocal Observation

High fidelity tape recordings are taken weekly[3] during the first 30
months of life of four first-born infants. Each observation consists of one-
half hour of tape and film of spontaneous activity of the child and any interaction in which she engages. Observations are made in the subjects' homes
with the mothers usually present.

In order to enable us to study the vocal sounds in original context, a
camera equipped with wide angle lens photographs the ongoing scene
every half second. This includes the child and her environment, her mother
when she is near enough, and the observer. Using a shielded microphone,
the observer dictates details of behavior at a finer level than the camera
records. The principal investigator, a psychiatrist experienced with both
adults and children, serves as observer in all cases. A stereophonic tape
recorder preserves these observations on a tape track parallel to the subjects'
track. The audio and cinema records are coordinated by a timer (masked
from the subjects) which gives a simultaneous coded audio and visual signal
at five-second intervals. This makes it possible to resynchronize the three
kinds of data.

We are using a field microphone masked by a "Hushaphone"[4] and
find that the observer's whispered voice cannot be heard by the subjects.
We have built a fairly compact and soundproof container for the camera
and timing devices. The camera is re-aimed only when absolutely necessary
to keep the child in view. The project is completely explained to the prospective parents. The mother is not expected to stage a performance but

---

[2] T. Berry Brazelton, M.D., and Mrs. Grace Young.

[3] The acoustic material from the first baby, born March 9, 1961, is augmented by a
second half-hour tape recording obtained each week. By coincidence, all the study babies,
chosen before birth, are girls.

[4] A device originally designed to mask telephones which we have now adapted to a
tape recorder microphone.

rather to do and say whatever she feels like while with her child. Although the situation is somewhat artificial, we have found that repeated recording sessions in the same household become routine. With mother and child in their own home we automatically sample the sound environment to which the child is ordinarily exposed. Our records contain the father's and mother's customary voices as well as other voices and noises which the child hears, e.g., pets, musical instruments, radio, TV, traffic noises, etc.

Under ordinary circumstances the observer and technician go to a subject's home as soon after nine A.M. as possible. The field equipment consists of a Tandberg 6 tape recorder and a Kodak Ciné Special camera packaged with timing and signalling devices. A tubular aluminum frame with panhead for mounting camera box and lower rungs to support tape recorder allows some flexibility in the field. While the equipment is being set up, the observer takes the opportunity to inquire of the mother about recent events in the household and about the baby's condition. The observation is started with the camera set up and the high fidelity microphone (Electro Voice 664) in operation. During the observation the technician keeps the camera pointed in the general direction of the baby, depending on the wide angle lens to catch the action, and monitors the tape tracks. The observer remains as near the subjects as possible without moving more than necessary so as to be able to report in detail items which the wide angle lens might miss or the film lose or distort, especially gaze, facial expression, and small movements at the extremities. The observer, while avoiding initiating action during the observation, is accessible to interaction initiated by the subjects. The film keeps track of the extent of participation of and in relation to the observer during the half hour's activity.

Each standard vocal observation produces three kinds of data: (a) 30 minutes of magnetic recording tape with audio material (taken at 7½ inches per second) from the subjects and environment, (b) 30 minutes of recording tape with dictated description, and (c) 90 feet (3600 frames) of 16 mm film of the observation (taken at two frames per second). Before the data from the standard session can be finally processed as a unit, each of these records undergoes individual processing and indexing.

Circumstantial information related to each observation is systematically recorded in two ways: (a) the technician makes notes on the time, temperature, equipment, and people present, and (b) after each session the observer dictates notes giving a general description of the observation, anything she considers important which might have been missed by the tape recorder or camera, and her general impression of the interpersonal situation.

Data Indexing and Processing

Whenever possible we index all three kinds of data from each standard observation within the day it was taken in order to keep track concurrently of significant changes in the babies' vocalizations so that we may be in a position to gather more data and test hypotheses when indicated. Furthermore, this enables us to reconstruct the situation while the experience is still fresh.

The audio track is audited and indexed by the technician, who enters on a worksheet items occurring within each five-second segment. These entries indicate source of the sounds: mother, baby, observers, objects, etc. Baby vocalizations are noted by a check mark corresponding to the appropriate time segment except in certain cases on nonlinguistic use of the vocal tract: cough, hiccough, etc. The descriptive tape track is transcribed by the typist and segmentation is indicated. The typescript is checked by the observer while auditing the tape. No further audit of this track is needed except to use the segmenting signals for orientation in detailed study of the audio track and resynthesis of the observations.

The film is viewed rapidly to review the events and activity occurring during the observation. A frame counter and visual signals on the film make it possible to analyze the subject's behavior in terms of observed motility. This specifies extent and direction of motion and distance between people, observer included. We hope to analyze the films in much greater detail when an analyzing projector becomes available to the project.

The behavioral data recorded during standard vocal observations on the film and on the observer's sound track will be coded in terms of categories describing gross neuromuscular patterns, facial expression, activity, and interaction with others.

INTERPRETATION

The audio material is studied in greatest detail.[5] A copy of the tape goes to the linguist for analysis. He is devising his own notation for infant vocal sounds and attempting to avoid the use of conventional phonetic transcription where it is obviously inappropriate, especially in the vocalizations produced during the first several months after birth. Several categories of vocalization are noted for these early months: "Whimper," "Tremble," "Cry," "Scream," which can be defined and contrasted in terms of duration, intensity, and pitch variation. These terms are given symbols (W, T, C, S) and noted on the data sheet at the appropriate time segments along with whatever diacritic additions are felt to be necessary. It is planned to attempt an acoustic definition of these terms and the additional terms which will become necessary for the analysis of later tapes, such as $<$ "opening," $B<$ "labial opening," $G<$ "velar opening," $>$ "closure," $>B$ "labial closure," etc.

---

[5] Since our oldest baby has only just passed her six months birthday at the time of writing, we are still concerned only with very early problems.

At the present time the tapes are being analyzed in roughly chronological order. Later they will be reviewed in reverse chronological order and compared in various ways in order to test the relevance of these categories to the development of the acquisition of distinctive speech units. Since the linguistic analysis is made mainly by the techniques of "impressionistic phonetics" (as opposed to instrumental techniques), it is planned to invite another linguist to review the data independently at the termination of the project.

RELATING METHOD TO AIMS

The work of the linguist brings out the natural development of vocal and verbal patterns. We plan to utilize acoustic analytic techniques when relevant as the project develops.

Emergence of the phonemic contrasts is studied by dividing the child's use and understanding of phonemic contrasts into three categories: (a) babbling, (b) purposeful use, and (c) discriminative comprehension. By being able to determine the situation in which the child uttered each vocalization, we expect to be able to follow in detail the progress from babbling to full command of language. We will attempt to relate the phonetic system which the linguist is developing for child vocalization to the phonetics and distinctive features of adult speech and also study these relationships by acoustic analysis.

Attention has been called to the observation that not only does the mother's vocalization influence the child's, but also the child's "baby-talk" influences the mother's speech. The vocalization of the child and the environmental speakers shall be related on two levels: (a) with reference to the habitual speech patterns of the children, and (b) in specific instances, closely neighboring vocalizations in the interaction. The acoustic record of the child's and the mother's vocalizations will be studied for evidence of imitation by listening and possibly by searching spectrograms. This information should enable us to study systematically the mutual effects at levels of magnification ranging from the level of fundamental pitch and distinctive features to that of content. Evidence of developmental achievement from examinations by our child development observation team (pediatrician and psychologist) and from MIH Study[6] examinations will be interpolated in the sequence and taken into consideration. The data on verbal development will be searched for evidence of consistent relationships with behavioral development in other areas. If any such recurring relationships occur in our limited series, it will be possible to test hypotheses on the vocal patterns accompanying specific developmental stages using a larger sample from the Collaborative Study.

---

[6] This is the local designation for the Collaborative Study.

CONCLUSION

For the field of linguistics, the introduction of modern technology and nonparticipant observation into the study of speech acquisition under essentially ordinary circumstances could contribute objectivity to an area still somewhat obscure. In the past, published reports have been based on studies of children within the investigator's own family, and, more recently, on institutionalized children. The main systematic studies by linguist fathers have started at an age when the child had already started to learn the language. This study is designed to use observers not otherwise involved in the child's language acquisition and to study the child's prelinguistic vocalizations in his natural habitat beginning at birth. By relating language development to the precise emotional and purposive situations in which it arises, we hope to understand the ways in which the utilitarian and affective aspects of speech become integrated. We expect that our study will test the hypotheses concerning the orderly acquisition of the distinctive features of the phonemes and other aspects of linguistic maturation.

While the order in which the distinctive features, phonemic patterns, and prosodic patterns are acquired is of importance to the linguist, the way in which they are learned could interest the psychologist, especially in regard to perception and category formation. If the normal order and patterning of verbal development can be established (and confirmed by later comparison with material from children developing in different language environments), the information could have application in other fields in which the knowledge of the structure of language is significant.

And finally in regard to the original purpose of our investigation of speech development, it is, of course, too early to make direct application to psychiatric problems. In the meantime we are collecting tape recordings of interviews with schizophrenic patients as a start toward developing a method of intensive study of their verbal communication.

FORMAL DISCUSSION

DELL HYMES
University of California

Bullowa, Jones, and Bever state their research concern clearly. They are studying the normal course of speech development in children now, so as to elucidate the verbal aspects of schizophrenia later. It is this relation between the present research and the later application that I shall chiefly discuss. My remarks apply, I think, to any study of speech development whose goal is a general understanding of its normal course, whether as a yardstick or detector of later regression or for some other purpose.

I should mention that the authors kindly sent me two statements of research plans besides the paper circulated for the conference, and, although all three statements are substantially the same, the other two do contain additional details of interest.

The project is still at an early stage. Beginning with cries at birth, it has followed its infant subjects at the most for six months, as of the time of writing the report. Thus it is too early to say much about the content of the data obtained, and, furthermore, the authors are committed to carrying through systematically with the design in hand. So far as the technological side is concerned, I am not particularly qualified by training or experience to say much about the details of recording and photographing or about the merits of the general research design. Some problems of obtaining data seem to have been met and solved, and the chief problem would seem to be handling the mass of data that is resulting in a manageable way. So far as the analysis of the data is concerned, I hope my comments will be of some value—that my background in the anthropological study of speech and my interest in the sociocultural context of speech may lead to some useful suggestions. With regard to this project, my comments may suggest the collection of some data supplementary to that now being obtained or at least suggest some additional analytic questions. With regard to projects that may be undertaken later or theories that may be developed from present research, I hope that my comments may direct attention to aspects of first-language acquisition that must ultimately be of concern to all who work in this area. What I say draws upon three papers, two published, one in press, which offer data and arguments in more detail than is possible here (Hymes, 1961a; Hymes, 1961b; Hymes, 1962).

Bullowa, Jones, and Bever stress that their data are obtained in a natural behavior setting, the babies' own homes, and that the behavioral context in which each of the babies' recorded vocalizations occurs is specified. At various points in their paper, and the other documents, they indicate their concern with the general subject of interpersonal communication and their concern, regarding verbal development, for its relation to behavioral development in other areas and to contexts of use. At the same time, their specific references are always to vocal behavior in the sense of the sounds of vocalization and the development of sounds into the phonetic and phonemic habits of a language. (The point emerges clearly in a March, 1960, document: "In order to bring out less obvious patterned aspects of the child's vocal behavior, systematic analysis by phonetic transcription and by machine will be made." Mention of "patterned aspects" leads directly and exclusively to mention of phonetic analysis by transcription and machine.)

Such a focus on the phonological aspect of verbal development is understandable. Phonology is a well articulated branch of linguistics, containing an important developmental hypothesis, that of Jakobson (1941). With regard to ultimate application of the research to psychiatric cases, there is reason to believe that schizophrenia has a phonological manifestation. Yet without prejudice to the study of the phonological aspect of language acquisition or of the grammatical aspect, I should like to maintain that a more general view of verbal development is necessary, a view more general at least than any in evidence in current consideration of the subject in linguistics and anthropology. The essence of this view can be indicated by saying that, whereas a study of phonology and grammar considers verbal development in terms of the acquisition of the referential function, verbal development itself is the acquisition of a complex of functions of speech among which the referential function has a special but not exclusive role. Another way of putting it is to consider verbal development in the first instance as the acquisition of utterances as well as of phonemes, morphemes, or transformations as such and as the acquisition of utterances not only as the output of or input for the operation of grammatical rules, but also as specialized in various functions, both as individual utterances and as participants in larger linguistic complexes, which we might term *routines* from the viewpoint of the participant and *repertoires* from the viewpoint of the situations. Just as reference itself is an intersection of utterance and context, an intersection of the range of meanings which the utterance can convey and the range of meanings which the context can support, so speech events generally, functionally viewed, are an intersection of the routines available to participants and the repertoires appropriate to situations. Here we must grant that Skinner's approach to verbal behavior (1957) has some merit. Although, as Chomsky has shown (1959), it makes the gross errors of ignoring the specific properties of language and of generalizing by analogy from nonlinguistic learning, still its focus on the engagement of utterances in situations is something we must come to if we are to comprehend adequately the verbal development of the child.

Bullowa, Jones, and Bever make in interesting statement with regard to this broader context of language acquisition, when they write: "By relating language development to the precise emotional and purposive situations in which it arises, we hope to understand the ways in which the utilitarian and affective aspects of speech become integrated." In short, they are concerned with the development in the child of differentiable functions of language. That is the area, I assume, that should ultimately be of greatest concern for the understanding of the genesis of schizophrenia, as well as for a theory of verbal development generally. The ideas of Bateson, Jackson, Haley, and Weekland (1956) on the development of schizophrenia through conflict between the referential and expressive functions (anticipated by

Sapir, 1949; De Groot, 1949; and others) certainly suggest this, and the work of Luria (1959) and his associates does the same. At the same time, this area of linguistic theory is the least well articulated, poorest in empirical grounding, most subject to preconceived opinion and a priori conceptualization.

Although the work of Bullowa, Jones, and Bever has some of its greatest promise in the light it may shed on the development of functions of language in children, the promise cannot be realized unless the authors give a great deal of explicit attention to the framework of such analysis, for there is not, as may be the case for phonological and grammatical development, anything like a satisfactory body of linguistic theory and method as to the terminal state. While a good deal may be learned without such a theory, and necessarily must be so learned, since the work in progress cannot be suspended until such an unpredictable millenium, it still would be a pity if the chance were lost for the interaction of the acquisition of data and the improvement of theoretical notions.

Let me complete my discussion by developing my argument in two ways: (a) by briefly stating the nature of the problem with regard to the terminal state of verbal development, (b) and by indicating what present and future contribution such fields as anthropology, sociology, and social psychology may be able to make to the solution of the problem.

The end result of verbal development is a child who can produce utterances characterized not only by grammaticalness, but also by appropriateness. Put otherwise, the child not only knows the grammatical rules of its language, but also its speaking rules or some portion of them. Its conduct shows some knowledge of expectations as to when speech is obligatory, when proscribed, when informative as an act by virtue of being optional. It shows some knowledge of a system of speaking, a system characterized partly by the fact that not all theoretically possible combinations of such various factors of speech events as senders and addressors, receivers and addressees, channels, settings, codes and subcodes, topics, message-forms can appropriately co-occur. It shows some knowledge of the hierarchy of functions which may characterize speech generally, or speech events particularly, in its society. And such knowledge is necessary, for of course it is not enough for the child to be able to produce any grammatical utterance. It would have to remain speechless if it could not decide which grammatical utterance here and now, if it could not connect utterances with situations.

There seems to be a developmental aspect of some complexity to the acquisition of this ability to function as a fullfledged member of the speech community. Luria's work and other reports suggest some independence from one another of the acquisition of referential, directive, and expressive functions. The work of Bernstein (1961) in England suggests major cognitive consequences dependent upon whether referential or expressive functions and routines predominate in the child's early linguistic experience.

When one scans the ethnographic literature, one finds little enough in the way of information. For various reasons of intellectual history, anthropologists have not performed their classic role of depicting relativity and cross-cultural variation so far as the development and the functions of speech are concerned. But enough can be gleaned to show that societies do differ in their beliefs about speech, the values they attach to it, the roles it serves in child development and social life generally, the ways in which it is implicated in other aspects of life affecting the child. What is transmitted verbally, for instance, differs radically as between ourselves, say, and the Kaska of Canada or some groups in Mindanao in the Philippines, where adult competencies are acquired by observation and practice without overt instruction. Sometimes neonates are believed capable of understanding adult speech (Mohave, Tlingit); sometimes their expressions are believed intelligible (Ottawa). Sometimes there are games and training of a metalinguistic sort, sometimes not. Sometimes a baby talk is imposed, sometimes discouraged (Comanche vs. Hidatsa). (See Hymes, in press.) Sometimes major socialization pressure intervenes at one level of communicative ability, at one juncture of psychosexual and linguistic development, sometimes at another. And so forth.

Of course, as Roger Brown (1958b, p. 258) has pointed out with regard to linguistic differences of the sort associated with Whorf, a good deal of the range of cross-cultural variation can be matched within a single society as diverse as our own. Psychologists and sociologists may contribute as much as anthropologists to an understanding of the aspects of verbal development sketched above. Two things are most needed: (a) To realize that the description of the terminal state in terms of factors and functions of speech events, an ethnography of speaking as it were, must be structural in the same sense as a modern grammar. Warrant for the existence of factors and functions as components of the speaking of a given community must be found, not imposed. The principle of contrast within a frame functionally relevant to the participants must continue to hold, and no list of factors or functions can be treated as an a priori "Latin model," needing only to be filled out. In Kenneth Pike's terms, (1954), the approach must be "emic," not "etic." (b) To develop as adequate as possible a comparative perspective, as background for the investigation of individual cases. Such a task would involve both the fuller gleaning of what insight cross-cultural variation, as reported in ethnographies, has to offer and the critical review of the various schemes of factors, functions, modes of discourse, and the like that have been proposed by philosophers, linguists, psychologists, and others. While none can be taken as absolute, many may prove heuristically valuable,

much in the way that a generalized phonetic classification and an acquaint-
ance with various phonemic systems prove heuristically valuable in getting
at the phonology of a new language, even though it must be described in
terms of its own system.

OPEN DISCUSSION

1. In the progression from vocalization to verbalization, a child acquires
phonemic contrasts, and the group thought it important to attempt to study
that process. One linguist said that there is a point, clearly, where one can
say that children have got phonemic contrasts. But it is extremely difficult
to say anything about the long period before this. The question of when
a child has a phonemic contrast depends on all sorts of complicated things
about the sentences he is producing: how differentiations come about at
the very early stages; with what consistency they are maintained under
repetition; what range of variability there is in each; and many other
questions.

Another linguist was impressed by the slow development of control
over the phonetic operations that underlie all language; i.e., vibration of the
vocal cords, lowering of the velum, and so on. This is clearly a development that depends on maturation. At the same time, presumably, the child
learns that these properties are used in the speech of parents to distinguish
words and that words are used according to certain rules. These several
processes are learned together, and so far have not been properly sorted out.
It is conceivable, however, that they are learned in some orderly way.

A psychologist said that he had long wondered what sorts of observations of child speech and behavior would justify one in crediting the child
with phonetic contrasts. He inquired whether there were not experimental
interventions that would provide some information about the child's control
of phonemic contrasts, interventions conceived in analogy with linguistic
field procedures. Consider, for example, the contrast between /p/ and /b/.
If the child says the word *pan*, he might be asked to say it again and again.
The investigator could determine whether *ban* was ever offered as a repetition or an equivalent of *pan*. The investigator could go on with, "Now I'll
say *pan*. Is this right: *ban*?" If the child sometimes said *ban* for *pan* and
accepted the investigator's *ban* as the same as *pan*, then it would seem likely
that the child did not have the contrast. Of course, the interventions would
have to be devised so as to distinguish between receptive control and productive control on the part of the child. A linguist agreed that these would
be very useful things to do, but added that they have not yet been done.

A linguist who is now working with children pointed out that, when a child has only a dozen or so words, he has no need for distinctive features or phonemes. The dozen words can simply function as a dozen distinct complex sounds. It should be possible to make absolute discriminations of a small number of sounds, but when a speaker has some thousands of words he cannot retain them as unique sounds. He must then have a small number of recurrent features or phonemes arranged in distinctive sequences.

It may be that *phonemic contrast* is not the right concept for the early stages in speech development, according to a linguist. One can hardly speak of the phonemes of deaf individuals' speech when they talk to one another in "sign language," and yet one might say that they "talk English." Similarly, it is possible that the child does not build up vocabulary on the basis of phonemic contrasts, but may use some other way of keeping his utterances apart. When a child has already developed some syntactic devices (that is, he has words, makes short sentences, and so on), he may still lack a morphophonemic apparatus and may use some other technique to differentiate utterances. If this is the case, argued a linguist, then the child's phonemic system would develop like the adult's only because of its position within the whole system of syntactic rules.

Even for adult speech, the theory of phonemics is not a settled matter. One linguist held that phonemes do not occur simply linearly and that it is not true that each of them corresponds to a certain physical part of a phonetic record. Therefore the technique by which a sequence of phonemes is mapped into a sequence of phones involves further information about the utterance in question and its syntactic organization. This is a fundamental source of problems in writing phonetic transcriptions of child speech, since one cannot describe the phonemics of a language independently of its structure. In order to arrive at the phonemes of the adult, it was argued, it is necessary to know something about the techniques by which they are producing sentences. The same may be true of the child.

2. An interesting point was made briefly in connection with Hymes' discussion of baby talk. It is possible that an extreme contrast could be found between societies in which children are never exposed to baby talk and societies in which there is a highly developed conventional baby talk. It would be worthwhile to compare the course of speech acquisition in the two cases. There is a possibility that baby talk functions as a kind of easy introduction to the language. Its simplifications may, for instance, facilitate the learning of syntax.

3. An idea often expressed at the conference received some clarification at this session. There must be some kind of distinctive mechanism, peculiar to the human brain, which is appropriate to the processing of speech. One must somehow account for the fact that, when children have heard a lot

of speech, they start to talk; whereas, if apes hear the same noises, they do not talk. A "language generator" must be built into the brain and set to operate independent of any natural language. The character of possible language, or the set of possible grammars, must somehow be represented in the brain. In the broadest sense, the language generator must contain the information-processing procedures which any human organism will use when exposed to some speech community. The language generator is either initially or through maturational processes primed to go off when suitable samples of speech are presented to it, and this has little to do with learning. This is not to say that man has *a priori* knowledge of any particular language. The particular language, particular grammar and phonological system, are *learned*. When we talk of language acquisition, it is often in the sense of the child's internalization of the particular grammar to which he has been exposed.

Experimental psychologists in general have seemed little interested in species differences. Now that we have arrived at the study of language, it is no longer possible to disregard them.

V

SPEECH AS A MOTOR SKILL WITH SPECIAL REFERENCE TO NONAPHASIC DISORDERS [1]

Eric H. Lenneberg

Harvard University and *Children's Hospital Medical Center*

Investigations of speech as a motor skill are relevant to a wide spectrum of interests. Speech, as much as ambulation and posture, is a synergism with central nervous system correlates. Clinicians have noticed for many years that certain mesencephalic and diencephalic lesions can produce disturbances in these mechanisms which are highly characteristic of certain diseases or insults to the nervous system. However, physiologists have not been able so far to describe the neurophysiological events that either lead to such disturbances or are responsible for the normal operation of the healthy mechanisms. On the behavioral side of the ledger our state of ignorance is well matched to that of the neurological side. It is relatively easy to classify disorders of speech or gait into vague groups such as "Cerebellar Speech" or "Tabetic Gait." However, objective description of symptomatology is totally lacking to date. Since we cannot review here the literature on efforts to describe gait (Drillis, 1958), it will have to be sufficient to state that, despite modern advances in electrophysiological and cinematographic technology, so far no important gains have been made towards interesting or revealing descriptions.

Speech, which may well be more complicated in some respects than gait, has an invaluable advantage over the study of gait in that it has acoustic correlates which today can be studied accurately. Since every acoustic modulation is directly related to some motor event, acoustic analysis is quite likely to lead to descriptions in which the temporal relationship of different events can be viewed easily and thus contribute to our knowledge of synergisms. The study of speech, then, is of fairly general interest and is thought here to be in some sense ancillary to neurophysiological investigations of highly complex coordinating patterns. Some 13 years ago Lashley

[1] Research carried out while the author was a USPHS Career Investigator in Mental Health. Grateful acknowledgment is made for financial support from the National Institutes of Health, Grants M-2921 and M-5268.

Research assistance of Freda Gould Rebelsky, Irene Nichols, Eleanor F. Rosenberger, and M. A. Whelan has been a valuable aid in this study.

(1951) discussed problems of what he called "serial behavior," and at that time he pointed out that we might speak of a syntax of motor patterns and that this would not be merely a metaphor but that there might be an essential (though not causal) relationship between grammatical syntax and motor syntax. The research reported here (still in its infancy) has been largely influenced by Lashley's reasoning.

The study of motor speech skills affords a longitudinal view of the acquisition of a motor skill by a child, the potential accuracy of which is unparalleled by any other longitudinal study. Moreover, the investigations sketched out below will be found relevant to learning theoretical models for the acquisition of speech. I hope to elucidate in some, however modest, way the relationship between speech as motor events and speech as psychological processes. If nothing more, I might at least be able to justify such a dichotomy and show that the separation of motor from psychological processes is not a mere theoretical fiction.

The work reported here is carried out under the auspices of the Speech Research Laboratory at Children's Hospital Medical Center in Boston. Since the project is still in its initial phase, the material below must be considered as research in progress; theoretical formulations are strictly tentative and may well have to be revised as the work progresses.

ONTOGENESIS OF MOTOR SPEECH SKILLS

Data

Samples of infant's vocalizations were tape recorded by either one of two methods. The vocalizations of infants of 3 months of age or younger were collected by a 24-hour sampling method. The technique and the specially devised apparatus are described in the Lenneberg, Rebelsky, and Chan article. The vocalizations of older children were recorded in a sound treated room at Children's Hospital at the occasion of visits for speech research. Following is a short list of the most striking acoustic features of early vocalizations. Although I shall confine myself here to a qualitative description, most of the data gathered lends itself to frequency of occurrence statistics and distribution studies relative to the children's age as well as to their maturation level such as can be determined by motor indices.

Ill-defined Formant Structure or Absence of Vowel Resonance

This is a constant feature in the vocalizations of the first three months. Figures 1 and 2a are examples. In the light of spectrographic evidence, it appears unjustified to speak of "frequency of occurrence of English vowels" at this age.[2]

---

[2] The frequency of the laryngeal tone in infants is, generally, considerably higher (ca. 350 cps) than in adults (ca. 250 cps for female voice). The Kay Electronic Sona-Graph,

Absence of Glottal Stops before Vowel-like Sounds

The virtual absence of glottal stops preceding vocalic sounds is a striking feature of children's vocalizations throughout the prelanguage period. (See Figures 2a and b, 3, 4, and 5.) When glottal stops are present, they tend to be of an exaggerated nature in comparison to standard English. In the repertoire of babbling sounds one gains the impression that the glottal stop is as much an autonomous sound as labial or palatal stops.

Discoordination in the Initiation of Vocalic Sounds

Figure 4 is an example of this feature. Notice that during the first 100 msec. formants move almost randomly up and down but begin to assume a definable pattern at point A.

Non-English Formant Distribution

Between 2 and 4 months the infant emits an increasing number of sounds that have more definite vowel color, but the formant pattern is only rarely identifiable as any particular English vowel. (See Figures 2b, 3, and 4.)

English Formant Distribution with Un-English Features

Figure 5 does show a distribution of formants which one might transcribe as the glide "yiai," but anyone experienced in the reading of spectrograms readily identifies several features which do not occur in our language such as the excessive amount of nasality and the slope of the second formant.

In articulatory terms these features reflect two peculiarities: first, events in the glottis are not as yet correlated with events in the oral cavity; second, the resonance producing deformations of the cavities of the vocal tract have a random aspect and unsteadiness about them that betray a poorly developed mechanism for steady control which is likely to be related to imperfectly specialized reafferentation mechanisms at this age, a hypothesis which still needs empirical verification.

Two other features are of interest because of their more definite relationship to somatic maturation.

The "Accordion Effect"

Figures 1 and 3 are good examples of this phenomenon. Notice that in each case the initiation of phonation is characterized by a constantly changing frequency rate of cord vibrations (each vertical stria corresponds to one phase of cord vibration). In the mature healthy voice, the vertical striae are seen to be equidistant, i.e., the cords immediately vibrate at a characteristic frequency. (Variations in pitch are reflected in slight variations in

---

however, was constructed to produce optimal display for the average adult voice and may therefore slightly distort visual distinctiveness of certain acoustic patterns in the vocalization of infants. The logical argument in this paper is not affected by this instrumental shortcoming in that it merely emphasizes the fact that there are dramatic acoustic differences between children's vocal output and that of adults.

cord frequency, but close inspection shows that, graphically, the striae continue to be fairly equidistantly spaced. This indicates that change in pitch is produced under good muscular control of tension of the cords.) What is peculiar about the instances referred to here is that for periods as long as one to two tenths of a second there is a constant change of frequency, the striae being irregularly spaced, indicating poor muscular control over the voicing mechanism. This feature is not seen in the mature, normal voice and cannot be reproduced at will. This as well as the next feature is of special interest because it makes spectrograms resemble those of the voices of adult patients with adventitious central nervous system diseases. Compare, for instance, Figure 3 with Figure 6b. The latter represents attempts at initiation of voice by an 11-year-old child with lesions in the dentate nucleus of the cerebellum and degeneration of the putamen and globus palidus. A more detailed discussion of this and similar phenomena may be found elsewhere (Lenneberg, 1962). Suffice it to say here that the feedback mechanism which controls the tension of the muscles that stretch the vocal cords is affected in both cases, even though the history of these disturbances is somewhat different for the two subjects. Such parallelisms between extremely immature behavior and behavior states produced by central nervous system disease are not uncommon in neurology. As the neonate moves from maturational stage to maturational stage, primitive reflexes are modified by and integrated with new sets of reflexes so that early life is in many respects characterized by reflex motor events which in the adult only reappear under conditions of disease where the ontogenetically recent or adult inhibiting reflexes have been blocked pathologically, releasing more primitive "strata" of reactions. Grasping, rooting, and plantar reflexes are typical examples in case. The spectrographic reappearance, in neurological patients with dysarthria, of motor speech phenomena that are only seen normally in small infants lends credence to the notion of *physical maturation of speech coordinating mechanisms.*

Tremor and Unsteadiness

Figures 1 and 2b show a periodic unsteadiness in the regions marked A which proceeds at a rate of up to 40 cps. There are no coordinated movements under the control of the central nervous system known to proceed at this high rate except for pathological phenomena in the adult such as fasciculations or in the immature such as quivering of the soft palate and chin in the neonate (Ford, 1960, p. 214). Figure 7 was produced by a 26-year-old housewife with an unlocalized but supratentorial lesion which resulted in a tremor of the diaphragm and/or intercostal muscles which is well reflected in the grossly abnormal pattern of interruptions in the higher harmonics in this spectrogram. The spectrographic patterns of small formant waves in Figures 1 and 2a or marbling aspect of higher harmonics in Figure 2b may be seen in distressed crying of infants up to the age of approximately 6 months, but eventually these patterns disappear entirely and they only recur in later life in stages of pathological voice synergisms.

At present we are analyzing our entire tape material in order to determine the relative frequency of occurrence of the spectographic features mentioned above as well as other articulatory phenomena.

Another facet of our research on speech motor skills has to do with determination of typical rates of articulatory movements in an attempt at discovering inherent rhythms in speech activity. A method for the completely mechanical determination of rate and rhythm in adult speech has already been devised and will be put to test shortly. The aim is to obtain some norms on these parameters of motor speech skills so that it will be possible eventually to trace the origin or appearance of "normal values" ontogenetically and to study the earliest vocalizations in the light of these perhaps speech-specific aspects of motor activity.

A Note on Imitation and Similarity

The discussion so far has made it plain that infant vocalizations throughout the first year of life are acoustically very different from speech sounds. This raises an important theoretical question. If it is true that the infant's earliest motivation for speech development is due to his discovery of the similarity between his own sounds and those made by his mother while attending to his needs, we would expect that the mother could with special effort reproduce the baby's sounds faithfully. Figures 8a and 8b show that this is not the case. They were obtained in the following manner. The cooing sound of a 3-months-old baby was recorded on a continuous loop so that it could be played back indefinitely and without switching the tape recorder back and forth. The mother listened through ear phones to her own baby's tape recorded noise with the instruction to practice imitation. When she reported that she had learned to reproduce the sound accurately, her own version was tape recorded. When mother's and son's spectrograms are compared, the objective differences become visually obvious. Once alerted to the difference, the two tape recordings also begin to sound very unlike each other. The same experiment has been repeated with other mothers always with similar results. We must conclude either that sound imitation is a mere fiction or, if the infant should indeed strive for imitation, that he is innately equipped to hear similarities between his and his mother's vocalizations where, objectively, there are definite differences.

Prerequisites for Language Acquisition: The Role of Motor Skills

Above I have given a rough indication of how articulatory skills of normal babies may be studied and profitably compared with dysarthric phenomena in older subjects. Now I would like to illustrate how a systematic study of children with various kinds of deficits may give us important insight into the process of language acquisition. I shall confine my comments to a few simple observations on the development of congenitally deaf children and of children with mongolism. In addition I shall briefly discuss a case of a child with severe somatic speech disability (congenital anarthria).

Deaf Infants

Deaf babies have been followed in the Speech Research Laboratory with a view to recording the history of their sound development. The procedure here was essentially the same as that used in the study of normal children. In order to include in our sample some neonate congenitally deaf babies, the City of Boston was canvassed for young couples where both parents were deaf. By this method I was successful in securing at least one congenitally deaf baby and making recordings at regular intervals since birth throughout the first year of life. Other deaf children were seen periodically beginning at ages as young as 18 months and followed through to their entrance into schools for the deaf. This study has revealed the following important fact. Neither deafness nor deaf parents reduces the sound activity during the first six months to any appreciable extent. Qualitatively, the sounds of the first three months are virtually identical among deaf and hearing children. From the fourth to the twelfth month there can be no question that a great number of sounds emitted by deaf children are very much like the sounds of hearing children; however, after the sixth month of life the total range of babbling sounds heard in the deaf appeared to be somewhat more restricted than those of hearing children. (Unfortunately, at this point I have no formal statistic in support of these impressions. The assertions are made on the basis of listening to the actual tape recordings. Nor is the number of subjects studied so far sufficient to present conclusive frequency distribution data.)

The speech education of the hearing-handicapped in the course of their schooling is also interesting. It is generally agreed that a child who is profoundly deaf in both ears and whose loss is congenital has an extremely poor chance of learning to use his voice and speech organs in the same way as normally hearing people do. To the members of this conference, who are sophisticated in linguistic analysis and phonological research, this may not come as a surprise; yet there is one particular aspect of the vocalizations of these school children that is surprising. It is an unassailable fact that these individuals will laugh and may even emit certain babbling sounds in connection with emotional states, displaying a perfectly normal voice with good pitch and loudness control. Yet in the course of their efforts to speak the quality of their voices changes entirely, frequently resulting in some ugly low or high pitched tone, completely devoid of pleasing intonation patterns and obviously uncontrolled by appropriate feedback. In other

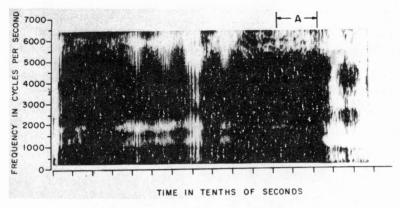

FIGURE 1—Spectrogram of 2-week-old boy, crying vigorously.

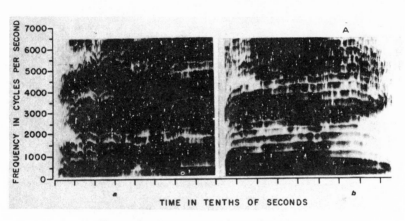

FIGURE 2a—Spectrogram of 6-week-old boy, crying vigorously.
Figure 2b—Spectrogram of 8-week-old boy, crying softly.

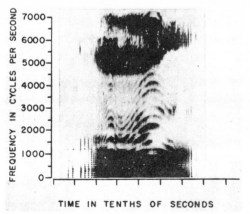

FIGURE 3—Spectrogram of
9-week-old girl, cooing.

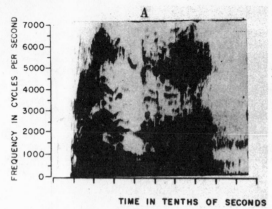

FIGURE 4—Spectrogram of 9-week-old boy, cooing in response to mother's talk (sounds like "ayeh").

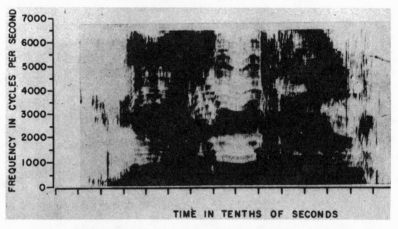

FIGURE 5—Spectrogram of 7-month-old girl, spontaneous cooing (sounds like "yiaiyai").

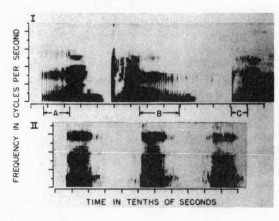

FIGURE 6a—Spectrogram of 11-year-old boy with Hepatolenticular Degeneration, saying "and cats get . . ." Bottom: Voice of healthy boy at same age.

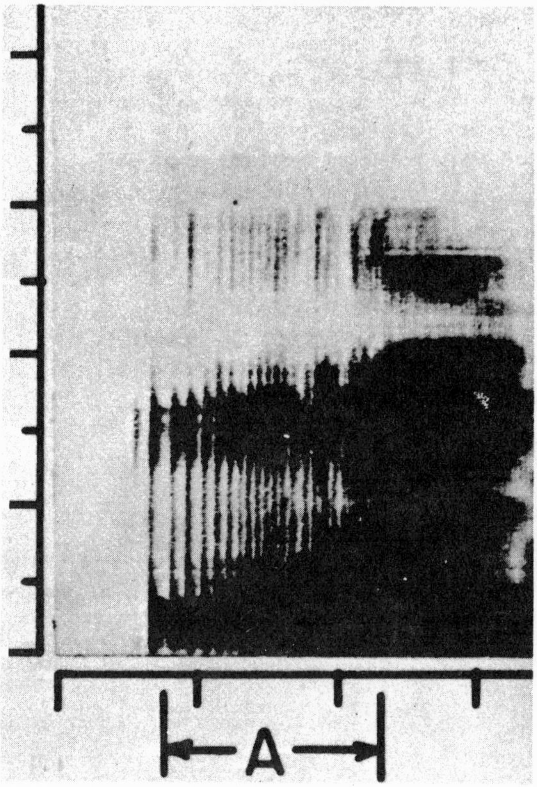

FIGURE 6b—Spectro-
gram of enlarged
detail of 6a.

FIGURE 7—Spectrogram of 26-year-old woman with unlocalized supratentorial lesion, saying "aaah."

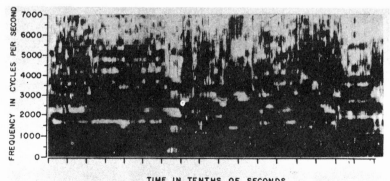

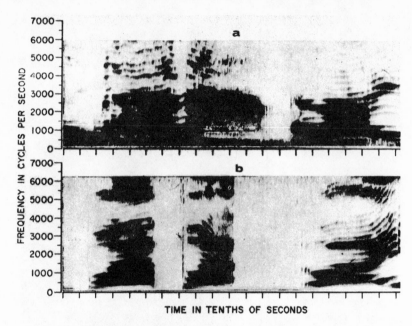

FIGURE 8a—Spectrogram of 3-month-old boy cooing.
FIGURE 8b—Spectrogram of mother imitating her child's cooing.

FIGURE 9—Spectrogram of 4-year-old boy with congenital anarthria; spontaneous sound "aaoo."

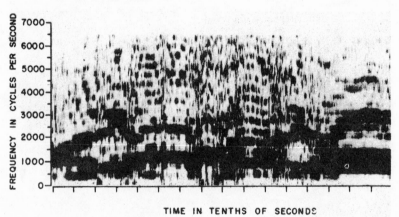

words, proprioception cannot take the place of auditory control, and no training procedures have been discovered as yet that would reinforce the use of normal voice and discourage the appearance of the abnormal-sounding pitch so frequently associated with deaf voices.

Language in Mongolism

A study of the language development of retarded children was undertaken in the hope that the retarded development would give us an opportunity to study the language acquisition process in slow motion. I had also hoped that this study would elucidate the question of the role of "biological intelligence" in the acquisition of language.

If it is true that there is a unique and orderly way of learning language, we would expect that certain stages of retardation are accompanied by certain definite stages of primitive language development and that each state should have some measure of consistency within itself. That is to say, there should be a correlation in the development of individual aspects of speech and language. For instance, we should not find a child who has learned to echo with great perfection but who is unable to generate grammatically correct sentences. Mongoloid children were chosen as subjects for this study because they offer a number of research advantages: the condition can be spotted at birth; and they constitute a relatively homogeneous test-population in that the condition produces a very consistent clinical picture which does not only extend over somatic symptoms, but also over behavioral ones. Thus, mongoloid children have typical mannerisms, typical ways of moving, typical ways of playing, and typical ways of communication.

For our study only children were chosen that are being raised by their parents at home. The vast majority of these children come from the middle income group, and the homes are frequently populated with other siblings. Since mongolism is not an inherited condition, these children come from normal stock which is further evidenced by the fact that their siblings have usually normal development.

My test population consists of roughly 60 children all of whom have been seen at least twice, most of them as often as three to six times. The research is observational and descriptive at the present stage. Tape recordings are made of spontaneous noises and speech; in addition a program of observations is followed which includes development of phonology (tested by the repetition method also used by Brown and Fraser), development of grammar with particular reference to the ability to concatenate individual words that are familiar to the subject, and syntactic development. Syntax is investigated both by the repetition method and by a scrutiny of the spontaneously emitted sentences. Further observations concern "semantic" development and the relative difficulties encountered by these children in learning the meaning of various types of words; we shall not concern ourselves at all in this paper with this last problem.

We have just finished making the first round of observations and are now in the process of analyzing the data; unfortunately, at the time of the present report final results are not yet available for this material. For the time being, the statements that follow ,can be corroborated only by playing typical tape recordings; the phenomena, however, are so dramatic that certain generalizations may be made with impunity about the over-all trend of the material. I shall confine myself to three important and obvious findings.

1. There is one stage—and some children's development is arrested at this stage—at which the subject is capable of repeating an English word only by rough approximation of the sound structure. When urged to repeat exactly what had been said to them, these subjects may, typically, improve the intonation and stress patterns of their response, but the articulatory skill remains consistently poor regardless of the number of repetitions. The disability has nothing to do with auditory preception of the word. In many instances it can even be shown that the subject is perfectly familiar with the word and knows its meaning. The deficit illustrates that a very special type of "understanding" is necessary in order to repeat the sequence of phonemes in a word following exactly the prototype. The understanding that I am referring to here has to do with understanding the *morphophonological structure* and rules. It can often be demonstrated that these children have imperfect acquisition of what Chomsky and Halle have called phonological syntax (unpublished seminar proceedings). Subjects may, for instance, have both a voiced and unvoiced interdental sibilant, but they may confuse these two sounds in the pluralization of nouns and not observe morphophonemic rules. Their utterances do allow of phonemecization; however, the phoneme structure is bound to be more primitive than the English paradigm, and, what is more important, the child will be consistent with himself in using the poorer phonemic system rather than having good enunciation of some, say, emotionally important words while using poorer enunciation for less important words. When we say glibly that learning to speak is "merely" learning to imitate, we forget that imitation actually implies the learning of analytic tools, namely grammatical and phonemic rules that can (and must) be applied to both the decoding and encoding of messages. This is even true on the level of so-called "simple phoneme sequences."

2. In a further stage of development some syntactic rules may have been acquired while others have not. At this stage children will repeat simple grammatical sentences corectly but make interesting mistakes in more complex ones even though the number of words remains the same as in the simpler constructions. A good example of this situation is the repetition of sentences in the active voice which for some children presents no difficulty, whereas to make them repeat similar sentences in the passive voice causes the child to make mistakes. Sometimes the mistakes indicate that

the child has not understood the sentence. At other times the child will produce a sentence that is grammatically correct but is put back in the active voice, often even preserving the original meaning. The same phenomenon occurs when these children are asked to repeat a question; they may repeat it with correct question intonation pattern yet without having performed the appropriate transformations. When we ask them to be very careful and repeat *exactly* what the experimenter has said, we find still the same failure prevailing and, even with the greatest effort, sentences will not be repeated correctly. The explanation for this extremely common phenomenon is quite simple. A sentence of 10 words contains an enormous amount of detail. It might consist of a sequences of some 60 phonemes, each one characterized by 9 to 12 distinctive features; each word in the sentence has well-defined intonation and stress characteristics; the sentence as a whole is the product of a male or female organ and bears acoustic peculiarities of age and idio-syncrasies of the speaker. "Blind" reproduction of all of this material, or even of the essentials, should be impossible, seeing that our memory is not even capable of reproducing a train of 10 random digits. Reproducing sentences in a totally unfamiliar language is difficult or even impossible because the sequence of phonemes strikes us as random. But when we understand a language, sequences of phonemes within words and sequences of words within sentences fall into familiar patterns that help to organize the stimuli and enable us to program the responses. The *sine qua non* for reproduction is, therefore, the ability to recognize the patterns—which is tantamount to saying the reproduction presupposes prior learning of grammar. When we are asked to repeat long sentences, we do not have to memorize the sequence of phonemes and their distinctive features, but as we receive the input signal we are capable of recoding the material in terms of a few principles, words, and their connections (Miller, 1956). We can now store this coded information which is simpler to do than storing the original, detailed information. When we are asked to reproduce the sentence, we reconstruct it by means of our knowledge of a few relevant rules. The output signal is now "our own way of saying what we heard" and is similar to the original only in terms of structural principles—not in individual phonological detail.

A child who has not acquired the complete grammar will fail to recognize the organization of symbols in a grammatically complicated sentence and is thus unable even to *store* the input signal without detrimental alterations. Apparently there are developmental stages at which recognition of certain grammatical patterns is possible without, however, being able to *use* the pertinent rules as yet. Thus a child may understand the meaning of a sentence couched in the passive voice, "The dog is fed by the boy," but, when asked to repeat it, the child will say "The boy feeds the dog."

(I may mention that my findings on the reproduction of syntactically complex sentences do, indeed, furnish some evidence in support of Chomsky's notion of "understanding a sentence" and are practical evidence against the recent criticisms levelled against Chomsky by Reichling, 1961, who doubted that it is true that we understand a passive sentence on the grounds of its relationship to its underlying kernel sentence in the active voice.)

3. There are children with mongolism who do attain an excellent control of the English language. These are children with IQs of 50 or better. They will apply rules of grammar on most grammatical levels correctly even though the subject matter of their conversation may not be very bright.

I have mentioned these facts in order to indicate that there are some cases where the motor skill itself (which is thought to be a prerequisite for the "proper response-shaping" into language) is definitely present, yet language does not develop properly in spite of conducive environments, motivation, and all other variables commonly identified with the necessary reinforcing conditions in a learning situation.

One of the conclusions we must draw from the study of speech development in mongoloid children is that babbling and making noises approximating English are insufficient conditions for the complete acquisition of language skills. Some central element is also necessary. There is the temptation to label this element simply as *intelligence*. However, this is not saying much in the absence of good definitions of this concept. An IQ of 50 is deficient enough to keep a child from learning the most elementary concepts (counting, social distance, rules of kindergarten parlor games), yet it is high enough to use correctly plurals, tenses, question transformations, etc. The general problem that emerges from these considerations, and which is central to psychological theories at large, is: Why are certain tasks easier than others for a given species regardless of stimulus variables (recency, frequency, intensity) or motivational variables?

Before relating the findings of mongoloid speech with those of deaf children, I would like to present one other case of speech handicap of an entirely different nature.

The Acquisition of Language by a Speechless Child

A detailed report of this case may be found elsewhere (Lenneberg, 1962). In brief this is an 8-year-old child with a congenital neurological deficit for speech articulation. He can make sounds like Swiss yodelling, but he has never babbled or made any attempts at word imitation. He is mildly retarded (IQ in the 80 to 85 range). Psychiatric examination is negative. Family and social history are unremarkable. When this child was first seen at Children's Hospital at 3 years of age, it was at once obvious that his motor-speech handicap had not impaired his ability to learn to understand English. Since then he has been examined repeatedly, and his "passive language ability" has been investigated thoroughly. I have recently made a sound film of this patient which documents the ease with which he can execute commands, and it shows also other dimensions of his language comprehension. He understands prepositions, number concepts, and the meaning of color words. He fails in distinguishing right and left, but he can answer questions without "situational support." He can answer questions such as: "Does ice cream feel cold on your tongue?" "Is a spider a light animal?" and so on. He knows the meaning of such words as *now, later, always, yesterday,* and he can answer questions about a story even when they are put in the passive voice, thus demonstrating a complex analytic capacity for linguistic structure.

Figure 9 is a spectrogram of a typical example of this boy's vocalizations. It shows grossly abnormal control over voice and organs of articulation and there is evidence of a continuing tremor which closely resembles that of the patient whose voice and speeech is reproduced in Figure 7.

Throughout the past 20 years traditional learning (conditioning) experiments have been performed on dogs treated with curare or similar drugs (Kimble, 1961, pp. 224f). The drugs render the animal totally paralyzed throughout the training period, and the objective has been to discover whether it could learn to adapt its motor behavior to certain new conditions even though it had been prevented from emitting motor responses during the training period. By and large the results of these experiments agree with each other and with a wealth of other data indicating that there is no need to assume an immediate and intimate relationship between a stimulus and a motor response in the course of the experimental acquisition of simple motor performances. In the light of these findings it is noteworthy that many learning theorists, when speculating about the acquisition of speech, either explicitly state or at least imply that this is a gradual process in which verbal responses of some primitive nature (e.g., babbling) are the essential prerequisites for language development. The difficulty (or actual impossibility) of teaching lower mammals to speak is attributed by these theoreticians to the animal's failure to babble.

The case reported here is evidence against this theoretical position. The learning situation here was very similar to that of the curarized animal, and the results of those experiments agree with the findings reported here. The case presented is an extreme example of a comparatively common clinical entity—severe congenital anarthria with unimpaired (or nearly unimpaired) intellect.

CONCLUSIONS

We have treated two distinct subjects: (a) the articulatory development of infant vocalizations and (b) the relation of speech as a motor skill to language as a psychological skill. We have briefly discussed the interdependence of these two skills during the acquisition of either. Table 1 sum-

TABLE I

Relationship of the Capacity for Making Speech Sounds to Understanding
Instructions as Illustrated by Children with Various Handicaps

UNDERSTANDING	MAKING SPEECH SOUNDS		
	Cannot	*Can but Does Not*	*Can and Does*
Does Not	Amented children (No language develops.)	Never observed	Feeble minded children (If IQ below 50, only primitive beginnings of language.)
Does	Congenital anarthria with normal cognitive development (Language can be acquired.)	Autistic and psychotic children (Some evidence for subclinical language acquisition is common.)	Normal children (Language is acquired spontaneously.)

NOTE.—The capacity for making speech sounds does not insure language development.

marizes the findings. It appears that understanding is more significant for language development than the capacity for making speech sounds.

Spectrographic evidence was adduced in describing the gross acoustic differences between the child's prelanguage vocalizations and mature language sounds occurring by the third year of life. The observations are of interest to psychological theories because they throw considerable doubt on the often heard assumption that the infant hearing himself babble notices the similarity between his own noises and those of his parents and that this similarity has the effect of secondary reinforcement, starting the child on his long journey towards perfect acquisition of speech skills. Since his own sounds are demonstrated to be objectively very different from those of the adults, the child must have some peculiar way of determining or recognizing similarities in the presence of diversifications. The descriptions are also of neurophysiological interest—even if only propaedeutic—in that relationships between immature motor coordination in the neonate on the one hand and discoordination due to central nervous system lesions on the other can be demonstrated.

A comparison of vocalization and speech behavior of deaf children, of children with mongolism, and of one child with congenital anarthria revealed the following important points:

1. The voice, intonation pattern and large part of the phonological repertoire of the profoundly deaf cannot be shaped into normal standards, despite the normal quality of these children's voices and sounds in their earliest infancy. Thus, training is of no avail here because of a peripheral interference with the nervous control mechanisms.

2. Mongoloid children with IQs of about 50 or less babble and produce approximations to English speech sounds but cannot be trained to develop full-fledged language because of a central deficit.

3. A child with congenital anarthria was described who has never been able to make normal babbling sounds and who has never acquired any motor speech skills, but who has perfect understanding of language.

From these observations we may conclude that motor speech skills are neither necessary nor sufficient prerequisites for the development of those psychological skills which seem to be an essential substrate for mature language. Certain aspects of motor speech development appear to be based on the innately given neurological mechanism controlling the voice box and vocal tract. Artificial shaping of random motor responses into controlled speech components meets—at least in the case of the deaf—with great difficulties.

SUMMARY

Sound spectrographic analysis of vocalizations during the first three months of life was presented and an automatic recording device for objective sampling was described. Language development was discussed in the light of these investigations and of studies of children with a variety of central nervous system deficits and peripheral deafness. It was found that language development may occur in the absence of motor speech skills and that the presence of motor speech skills is no insurance for language development.

APPARATUS FOR REDUCING PLAY-BACK TIME OF
TAPE RECORDED, INTERMITTENT
VOCALIZATION [1]

C. H. CHAN

Belmont, Massachusetts

ERIC H. LENNEBERG *and* FREDA GOULD REBELSKY

Harvard University and *Children's Hospital Medical Center*

Tape recording of verbal transactions is an increasingly used research tool. However, the problems of analyzing tapes are often enormous, and much time is wasted listening to recorded silence and timing taped sequences in order to get quantitative measures. The present apparatus was developed in order to reduce play-back time and to simplify quantitative

[1] Grateful acknowledgment is made for financial support from the National Institutes of Health, Grants M-2921 and M-5268.

analysis. It prevents the recording of silence but provides a graphic record of the distribution of noise over given periods.

The authors have used it successfully to investigate the vocalizations of human infants during 24-hour sample periods. Other uses for the apparatus will readily suggest themselves.

The equipment consists of an assembly of three units (Figure 1):

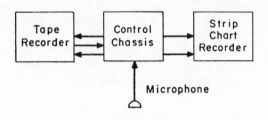

FIGURE 1—The equipment set-up.

1. A tape recorder with remote control transport (Uher model "Universal").

2. A control chassis (Figure 2) to operate the tape recorder and the strip-chart recorder.

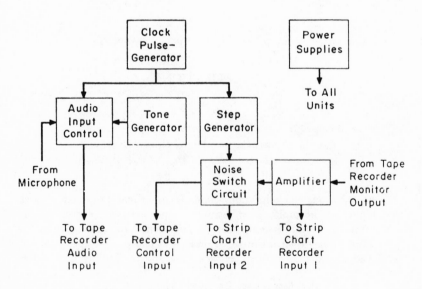

FIGURE 2—The control chassis.

3. A two channel ink writing strip-chart (polygraph) recorder (Brush Instruments Oscillograph model RD 2322 00) which registers the tape recording activities and time in hour-step signals.

The instruments are so connected that the tape recorder is turned on by any noise in the environment (with negligible delay) but shuts itself off after cessation of the disturbance. The strip-chart (polygraph) runs continuously, recording in one channel the time and the on-off activities of the tape and in the other channel the rectified acoustic input signal irrespective

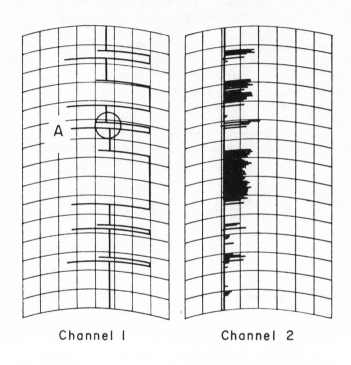

Channel I   Channel 2

Channel I. Record of off-on positions of tape recorder.

Channel 2. Record of noises in sound field of microphone.

A shows point at which baseline moves to indicate a new hour. Paper speed 6.5mm/min.

FIGURE 3—Sample of strip-chart recording.

of whether its volume is above or below the threshold for turning on the recorder. There is a time lapse between cessation of noise and stoppage of tape transport which can be varied manually from a short delay of .5 second to a maximum delay of 10 seconds. Periodically (for our study, every 60 minutes) a clock pulse-generator gates on a tone generator to produce a short beep signal of 1.5 seconds duration. This signal is recorded on the tape so that the final tape recording is segmented into periods marked by beeps to help orientation during play-back. The hour information is also clearly marked on the strip-chart as hour-step signals (see Figure 3).

Since the tape stands still during silence, it produces an economically "packed" tape. In the case of our research on baby-noise it was possible to reduce the 24-hour observation period to three to four hours play-back time. Yet the distribution of these noises over the baby's day are accurately preserved on the strip-chart which was left running continuously throughout the day. Synchronization of noises heard on the tape with signals seen on the strip-chart is easy because of the recurrent hour marks in both records.

The apparatus makes little noise and can be removed completely from sight and hearing range of subjects by using a microphone with a long cable.

FORMAL DISCUSSION

MORRIS HALLE

Massachusetts Institute of Technology

Two separate functions are involved in language; there is the function involved in computing an utterance, and that involved in actualizing it or speaking. I call the latter the print-out stage.

Lenneberg's paper clearly and strikingly separates the computation and print-out stages of language. He demonstrates that the ability to compute an utterance does not depend on having available a print-out device that can make the utterance physical.

I was therefore somewhat surprised that in the first section of his paper he tried to prove that children who can make sounds but cannot speak do not utter English sounds. When I asked him why he had chosen to argue this self-evident point, he replied that many people believe the contrary. As I told Lenneberg then, I believe that all such argument is about as useful as trying to argue with an archaeologist who, on finding a thin piece of metal in a Roman grave, publishes this as proof that telegraphy and telephony were already known in classical antiquity. To prove to such a person that what he had found could not possibly transmit electrical impulses would be entirely useless, for it would almost certainly provoke the reaction that, if no wire was found, then it is clear that the Romans had wireless telegraphy.

I have a suggestion to make about the spectrograms which are presented in the paper. It is an unfortunate characteristic of the Sonagraph that it produces very bad spectrograms in cases where the band width of the analyzing filter and the fundamental frequency of the voice of the person speaking are less than a factor of two apart. The band width of the analyzing filter on the Sonagraph is 300 cycles, and the pitch of children's speech is around 300 cycles. In the Sonagrams presented, some things are artifacts due to this unfortunate coincidence. For example, Lenneberg states that in Figures 1 and 2a there is not a clear formant structure. I would say that one cannot tell, for with a wider filter one might actually get formants. I would suggest, therefore, using a wider filter or a different method for displaying the results.

FORMAL DISCUSSION

Hans-Lukas Teuber
Massachusetts Institute of Technology

There is one fact that both Lenneberg and I would wish to make clear: we do not know the neurological basis for speech movements. It was the main point of Lashley's Hixon Symposium paper (1951) that we do not know how serially patterned movements get themselves serially organized. What we have in neurophysiology is so inadequate as to obscure the very existence of the problem. The chaining of reflexes, any kind of reafferent theory that goes via the output, must be inadequate for the explanation of sequentially patterned movements, from walking or swimming to speech itself. While speaking, walking, and swimming are all serially patterned, speech offers additional complications which we can illustrate by discussing what Lenneberg has said.

Lenneberg was talking about problems of language acquisition in the presence of three sorts of deficits: (a) sensory deficits as in deafness; (b) motor difficulties due to disease; (c) central deficits of the kind usually called defects of intelligence. I would like to discuss these three points in the order in which I have given them here.

Sensory Deficits

Suppose it is true, as it appears to be, that there is no speech acquisition in the total absence of auditory input, unless, of course, the input is presented through a different channel. If this is the case, i.e., if congenitally deaf children or children who became deaf within the first two years do not acquire speech, then there seems to be a difference between speaking and such movements as walking and swimming. In lower forms there is increasing evidence that such serial patterns as walking and swimming are to a large extent autonomous; they unreel themselves in the absence of specific sensory feedback.

Of course most of the experimentation has been done on lower vertebrates. If you cut all the dorsal (sensory) roots in a fish and cut his spinal cord at the neck (which of course is not a major operation in the fish) and then put him in warm water, he will start swimming again, after a fashion. That is, he will develop extremely intricate rhythmic movements of the appendages; these have been recorded and analyzed in great detail by von Holst (1939). The motor system "plays its score," as Paul Weiss (1941) would say, even though the audience has gone home. A similarly striking automatism or spontaneity of centers can be shown for breathing movements. One can take the breathing centers, in the brain stem, out of the goldfish, throw away the goldfish, and record from the medullary neurons, getting essentially the same wave-forms as in the intact fish (Adrian and Buytendijk, 1931). The pattern is emitted by itself, without the peripheral feedback that is provided in the normal animal.

This of course is true at lower levels; fish are the lowest vertebrates. If you go a little higher, it becomes a bit more complicated. People have repeated the Holst-type radical de-afferentation experiment and studied walking and swimming movements in toads (Gray and Lissman, 1946-1947). Some say that von Holst is "wrong" because one dorsal root has to be left intact. Yet note that this is in toads—not fish, and it can be any one root at that, up and down the toad's spinal cord; and that is still fairly close to von Holst's result. A toad that has one root open—one sensory input, with motor roots intact—will walk on a solid substrate; if he comes to the edge of a pond set up in the laboratory, he will plunk into that, and will then swim. Thus, the movement shifts appropriately from walking to swimming pattern, and all that with one root—any one—providing a nonspecific input. The toad becomes quiescent when that last root is cut off (Gray and Lissman, 1946-1947).

If we follow Lashley—in going from this kind of pattern on to speech —I think we miss an interesting difference: the afferent patterns are much more crucial in speech than they appear to be in such autonomous, rhythmic, repetitive movements as walking and swimming. There is some question of how far one can generalize from the fish and toad to the monkey and man (Teuber, 1961a). But in the monkey, for instance, if you de-afferent a limb, the limb is not used (Mott and Sherrington, 1895). It looks paralyzed and just hangs limply. But if you excite the animal, he can now move that limb quite adequately, usually in unison with the other limb, like a mirror image: a flexing movement on one side is accompanied by flexion on the other side; extension is coupled with extension. By contrast, the very crux of good articulation in human speech is independent movement in several parts of the articulatory organ. In the early stages of speech development in the child, and later on, in decomposition of movement in acquired motor disorders, the characteristic picture is that of forced obligatory association of movements, i.e., movements have to go together that for proper enunciation would have to come apart and would have to be modulated independently of one another.

I understand Lenneberg to be saying that severe sensory deficit is quite damaging for speech, and this I think would set it apart from such built-in patterns as swimming and walking. In speech we have an extremely intricate movement of the mouth organs and throat which is not necessarily rhythmic and repetitive as are breathing, swimming, and walking. Speech is different, depending on the language community in which one grows up; it is critically dependent upon a particular patterned input—not just on an energizing input like the one dorsal root giving a kick every once in a while so that the apparatus doesn't go quiescent.

There is one further observation I should like to make about the implications of sensory deficit for speech acquisition. I feel that it should somehow be possible to get through to the deaf child who does not acquire proper speech. Of course there have been many attempts to do just this—attempts going back to Alexander Graham Bell. The issue behind the success or failure of such attempts lies in the comparability of different sense modalities—the possibility of cross-modality transfer without special training. In recent years—influenced by the new empiricist tradition, by von Senden (1932) and Hebb's interpretation of von Senden (1949)—we have gone a long way toward disbelief in the possibility of such transfer. Too far perhaps. For 15 years now I have been reading and rereading von Senden's library dissertation; he did not see cases but interpreted the reports of others. I have never quite understood—never quite believed what he says (Teuber, 1960; Teuber, 1961a; Teuber, 1961b).

Consider this instance from a case report by Dr. Richard L. Gregory from Cambridge University (unpublished). The patient was a man who had been blind for over 50 years; he was 52 when his opaque corneae were removed to render him able to see. Dr. Gregory, in examining this patient in the hospital, picked up a magazine and pointed to the word "Everybody" on the masthead. It was printed in a peculiar way—a combination of block letters and lowercase letters. The patient read this word correctly as "Everybody," but insisted that he could only make out the block letters; he said he was guessing those printed in lowercase. In explanation, the patient reported he had been taught, in his school for the blind, not only to read braille, but also to palpate block letters, so that he might be able to decipher the embossed name plates at doctors' offices.

Now this observation—if my recollection of it is correct—runs counter to most of von Senden's case histories: the observation of Dr. Gregory's implies an almost immediate visual-tactile transfer. Perhaps we have to reconsider these issues: generally, the evidence for cross-modality transfer may not be as bad as von Senden makes it seem. The issue is of considerable importance; because, if there is some transmodal transfer, then we can expect much more effective substitution of a remaining sense modality in the deaf for a missing one.

MOTOR DEFECTS

In addition to studying sensory deficits, Lenneberg has explored the consequences of motor defects for language acquisition. His case study denies that response emission is important for the understanding of input: a child may learn how to listen to speech sounds made by others, and to understand them, without having learned how to speak. Ervin made a similar point; in her experience with normal children, the understanding of grammar appears to antedate the proper production of grammatical contrasts. These observations have important implications for the theory of perception. It bears on the ideas developed by the Haskins Laboratory group in their work on speech analysis and synthesis. Their working hypothesis invokes "articulatory reference" as the basis of speech perception; when I hear a phonetic distinction, it is because I have made the distinction implicitly (see, e.g., Liberman, 1957). The strong form of this hypothesis requires that we go through the overt motor sequences at first, and then put them gradually inside our heads, so to speak. But if it can be proved that we do *not* need to be able to produce the phonetic distinctions that we can detect, then I think this type of motor theory of perception is called into question.

However, there may be an intriguing alternative: the motor systems may be able to "inform" the sensory systems directly via a central discharge, and without the peripheral loop invoked in the ordinary reflexological notions of peripheral feedback from motor output to sensory centers. The possible role of a direct discharge from motor to sensory centers is being considered by an increasing number of people, including the same von Holst I have mentioned before, together with Mittelstaedt (see, e.g., von Holst and Mittelstaedt, 1950). Simultaneously, and independently, Sperry has come to the same conclusions about the bases of sensorimotor coordination (Sperry, 1950); essentially analogous proposals were made by MacKay (1956), by Held (1961), and by myself (1960; 1961a; 1961b). This postulated central discharge—we call it the "corollary discharge" (Teuber, 1960) —is thought to be emitted each time we make a voluntary movement. Thus, as the efferent signals move out, from the motor system to the peripheral effectors, there is concomitantly a massive discharge from the motor to the sensory system within the central nervous system, and prior to any return signal from the periphery. In fact, these return signals—the re-afferent streams that move back up into the central nervous system—have to be compared, centrally, with the expectation of the changes in the input that result from the movements our body is about to make. This postulated central discharge, which represents the expectation of a normally occurring change in afferent patterns, can handle such classical problems as why the world stands still when we move our eyes voluntarily. We are now getting a certain amount of physiologic evidence for this "corollary discharge"; for instance, we now know that some fibers of the pyramidal tract discharge directly into the dorsal column nuclei, the relays of the somatic sensory system. The anatomical evidence for these connections has been available since 1903 (Probst), but nobody remembered it, since it made no theoretical sense. More recently, experiments involving both macro- and microelectrode recordings have shown that every time efferent discharges descend in the pyramidal tract—the classical motor tract—there is modulation of activity in the major brain stem structures that transmit sensory impulses upward into the forebrain (Magni et al., 1959; Towe and Jabbur, 1961).

If our assumptions about the hypothetical role of these corollary discharges are correct, then we might be able to make a word honest that has been taboo, and that is the word "voluntary." In a sense, we would have a physiologic basis for distinguishing voluntary from involuntary movement. A voluntary movement now would be one in which there is a corollary discharge, by which I reset my central sensory mechanisms for the anticipated change. An involuntary or passive movement would be one in which no such corollary discharge meets with the ascending input.

Incidentally, these notions do not fit at all into current S-R theory, and that's why I think these notions may bear on studies of speech and language. After all, it is in the approach to language learning that S-R theory fails so utterly, and S-R theory—as Lashley never tired of pointing out—is only traditional reflex-physiology "psychologized."

CENTRAL ("INTELLECTUAL") DEFECTS

This brings me to the third point implicit in Lenneberg's remarks—the deficits in language that can not be traced, either to clearly sensory or to clearly motor troubles, but to some central deficiency that we consider intellectual. Let me turn therefore to work on mongoloid children and those with other forms of severe mental deficiency. I would like to bring out some rather striking features of visual discrimination learning in these defective children. Such unusual features are best obtained by using nonverbal tasks, or, as we like to call them at our laboratory, "monkeyfied" tests, that is, tasks derived from work with nonverbalizing (infrahuman) organisms and adapted for use with human subjects. These experiments were done by my former student and present collaborator, Rudel (1957; 1958; 1959; 1960). The results point to certain serious shortcomings of the S-R approach and, indirectly perhaps, to the question of those stages in perceptual development that either antedate or accompany the acquisition of certain forms of language.

The experiments in question deal with the classical problem of "transposition of response" in discrimination learning. Köhler (1918) was the first to show this phenomenon for chick and chimpanzee. After training a subject to choose the larger (or brighter) of two targets and then presenting him with another pair of targets still larger (or brighter) thus:

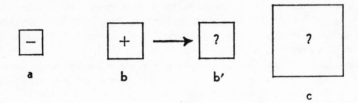

one often elicits choices of the largest target (c), as if the subject had learned to respond to the relationship ("larger-than") rather than to the previously rewarded "absolute" target (b'), which is now the smaller one in a new pair. As you all know, S-R interpretations of this seemingly "relational" form of responding have invoked the postulation of "gradients" of positive and negative response-tendencies, which are said to interact in such a way that one can predict both the occurrence of transposition under certain conditions and its failure under other conditions, e.g., with very large stimulus differences (Spence, 1937).

However, one can show the inadequacy of this view quite simply by taking three rather than two discriminanda and by requiring the subject to find a reward—say a raisin—under the target of intermediate size. In such intermediate-size problems, transposition can no longer be attributed to interacting gradients, since the negative gradients around the largest and smallest stimuli should tend to balance each other, thus leaving the position gradient around the middle-sized prepotent. Thus, there should not be any transposition: according to S-R theory; the response should be made to b'.

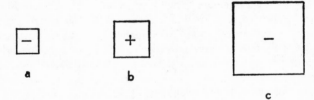

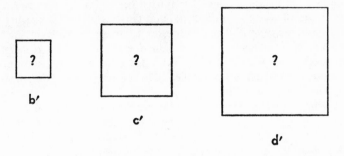

In cases where transposition of response does occur (response to c′), S-R psychologists have invoked language as the mediator of such a response: the subject instructs himself audibly or sotto voce: "It's still the middle-sized object!" In extensive tests of performance on tasks involving the intermediate-size problem, Rudel has been able to show that transposition of the intermediate-size relation occurs readily and well before there is any indication that the child can verbalize the relationship in question. In fact, it is the response to the absolute stimulus that seems to be harder to obtain and difficult to remember. The child's choices are therefore likely to be relational (rather than absolute) if the initial stimulus differences are small or if one lets three hours elapse between training and testing (Rudel, 1957; Rudel, 1960).

Similarly, working with the severely retarded mongoloid children, Rudel could show (1959; 1960) that they tended to react to a training situation involving large size-differences ("easy" discrimination) as did the normal children to a training situation with small differences or with three hours interpolated between training and testing. Thus, the mongoloid children reacted relationally in situations where the normal children produced absolute responses. The performance of the brain-damaged children, incidentally, fell between that of the normals and the severely ("endogenously") retarded (Rudel, 1960).

On the surface, these results look as though the mongoloids displayed a superior ability to "abstract." However, the relational response on tests of transposition of this sort is *not* identical with any complex, generalizing abstraction (Klüver, 1933). It is rather the absolute response, under these conditions of testing, that is more difficult to achieve and maintain, since it depends on proper utilization of opportunities for comparison during training and testing. It is therefore not at all surprising that relational responses, as seen in transposition, can be obtained by nonverbal means at a stage in child development that is prior to the appearance of any ability to verbalize "middle-size."

To make the relational response depend on language seems to us to put the cart before the horse. As Rudel points out (1960), generalization proceeds on several levels; the "undifferentiated generalization" (Klüver, 1933) of the relational response (in transposition tests) is not to be equated with the differentiated generalization involved in language and thought. Actually, Brown (1958b) has made a similar point for the acquisition of language. Before a child can abstract the idea that all daddies are men, he must first have ceased to call all men "daddy." The latter generalization does not presuppose the former (Rudel, 1960).

An intriguing difference between the performance of normal and defective children was noted during the presolution period on the intermediate-size problem; particularly where the size-difference between stimuli were small ("difficult" discrimination), the normal children tended to err by confusing middle-size with midposition, i.e., they selected that stimulus, among the three, that happened to be in the middle of the array. Curiously, this kind of confusion did not appear under our conditions of training among the retarded children; their errors were thus less systematic. It is not clear from the experimental results whether attempts at verbalization by the normal children helped or hindered them in finding the correct mode of response. These early verbalizations were frequently of a personifying sort, so that the child would call the three stimulus boxes: "papa, mama, and baby bear," and declare "I know it's in the mama bear," or insist that the reward was in the "almost grown-up one" (Rudel, 1957).

It may be worthwhile to investigate systematically what levels of individual language development "go" with what levels of performance on these essentially nonverbal ("monkeyfied") tasks. Some hunches can be derived from the almost complete absence of "absolute" responses on the part of the mongoloids; this lack seemed positively correlated with their retarded language development.

OPEN DISCUSSION

1. The discussion opened with a challenge to learning theory. The conditions determining whether or not language will be acquired are not exhausted by such variables as the amount of practice and the schedule of reinforcement. It is, in the first place, necessary that the animal exposed to language be a member of the species *homo sapiens*. Chimpanzees have been raised by human adults as if they were human infants; in fact, they have been raised with far more explicit attention to language than the average human infant enjoys, but chimpanzees do not learn language. They have been exposed to all the noises and treated with full parental solicitude, but these alone were not enough. The organism must be human. It is also probable, in the opinion of Lenneberg and others, that the infant must be of a certain age.

2. The evidence and argument presented by Lenneberg and others strongly suggest that the years between 2 and the early teens constitute a critical period for the acquisition or recovery of language, a period that is presumed critical for biological reasons. However, the social scientists in the group observed that the biologically critical years are also socially critical. There are age-graded role changes of considerable importance between infancy and adolescence. The years of early childhood are years of maximal dependence on others, and this dependence may make a child especially susceptible to influence. It is in early childhood, also, that the human being is best able to devote a large amount of time to the practice of linguistic skills. The child's accomplishments between 2 and 3 are genuinely dazzling; but, in comparing what he does in one year with what a college student does in his course in Conversational French, we should remember that the child puts in a full working day. When children are first learning to name things, for instance, they go about the house all day saying over and over again the same small stock of words. Finally, it is expected that a child will make speech errors and he is not ridiculed for them. Adults learning a foreign language are frequently unhappy about the fact that they must "become as little children" again. One of the personality factors determining whether or not an adult in a foreign country will pick up the language seems to be the individual willingness to go ahead and talk, however clumsily, however ungrammatically. In short, it is not just biology that makes 2 through 13 years a good time for acquiring language.

VI

MEDIATION PROCESSES AND THE ACQUISITION OF LINGUISTIC STRUCTURE [1]

JAMES J. JENKINS *and* DAVID S. PALERMO

University of Minnesota

> It is futile to inquire into the causation of verbal behavior until much more is known about the specific character of this behavior; and there is little point in speculating about the process of acquisition without much better understanding of what is acquired (Chomsky, 1959, p. 55).

When psychologists have addressed themselves to questions concerning mediation and language, they have dealt in the main with two general classes of problems: (a) language as a mediating behavior and (b) non-linguistic mediating responses as explicators of the meaning of lexical items. In the first case, exemplified by the work of Birge (1941), Kuenne (1946), Jeffrey (1953), Cantor (1955), Shepard (1956), Spiker (1956), Spiker, Gerjuoy, and Shepard (1956), Shepard and Schaeffer (1956), and Norcross and Spiker (1958), language is treated as of special importance because it furnishes a label, tag, or response which may be elicited in common by diverse members of some stimulus class.[2] Here it appears possible to show that such an intermediary response (whether overt or covert) serves an important role in the other, sometimes nonlinguistic, behaviors of the subjects.

In the second case, investigators such as Osgood (1953), Osgood, Suci, and Tannenbaum (1957), Bousfield (1961), and Staats and Staats (1957) have been concerned to show that "meanings" of items may be accounted

---

[1] This paper was prepared for the Conference on First-Language Acquisition sponsored by the Social Science Research Council, October 27-29, 1961. Dr. Jenkins' research in mediation processes is supported by the National Science Foundation. Dr. Palermo and Dr. Jenkins are jointly supported in their study "Word Associations: Grade School Through College" by Grant M-4286 from the National Institute of Mental Health, United States Public Health Service.

[2] It should be noted that some of these studies experimentally introduce and manipulate the mediator within the experimental setting while others infer the use of a verbal mediator on the basis of other data.

for by a theory which supposes that the occurrence of the item is accompanied by implicit, covert responses assumed to have been attached to the items by simple conditioning procedures earlier in the experience of the subject.

We feel that both of these areas of research are extremely important and need much further research and thought. In this paper, however, we would like to direct the reader's attention to a new area in which we think mediation theory has an important role to play: the area of linguistic *structure*. Strangely enough, this obvious aspect of language, the fact that it is structured, seems to have escaped psychological analysis to any appreciable degree.

In 1936, Kantor wrote *An Objective Psychology of Grammar* without more than casual reference to the facts of linguistic structure. One gathers, indeed, that he seems to have thought of "structure" as an insidious creation of the linguist to be abolished, along with other nonbehavioristic ghosts, rather than considered as a part of the description of behavior. The major point of the book seems to be that language behavior must be thought of as an adjustment of the organism, subject to the same laws as any other behavior. In the effort to make this laudible point clear, the description of language provided by grammar was to a great extent neglected.

In 1951 Lashley specifically pointed to the structured nature of speech as an example *par excellence* of the general problem of the serial ordering of behavior. He wrote, "In spite of the ubiquity of the problem, there have been almost no attempts to develop physiological theories to meet it. In fact, except among a relatively small group of students of aphasia who have had to face questions of agrammatism, the problem has been largely ignored" (1951, p. 113). Lashley pointed out that the phonetic elements were unpredictable at their own level, being determined by the words, and the words themselves were unpredictable in a left-to-right sequence since they were in turn determined by higher levels of organization. This led him to assert specifically that combinations of associations between words in sentences could not account for grammatical structure. He argued for a series of hierarchies of organization but confessed that he had not been able to systematize a set of assumptions concerning selective mechanisms which "was consistent with any large number of sentence structures" (1951, p. 130).

In 1953 a group of psychologists, linguists, and anthropologists met to discuss problems of psycholinguistics (see Osgood and Sebeok, 1954). This group explicitly recognized the problems faced in the area of grammatical structure but failed to deal with it effectively. The predominant approach of the entire section of the psycholinguistic monograph devoted to sequential organization seems to be built on the left-to-right assembly pattern or Markov process which Chomsky (1957) has since attacked with compelling success. The idea is presented that there need to be several levels of organization (skill level, integrational level, and representational level), and analysis by immediate constituents is introduced but no general fusion of the psychological theories and the linguistic analysis seems to have been achieved. Even in the analysis of word association phenomena where it was seen that the predominant organization of associative responses is in terms of agreement in form class with the stimulus, there is a vague suggestion that sentences are organized in terms of sequential associations (manifestly a contradiction of the first statement), and several research proposals related to that idea are offered.

Miller, Galanter, and Pribram (1960), in the main, avoid the problem of linguistic structure by accepting it as the *Plan* by which sentences are constructed. They take the grammatical model advanced by Chomsky and, approving of it, install it. Unfortunately, they do not tell us how Plans are acquired or how they are executed with the result that an independent explanation of grammar in terms of traditional psychological constructs is little advanced.

While other examples could be cited, the above are sufficient to indicate that psychologists have for the most part ignored, avoided, or mishandled the problem of accounting for grammar in particular or structure in language more generally.

The writers believe that it is clear to even a superficial analysis that the systematic nature of language is at the heart of its enormous utility. What it means to "understand" a sentence one has never heard before or to utter a sentence which is "novel but appropriate" (to borrow Brown's happy phrase) must rest on a psychological explication of the properties of *systems* in both stimulus and response roles. It will be the attempt of this paper to take a small step toward such an explication.

The reader should understand that the account to be given here is speculative in the extreme and little data are available which can be used to support it. The writers' apology is as simple as it is weak: the paper is premature. Our justification for presenting it at all is that research must begin somewhere and this is where we are beginning. Our current thinking and proposed research should both change and improve as our colleagues from several fields consider this material critically.

LANGUAGE IS STRUCTURED

What does it mean to say that language is structured? Most psychologists writing about language seem to feel that this can (and must) be said, but it is not quite clear what is meant by that sentence or what importance should be attached to it. A series of related quotations may provide certain guidance:

Dollard and Miller, *Personality and Psychotherapy* (1950):

> . . . a person can learn to respond to specific combinations of stimuli or rela-
> tionships among them and to make different responses to the same cues in
> different contexts. This is called patterning. A person's responses to the words
> that he hears someone else speak obviously involve patterning. Thus a parent
> will respond quite differently to the following two reports containing the
> same words in different sequences: "Jim hit Mary" and "Mary hit Jim." . . .
> it is obvious that man's great innate capacity and rigorous social training
> have produced marvelously intricate and subtle patterning in his responses
> to spoken language (p. 100).

Carroll, *The Study of Language* (1953):

> The central concept in linguistic analysis is *structure* by which is meant
> the ordered or patterned set of contrasts or oppositions which are presumed
> to be discoverable in a language, whether in the units of sound, the gram-
> matical inflections, the syntactical arrangements, or even the meanings of the
> linguistic forms (p. 14).

Hebb, *A Textbook of Psychology* (1958):

> What puts language on a higher level than the purposive communication
> of dog or chimpanzee is the *varied combination* of the same signs . . . for
> different purposes. The parrots and other talking birds can reproduce speech
> sounds very effectively—but without the slightest indication of transposing
> words, learned as part of one phrase or sentence, into a new order, or making
> new combinations of them (p. 209).
> The fundamental difference between man and chimpanzee in this respect
> seems to lie in man's capacity for having several sets of mediating processes
> at once, relatively independent of each other (pp. 209-210).

Brown, *Words and Things* (1958b):

> There is a refrain running through descriptive linguistics which goes
> like this: "Language is a system." . . . when someone knows a language he
> knows a set of rules: rules of phonology, morphology, reference, and syntax.
> These rules can generate an indefinite number of utterances. . . . The most
> important thing psychology is likely to get from linguistics is the reminder
> that human behavior includes the response that is novel but appropriate
> (p. viii).

From a set of statements like these it may be concluded that "language
is structured" involves at least two ideas: (a) that structure has something
to do with interrelated combinations and patterns which are differentially
uttered and differentially responded to and (b) that language structure
exists at several levels, at least at the levels of phonology, morphology, and
syntax. What "structure" is, whether the same thing is meant by "structure"
at each level, and whether there are general psychological explications of
"structure" remain to be explored.

For our specific target we will take that aspect of structure which is
called syntax or grammar. Within that area we will accept a phase structure
grammar, such as the model given by Chomsky (1957), as our ultimate

target, though we can make but the most meager beginning in this paper. For our mode of analysis we will take a simple notion of stimulus-response learning and the ramifications possible when one permits implicit responses having stimulus properties. To the elaboration of our simple tools we must next turn.

MEDIATIONAL PROCESSES

A decade ago it seemed to be the hope of the workers in the field that language assembly would turn out to be the general nature of the Markov chain model. For the S-R psychologist this would have been nearly perfect as far as explaining the formal system of language was concerned. Essentially, the cumulation of steps in the chain could account for the particular "state" of the speaker, and his behavior from that point on could be viewed as a probabilistic matter depending on habit strengths. Two difficulties which immediately arise (see Chomsky, 1957, and Miller, Galanter, and Pribram, 1960) are that this approach requires an enormous amount of learning on the part of the organism to acquire all the probabilities which would be needed to make even a small set of the sentences he would require in his daily life, and, secondly, it can be shown that many English sentences are made up of sets of "nested dependencies" rather than serial dependencies. Thus, in almost any English sentence one may find several places at which the sentence may be "opened up" and a whole new set of material introduced. Thus, "The boy runs" may be expanded almost without limit: "The boy . . . who lives in the big white house across the street from the curious looking bank that you saw when you first entered the town by the main highway . . ."

Some variety of phrase structure grammar seems to be required, and, as Chomsky points out, when one starts working with such a grammar, one finds lawful transformation rules from one basic set of kernel sentences to other sentence forms. These encouraging higher-order regularities make it all the more necessary that psychologists deal with phrase structure grammar seriously and attempt to explicate two problems: (a) how do verbal utterances become members of classes such as "noun phrase" and "verb phrase" (especially when the speakers may not be able to tell the investigator that there are such things as nouns and verbs) and (b) how can sequences be formed of materials in classes.

Before attempting to attack these two problems within a mediation framework, some minimal statements of operations which lead to mediational phenomena must be made. These may be much more elaborated, but for purposes of this paper they will be summarized briefly in the form of a few principles.

1. If there are two S-R contingencies such that the response to the first one is "the same" as the stimulus for the second one, then the first stimulus will acquire a tendency to elicit the second response.

That is:

Given that: A elicits B;
and that: B elicits C;
Then: A will tend to elicit C.

This is the classic treatment of stimulus-response chaining and scarcely needs to be elaborated here. We know that it holds under a variety of conditions for men and lower animals. A very simple example is provided by "avoidance" conditioning with rats as in the classic experiment by May (1948). We can match the paradigm by letting A stand for a buzzer, B stand for a shock, and C stand for escape behavior. It is easy to establish a B-C connection, i.e., the animal readily learns to escape from shock. Now the animal may be penned and given the buzzer as a stimulus followed by shock where escape is impossible. Here the A-B connection is established. If the animal is put into the original situation, he will show escape behavior, C, when the buzzer, A, is presented. Similarly with children (see Norcross and Spiker, 1958), it has been shown that the verbal learning of a sequence such as *tree-pony* followed by the learning of *pony-doll* will facilitate the subsequent learning of *tree-doll*.

With respect to this paradigm we must add the caution that the chaining may not be wholly automatic (i.e., it can be inhibited, facilitated, or interfered with by various activities of the subject), and in the animal case at least (see Gough, 1961) the order in which the first two stages occur may be very important.

This paradigm is usually regarded as a *mediation* paradigm because the traditional S-R analysis assumes a mediating response in the last stage:

A-B learning;
B-C learning;
A-(B)-C.

The argument is that when A is presented in the last stage it is sufficient to elicit (B) as an implicit response. It is further argued that the stimulus consequences of (B) are sufficiently like the stimulus consequences of B presented as an explicit stimulus that C is elicited.

It is very important to notice that the outcome of this paradigm is a "chain" from A to C. This does not imply that a chain similarly exists from C to A. The association may be expected to be asymmetrical. (In many cases a reverse chain would be simply impossible. In the animal example given above we expect that the rat will run in the presence of the buzzer but not that he will buzz every time he runs.) While the human data are far from complete, there is a suggestion (Horton and Kjeldergaard, 1961) that real asymmetries may be observed even in the paired-associate situation in spite of the fact that the paired-associate situation probably maximizes the chance of observing reverse chaining (see Jenkins, 1961).

2. If a stimulus elicits two responses, the responses will acquire a tendency to elicit each other. That is:

Given that: A elicits B;
and that: A elicits C;
Then: B will tend to elicit C and
                C will tend to elicit B.

This may be called the "response equivalence" paradigm (see Jenkins, 1959). There is abundant evidence that this paradigm can achieve the equivalence result in laboratory experimentation with humans. (See Mink, 1957; Martin, 1960; Horton and Kjeldergaard, 1961.) There is little evidence that the paradigm may be found to be effective with lower animals, but this has not been systematically studied.

An example in the case of paired-associate learning would be the learning of *zug-dol* followed by the learning of *zug-gex* facilitating the learning of *dol-gex*. Using other materials, it has been possible to show that, if one has a strong A-B association and learns an instrumental response C (such as a lever press) to A, the response will generalize to B (Mink, 1957).

Here again we must add the caution that the equivalence may not be automatic (it can be both facilitated and interfered with by various activities of the subject) and that it may have a directionality component in the association depending on the order in which the steps were learned and on the nature of the stimuli and responses involved. In general, however, if the order of the first two stages is mixed or alternated, we anticipate bidirectional associates if such would be compatible with the nature of the stimuli and responses.

We talk of this as a mediational paradigm because it too may be derived from simple S-R associations given the use of the implicit response:

A-B learning;   A-C learning;
A-(B)-C learning;   A-(C)-B learning;
B-C results.   C-B results.

That is, over-all, with varying order of the first two stages: $B \leftrightarrow C$.

That is, if we sometimes have A-B followed by A-C and sometimes A-C followed by A-B, the terms C and B should come to elicit each other, $B \leftrightarrow C$. The key to this paradigm is of course in the second stage. It is assumed that A as a stimulus elicits (B) as a covert response. The stimulus consequences of (B) then have an opportunity to become attached to the response C. Similarly, in the other order of the first two stages, the stimulus consequences of (C) become attached to the response B. Thus, if both orders are experienced, B and C come to elicit each other.

(It is clear that this paradigm also offers an opportunity for [B] or [C] to become extinguished or inhibited which is an alternate possibility [see Jenkins, 1961]. We will assume, however, that the individual items are returned to full strength repeatedly so that B and C are held simultaneously and become associated.)

If B and C are two verbal responses to A, it can be argued that we may build up strong verbal associates, a class of responses, without ever practicing the elements together explicitly. As we shall attempt to demonstrate later, we feel this possible outcome to be of great importance in building classes which may enter into the syntax.

3. If two stimuli elicit the same response, they may be said to become "functionally equivalent" stimuli; i.e., if a new response is attached to one stimulus, the other stimulus will acquire a tendencey to elicit it. In diagram:

Given that:	A elicits B;
and:	C elicits B;
If learn:	A-D;
Then:	C will tend to elicit D.

This paradigm expresses the notion of "acquired stimulus equivalence" developed by Hull (1939) and exemplified in the experiments of Shipley (1935), Birge (1941), and Wickens and Briggs (1951).

This is regarded as a mediation paradigm because of the assumed mediating responses occurring in the third and fourth stages.

A-B;
C-B;
A-(B)-D. A elicits the implicit (B) the stimulus properties of which become associated with the D response.
C-(B)-D. C elicits (B) which in turn tends to elicit D via the presumed learning in the third stage.

An interesting characteristic of this model is that, as A and C function as equivalent stimuli, B and D become equivalent responses. Thus, this more elaborate paradigm contains the response equivalence paradigm within it.

Using both verbal and motor mediators, Birge (1941) has demonstrated the full stimulus equivalence paradigm using children as subjects. It should be noted that it was necessary for the mediating response to occur explicitly in the third and fourth stage to provide strong evidence for the phenomenon. (As was mentioned in the case of the response equivalence paradigm, the extinction of the mediator is a possible occurrence during the third stage of this paradigm resulting in a failure to obtain equivalence results.) By requiring the overt occurrence of the mediating response prior to the making of the new response, Birge obtained the expected results which were not apparent when the subjects were left to their own devices.

More recently, Greeno and Jenkins (unpublished research) have demonstrated with natural language materials the full stimulus equivalence paradigm. In this case, the subjects were presented with a paired-associate learning problem of exceptionally high difficulty unless use was made of common mediating associates of groups of stimulus words which required the same nonsense syllable response. Eighteen words used as stimuli were paired with six nonsense syllable responses in such a way that the three stimulus words paired with a particular response were related by a single word presumably used as a mediator, i.e., *iron, copper,* and *steel* were paired with one nonsense syllable with the expectation that the mediator would be *metal.* After learning was complete, it was demonstrated that excellent transfer could be obtained in new learning to other stimuli which called out the same mediator as the presumed one in the first learning or to stimuli which were the inferred mediating stimuli themselves. Thus, in the above example, regardless of whether *tin* or *metal* was used as a stimulus in the second task the transfer was very strong.

The general paradigm, of course, is the one ordinarily used for the explanation of concept formation via mediation.

APPLICATION

Now, given the processes of chaining, response equivalence, and stimulus equivalence, how are they to be applied? What constitutes a unit or element in one of the paradigms? Certainly we do not want to hold that the paradigms apply only to nonsense syllables or to discrete lever presses. Nor do we wish to limit ourselves to items taken two at a time. At the risk of making the processes inapplicable, we must say that they apply to any functional stimulus classes and any functional response classes at any level of complexity made up of any number of items and that all processes may operate on all levels at the same time. In essence we are saying that subjects have integrated both stimulus and response units at many levels and that these processes may apply to all of these units.

Let us look at some examples of application in limited domains to furnish illustrations of what we mean.

Application in Paired-Associate Learning

Following ordinary paired-associate learning, we observe that the subjects can give us the list of responses without having the individual stimuli present (Cunningham, Newman, and Gray, 1961). Their ability to do this much exceeds their ability to report the specific stimuli (in the experiment under discussion the advantage was of the order of 3.5 to 1.0). One wonders why this should be true. The subjects were not instructed to learn the responses as a group; on the contrary, they were required to learn the set of pairs a-b, c-d, e-f, etc.

We assert that this response-group learning behavior follows from the response equivalence paradigm. All of the response items in the paired-associate learning task were responses which had to be used in "situation X" (the complex of stimuli making up the entire learning situation); hence we have the X-B, X-C, X-D, etc. paradigm, and it follows that the responses should come to elicit each other, as they in fact do.

It can be seen that the most general order of learning in this experiment is to acquire the responses to "situation X." As the experiment proceeds and specific contingencies are built up, the responses become progressively more and more under the control of a particular element of "situation X"; that is, they will be controlled by the nominal stimulus and therefore "correctly" emitted. (See McGeoch and Irion, 1952, and Underwood and Schulz, 1960, on this point.)

We must also observe in this experiment that the learning of the so-called S-R pairs shows that the subject is capable of narrowing the range of stimulus conditions under which he will emit the response; i.e, he can select some aspect of the total stimulus situation. In this case, it is the one we want him to consider, the term (or picture, or color, etc.) presented on the left-hand window of the memory drum. Once one has accepted the notion that the subject may in some fashion select elements of the stimulus situation, it is easy to admit the converse of this; namely, the subject may not respond to all the stimuli presented to him. Thus, we may find that the subject is not responding to the left-hand term in its entirety but rather to some fraction of it. Underwood and Schulz (1960) report that their subjects often volunteer that they attend to only one letter of the stimulus cluster (when this is possible in an experiment). Recently, Jenkins and Allen (1963b) confirmed the Underwood and Schulz statement in paired-associate learning by using as stimuli triple consonants which were totally independent from one stimulus cluster to another. The responses were single digits from one to seven. Transfer tests showed that subjects tended to respond correctly to first letters of the triples, next best to the last letters, and poorly to the medial letters. In other words, selection of stimuli had taken place although all stimuli had been available all the time. Position of the letter was not, however, the only variable involved. In part, idiosyncratic relations of the particular stimulus-response pair appeared to be important; for instance, if the middle letter rhymed with the number (e.g., "q"-"two"), it was likely to have been selected for attention as the functional stimulus.

Recent work of Underwood and his students (see Underwood, 1961) showed that, given multiple stimuli, subjects tend to learn the response to the most "meaningful" aspect of the stimulus complex. When the stimuli are real words and colors, the response is learned to the words and not the colors; when the stimuli are difficult nonsense letters and colors, the responses are learned to the colors and not to the letters. Jenkins (1964) followed this with a replication of the second part of the study plus the use of the names of the colors as a test of mediation. In this experiment, although the subjects had been instructed to learn to respond to the letters and had, in fact, been required to read the stimulus letters aloud on every trial, the subjects learned to respond to the colors and not the letters as indicated by the fact that there was almost perfect transfer to the color *names* which up to that time had not appeared explicitly in the experiment. Thus, we have good evidence for the selection of aspects of the stimulus to be used as the functional stimulus and transfer to the name of that aspect of the stimulus.[3] Since this is a natural language case and we do not have the histories of the relations between the colors and their names, we cannot decide unambiguously which paradigms are operative here, but it is obvious that verbal mediation is enormously successful.

Just as the stimulus side of paired-associate learning may be separated into gross and specific stimuli and aspects of particular stimuli, so aspects of response structuring should be considered. If, in simple learning, the subject is asked to respond with the series of letters "w-a-t-c-h," he has a unitary response available from past learning, saying "watch." If he is required to spell it as a response, we have every reason to believe that he says it implicitly, and he runs off already-learned spelling habits. This is in marked contrast to his behavior when he is asked to respond with *hctaw,* which he cannot pronounce, cannot remember as a unit, and cannot run off from the usual letter contingencies in English writing. (We have in fact in our laboratories used pronounceable syllables as *volvap* and found them appreciably more difficult for psychology students to learn than the familiar *Pavlov* from which the nonsense term was derived.) To refer to this phenomenon, workers in verbal learning use the term *response integration.* Well-integrated responses are more easily learned than less well-integrated responses, presumably because they are single units and the subject needs to learn only when to emit the unit. Less well-integrated responses must first be "knit together" before they may be given in the presence of the correct stimuli.

It should be noted that we do *not* expect these processes to run off in an orderly fashion; i.e, first the subject integrates all the responses he is going to use, next he associates these with all the stimuli in the situation to form a response pool, next he selects what particular aspects of narrow stimuli he will respond to, and finally he "hooks up" the narrow stimuli to the particular responses. Instead, it is clear that for a given learning task some parts of the material may be at quite different stages of the various processes at the same time. In addition, the processes may overlap for a single item as in the case of a subject who is still mispronouncing a response but knows its appropriate stimulus. Now, if we further complicate this description by giving you the additional information that this learning task is the second

---

[3] To talk of the "functional stimulus" suggests that there will be a dangerous circularity and looseness in any subsequent formulation, but we think this constitutes no danger. It does mean that the search for the determinants of stimulus selection must be added to the task of the S-R psychologist, but even the early experiments seem to promise lawfulness and regularity.

stage of a mediation model and that the stimuli are eliciting implicit responses with their associated stimuli which are becoming associated simultaneously with responses which are evolving in the experiment (and that at the same time the implicit responses are probably being extinguished because they are not being specifically reinforced), you have some idea of the confusion which attends a mediational explication of almost anything.

Application to a Simple System

Let us become one step more specific. It seems to us that a good place to begin is with a simple system which has been studied experimentally in the hope that we can pull ourselves up by the bootstraps and improve our ideas of structure and our understanding of the psychology of structure as we go along. The simplest structure we know of is one studied by Esper, one of the first American psycholinguists. Esper's first experiment (1925) was as follows:

Three groups of subjects were given learning problems with the same objective reference matrix (four shapes in each of four different colors). Group I had "names" for the stimuli which were "structured"; the first syllable of the name was constant for a given color, and the second syllable was constant for a given shape. Group II had the same arrangement except that the color-shape order of the response was reversed and the division was no longer at the syllable boundary. Shape was denoted by the initial consonant and vowel while color was denoted by the medial consonants, second vowel, and final consonant, i.e., CV (shape) – CCVC (color) as contrasted with CVC (color) – CVC (shape) for group I (see Table 1 for the design). Group III received different names for each stimulus compound. In each

TABLE 1

First Esper Experiment (1925)

Color	Shape A	Shape B	Shape C	Shape D
Group I				
Red	nasling*	naschaw	nasdeg	——
Green	wechling	wechchaw	wechdeg	wechkop
Blue	shownling	shownchaw	showndeg	shownkop
Yellow	royling	——	roydeg	roykop
Group II				
Red	nulgan*	doylgan	pelgan	——
Green	nugdet	doygdet	pegdet	wigdet
Blue	nuzgub	doyzgub	pezgub	wizgub
Yellow	numbow	——	pembow	wimbow

* These are approximations of the Esper names.

group two of the 16 possible color-shape combinations were never given in the training trials but were presented on test trials to observe how the subjects extended the "language system" to deal with these "new" stimuli.

The results are intuitively predictable. Group I learned most rapidly; group II learned much more slowly and showed great interference between terms; and group III learned about as rapidly as group II but showed little interference. When the two stimulus combinations which had been withheld were presented for naming in the context of the other stimuli, the group I subjects named them correctly almost as frequently as they named the training stimuli correctly and in general *showed no awareness that the stimuli were new*. Group II subjects never did well on synthesizing the names for the new stimuli. Group III subjects tended to apply the name of a stimulus of the same color or the same shape (in this group, of course, there was no "correct" synthesis to score).

What descriptive generalizations seem to be justified here? First, with respect to group I it is clear that a "system" was learned. The order of elements (color referent-form referent) and the point of division of the element (by syllable) in the response agreed with the subjects' experience. We must assume that the subjects fractionated the stimulus and responded separately to its components, associating these components directly with the familiarly divided elements of the response. This may be argued from the grounds that they could not identify new combinations (though they responded to them correctly) and also from the fact that the number of color-shape terms correctly given in each learning trial is almost exactly predictable from the product of the proportion of correct color responses and the proportion of correct shape responses. It would appear here that we must be prepared to deal both with the matter of analysis of the stimulus and segmentation of the response as well as a combination rule. It is not implied that any of this is "naturally given," of course, since in this case both the stimulus divisions and the response divisions and ordering are in accordance with the natural language habits the subject brings to the experiment with him.

In the case of group II we must conclude that there is little evidence that the system was learned. The novel but appropriate response to the new stimuli failed to appear just as the learning of the rehearsed responses failed to exceed the learning of unsystematized responses in group III. The correct responding to individual color-form stimuli, trial by trial, steadily exceeds what would be predicted from the hypothesis of independent learning of the color and shape stimulus-response habits, indicating that individual responses were being slowly and tortuously memorized. Whether the system would have emerged had learning been carried to higher levels is unfortunately unknown (at the end the subjects were getting only about 50 per cent of the items correct as contrasted with 88 per cent correct responding being achieved midway through the experiment by group I). It is clear that the unusual segmentation of the response, or its unusual ordering, or both, seriously hampered the development of the linguistic system. A consideration of the very large number of errors made by the subjects suggests that they were "trying" to make an old familiar system work in an inappropriate place or, more simply, that old habits of response segmentation and ordering were interfering with the learning of the system. It is important to note that the semantic aspect of the system for group II is exactly the same as for group I. The stimuli may be fractionated in exactly the same manner, and each stimulus aspect may be unambiguously related to an aspect of the response. The difference is that one response is familiarly divided and ordered and one is not. The conclusion must be that the development or discovery of the system depends heavily on the active participation of the subject and his past learnings and habits with respect to his natural language system.

How shall we approach the Esper experiments? Let us start with group I. In this situation we have stimuli which are highly discriminable. Certainly the instructions[4] plus the visual presentation of the stimuli strengthen the responses of color and shape. We expect that the subjects would say (if asked to name the stimuli), "There's a red jagged one," "There's another jagged one and it's yellow," "There is a green lump with a square corner," etc. The responses which are provided to the subjects as auditory stimuli from the experimenter are familiar in structure and easily echoed. We assume that the subjects are well trained in English adjective-noun structures such as "red square," "green circle," etc., and that they expect (from both their experience and the instructions of the experiment) that stimuli of the same shape will be called by some common name and stimuli of the same color will be called by some common name. We further assume that they are actively trying to link their own linguistic responses (which are implicit here) to the artificial responses the experimenter requires. Simple contingencies of implicit and explicit responses will account for the remainder of the experiment. The diagram may be seen in Figure 1.

When any red figure is presented, we assume that the implicit naming response "red" is made by the subject. At the same time the experimenter says "nas ——" and the subject echoes "nas ——." This sequence sets up a virtually perfect chain from the color of the object to the implicit response and from the stimuli produced by the implicit response to the overt response itself. A similar argument may be made for any particular shape becoming associated with a particular second syllable through the implicit shape

---

[4] "This is not an intelligence test. It is an experiment to determine how quickly you can learn the names of certain sacrificial objects in the Morgavian language, a language spoken on the northern slopes of the Himalayan Mountains. As each object is shown, I shall pronounce the name. You will immediately repeat the name after me aloud."

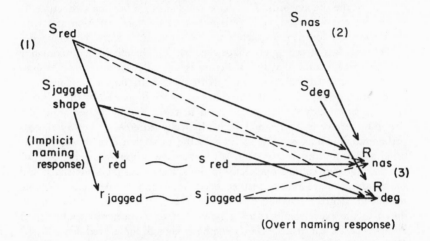

(Visually presented figure)   (Auditorially presented "name")

(Overt naming response)

FIGURE 1—Mediational description of Esper experiment I (1925) for group I.

1. A complex visual stimulus. Color and shape are assumed to be two aspects of the stimulus which have high likelihood of eliciting naming responses.

2. Stimulus presented as one utterance. We assume that it is fractionated by the subject into two syllables as a result of his experience with English.

3. A complex response matching the auditory stimulus. We assume that it is fractionated as a result of the subject's experience with English.

4. Solid lines represent relationships which are assumed or observed to occur with very high probability, approaching $p = 1.00$. Dashed lines represent contingencies assumed or observed to occur approximately one quarter of the time, $p = .25$.

naming responses. It is clear then that for any color one nonsense syllable in one position will become overwhelmingly dominant, and that for any shape a nonsense syllable in the other position will become dominant. The dependencies between members (syllables) of "an utterance" will not be great because they will be essentially equal for all members of one class to all members of the other class. The classes formed, however, should be a considerable strength, e.g.,

$Color_1$-$Shape_1$	$Color_2$-$Shape_1$	$Color_3$-$Shape_1$	$Color_4$-$Shape_1$
$Color_1$-$Shape_2$	$Color_2$-$Shape_2$	$Color_3$-$Shape_2$	$Color_4$-$Shape_2$
Etc.	Etc.	Etc.	Etc.

This furnishes a sufficient condition to make the color names functionally equivalent responses to the total situation and functionally equivalent stimuli for the shape words. The shape words in turn become a functionally equivalent response class, both with respect to the total situation and with respect to the colors as immediately preceeding stimuli. Since the occurrence of the color class preceding the shape class has a probability of approximately 1.00, we may assume that this structure is virtually perfectly learned once the classes are established and serve as functional stimuli and responses.

Because the experimentally relevant classes are supported by the subject's language history, by the extra-experimental world, and by the semantic support they receive by correlation with physically different aspects of the experimental situation, everything leads to the formation of a strongly structured miniature linguistic system. When the new stimuli are presented, we can see that they conform perfectly to the system (i.e., the same shape and the same color have already been encoded) and hence are perfectly adequate stimuli to elicit the response. If a new member of either aspect were introduced to the experiment (either a new color or shape), we would expect an appropriate construction, a "something jagged" or a "red something." We would predict that the subject would never respond with a monosyllable.

The experience of group I overlaps so much with natural language that it is difficult to find much to explain that is not firmly rooted in habit already. The experience of group II, however, departs in two respects from English and does not permit us to assess unambiguously the "weight" of each deviation. Here the order of construction is violated (if the subjects do indeed think of the stimuli as colored things), and the response units are not those which the subject has integrated. We are virtually certain that the second alteration generated much more severe difficulty than the first.

Semantically the problems facing these subjects are the same as those facing the subjects in group I. However, when the subject begins forming associations between the implicit responses he is making (in English) and the echoes he is performing in the artificial language, he cannot achieve success. He has brought with him from English a set of well-integrated response units. He cannot even know that these units are inappropriate in the experiment. But even if he were to be given the "correct" responses for colors (e.g., *lgan, gdet, zgub, mbow*), he would find them unpronounceable and difficult to remember. The "units" cannot enter into the system because they are not units for the subject and would be extremely difficult to utter even if he were told that they were.

But the situation is even worse than it appears at first, for we may assume that the model for the color term would be much like the one given before, except that the order is incorrect and that the subject would not divide the response term properly.

Any Red Object

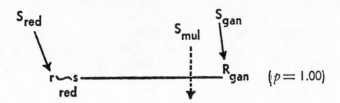

With the confirmed contingency for the R_{gan} syllable and "red," we would expect the subject to continue making this connection and direct his attention to the shape variable. What he is doing appears "correct" to him since the second syllable varies perfectly with the color. It will not be scored correctly, however, and he will not make correct total responses because the consonant preceeding the syllable will tend to be incorrect more times than it is correct.

With respect to shape, the subject will (both by elimination and by contingency) attempt to match the first syllable.

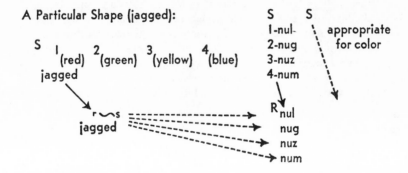

But note the conflict. The subject isolates *nul, nug, nuz,* and *num* for this shape. All will have some habit strength. Any one he says will be likely to be incorrect unless he also is using the color as a conditional stimulus. Thus the subject finds himself in doubt as to the first syllable which he is assigning to shape. As the experiment is scored, any response from this class will be scored as correct for shape but has three chances out of four of being wrong for color. If we examine the error list presented by Esper (which is not complete since he wished to illustrate only associative aspects of errors), we find that the last syllable in each of these "errors" is correct for the color in 40 of 54 cases and the initial consonant and vowel are correct for shape in 42 of 54 cases. The vast majority of the errors reported (even though they were selected to illustrate another point) are errors associated with the third consonant position.

We might argue that the strategy of the subjects was wrong. The fact is that they were probably (from their point of view) achieving almost complete success as to color names and coming very close (but missing for some mysterious reason) on the shape names, which from Esper's point of view was exactly the opposite of what was occurring. In the last analysis their learning was just as difficult as the learning of completely arbitrary names, because from the natural language syllable point of view the aberrant consonant at the end of the first syllable could only be given successfully when the color-shape pairing was used as the cue. This is apparently as difficult as learning a whole word for each color-shape pairing as the subjects in the third group were doing.

Finally, we should note that, despite the experimenter, the subjects in this portion of the experiment have learned a system. The syllables comprising the shape class have become functionally equivalent responses to the total situation and functionally equivalent stimuli for the color syllables. The color syllables, in turn, have become a functionally equivalent response class both with respect to the total situation and with respect to the shapes as immediately preceeding stimuli. The color syllables are appearing where they should and the shape syllables where they should although it is the reverse of the natural language. The only real difference in the systems of the experimenter and the subjects lies in the response unit being used.

Another experiment by Esper (1933) may also be fruitfully examined here. In this experiment a specific vocabulary was set up for a particular referential field, and then the referential field was enlarged. The experiment

TABLE 2

Diagram of Stimuli Presented in Esper (1933) Experiment

| Area of Figure | SHAPES OF FIGURES PRESENTED | | | |
	Shape A	Shape B	Shape C	Shape D
8 sq. cm.	——	B-1 (Name)	C-1 (Name)	D-1 (Name)
16 sq. cm.	A-2 (Name)	——	C-2 (Name)	D-2 (Name)
32 sq. cm.	A-3 (Name)	B-3 (Name)	——	D-3 (Name)
64 sq. cm.	A-4 (Name)	B-4 (Name)	C-4 (Name)	——

was designed to discover how the vocabulary would be shifted to cope with the larger referential system.

Sixteen stimuli were constructed. Four basic nonsense forms were chosen each of which was cut out in each of four sizes (8, 16, 32, and 64 sq. cm. in area). Four of the figures were removed from the set, and names were assigned to the remaining 12 figures. The names were nonsense monosyllables chosen so as to be easily discriminable. The experiment is diagrammed in Table 2. Appropriate names for the 12 figures were very thoroughly learned by the subjects over a period of months. An association test was given which included the names of the figures as well as English words. Test trials were given repeatedly over another period of months with all 16 figures present. Subjects were required to name all the figures which were presented four times each, three days a week, for approximately three months. No information was given as to correctness or incorrectness of their responses. At the end of this extensive testing period, stable naming systems had developed for the subjects.

Over all it was clear that the semantic system became stabilized by dividing the 12 terms among the 16 forms in such a way that there were individual names for each of the smallest and largest forms and a name in common for the two middle-sized forms in each shape series. The resolution and the shifts necessary for it are shown in Table 3.

TABLE 3

Resolution of Naming Problem When All Forms Were Present
(from Esper, 1933, Experiment)

| Area of Figure | SHAPES OF FIGURES PRESENTED | | | |
	Shape A	Shape B	Shape C	Shape D
8 sq. cm.	A-2 *	B-1	C-1	D-1
	↑			
16 sq. cm.	A-3	B-3 *	C-2	D-2
	↑	↑	↓	↓
32 sq. cm.	A-3	B-3	C-2 *	D-2
				↓
64 sq. cm.	A-4	B-4	C-4	D-3 *

NOTE.—Symbols * indicate name assigned in the final resolution. Arrows show source of name.

The study of the association pattern after initial learning showed that the names for forms of the same shape and adjacent size were most frequently associated. These, of course, were precisely the terms which had been hardest to learn and which had produced the most errors. After the new system had stabilized, the same finding was true, with the addition that now the terms for the middle-sized figures tended also to elicit one another across the shape categories. Esper was so impressed with the associative findings that he devoted considerable space to their discussion and formulated a series of principles which seemed to govern the establishment of verbal associations. Several of his conclusions bear directly on our equivalence paradigm:

> The greater the possibility of confusing an object, *a*, with a specific other object, *b*, and the less the possibility of confusing it with any other specific object, *c*, *d*, etc., the firmer and more universal does the verbal association between the names of objects *a* and *b* become (Esper, 1933, p. 359).

> When a given object is subject to confusion with a number of other objects, its name tends to become an alternative response to these other objects and an associative response to their names, and consequently to become the most frequently elicited name in the category (*ibid.*, p. 361).

Esper showed that subjects who responded very rapidly in the first period and made many errors, especially multiple errors (giving a wrong response and then rapidly correcting themselves and giving the correct response), tended to be fast in the association test and to give highly common responses to the nonsense stimuli. It also appears that subjects who were appreciably faster in their naming reaction times in the second period than in the first period were rapid on the association test, gave common responses in association, had little scatter on repeated association, and tended most markedly to shift the entire naming structure into the "small," "middle-sized," and "large" pattern.

Finally Esper foreshadowed the present paper with:

> . . . this readiness to respond to an object not only with a uniform verbal response but sometimes also with the responses usually made to somewhat similar objects, undoubtedly is the behavior tendency which has been responsible for most linguistic (and logical) organization. Its end-products in language are semantic and phonetic word groups. "Errors" of this type, particularly the semantic shifts which follow the introduction of the n-figures (new figures) . . . represent a progressive change in behavior and *interconnection of response units* which are to be regarded as a very important form of human learning (*ibid.*, p. 372).

This experiment fits easily into our framework of explanations and, in addition, provides supplementary data for our response equivalence paradigm. To begin with, we may assume that all responses in the experiment form an equivalence class of the broadest sort. That this is the case is shown by the fact that in the association test (where certainly other responses could have been made because all of the practice words and half of the test stimuli were meaningful English words) eight of the 12 subjects responded exclusively in the artificial language when the stimulus was in that language.

We would anticipate on grounds of primary stimulus generalization that the members of each stimulus form category would tend to elicit all the responses appropriate to the category and thus that these could form sub-classes. The more likely the stimuli were to elicit a particular pair of responses in a subclass (say, the next-to-smallest stimulus eliciting both the small and middle-sized names) the more these terms would become related. We would suppose, finally, to keep the stimuli distinct (acquired distinctiveness of cues), that the subjects would introduce implicit terms such as small, middle-sized, and large. When the shift in reference items occurs, we would expect the subjects to continue naming as before, but now the names would mediate the shift of responses to the new structure which finally becomes stable.

Example:

Period I		*Period II*	
A-2 (small ✕) ...... name 1		A-1 (small ✕) ...... name 1	
A-3 (middle-sized ✕) name 2		A-2 (middle-sized ✕) name 2	
A-4 (large ✕) ...... name 3		A-3 (middle-sized ✕) name 2	
		A-4 (large ✕) .... name 3	

Here the implicit responses, which may be presumed to have introduced order and clarity into the first system, are seen to mediate a change to a new but similarly structured system when the referential field is expanded. The specific changes are of course capricious, unless one views the system as a whole or studies the probable mediators. In essence, including the implicit response of the subject as a functional stimulus allows one to deal with the relations existing in the stimulus field, insofar as they are available to and responded to by the subject. (This is always of course subject to the proviso that one can show that the subject has such experience in his history and can make this response to the situation. As stated above, this extends the S-R researcher's task and responsibilities if he wishes to pursue such explanations.)

Application to Natural Language

The above examples have been simple exercises to warm up our tools, so to speak. Does the laboratory psychologist have anything to say about the acquisition of real language in all its complexity when it is first encountered? This is difficult to deal with for three reasons:

1. No one has provided us with the precise description of language acquisition that we need before we know what it is we are to explain. The material in McCarthy's (1954) excellent summary is of virtually no use if one wants to know the behaviors emitted by a child or the stimuli impinging on a child as he acquires language. The exciting work of Miller and Ervin and Brown and Fraser is just becoming available and is still far from complete even for one child. In a sense the Chomsky quotation which leads this paper is substantially correct.

2. Too much happens in genuine first-language learning, and it happens at all levels and all at the same time. To attempt to talk about first-language learning in all aspects is patently impossible.

3. Because we are dealing with first-language learning rather than the behavior of mature speakers of some language like first graders or college students, we lose our favorite salvaging device: the subject's talking to himself and providing just the stimulus we need at each crucial point.

The reader is reminded that the account is speculative, that we will attempt to speculate only about the formation of classes and the development of syntax, and we will have to do our best to defend the account without the self-stimulating verbalizations attributable to more advanced users of language.

How does language get under way? We think that children imitate the speech around them. They imitate because it is a functional property of the nervous system, because they are reinforced for imitating by other humans, because imitation is secondarily reinforcing, and because very soon the behaviors involved have functional properties for them as instrumental acts.

We believe that associative correlates between verbal behaviors and events in the world around the beginning speaker rapidly appear through simple S-R laws and that labeling or naming in its broadest sense ought to be one of the earliest forms to appear. (It will be understood that the label may be used descriptively, as in simple naming, or as a request, an announcement, a demand, etc.) It is clear that many general classes of behavior are present before the speaker learns labels for the salient objects and events involved, and we assume that the labels are readily used as instrumental acts within already-developed behavior repertoires. It seems reasonable to suppose that these early labels are attached to the functional properties of the situation which are of importance to the child as a result of his experience with the world or to properties which are "salient" in his stimulus field as a result of the way his nervous system is "wired." In other words S-R contingencies are developed where the functional stimulus is of the "acquired distinctiveness" sort, as well as where the functional stimulus is of the "figure-ground" sort.

We presume that at this early stage language behavior is too unstructured to speak of classes of utterances or of utterance units but that some contingencies would be observed (as a result of the groupings of stimuli in the external world if nothing else) which would form "proto-classes." One would merely expect that some elements are more likely to occur in the same time span than others.

When more than single word utterances appear, it is asserted that the development of classes begins in earnest. The simplest structure we have imagined (and, of course, the paper by Miller and Ervin reinforced this belief) would be some sort of "operator" plus the existing labels. Whether the operator precedes or follows the label makes little difference at this point; in either case the labels by our mediation principles will begin to form a class. Both reinforcement and primary stimulus generalization begin to play a part here as the grouping emerges. If the child makes a construction which is like the adult construction (within whatever weak limits we wish to specify "like"), we assume that this: (a) has a greater likelihood of being praised by others; (b) has a greater likelihood of inducing others to respond linguistically, which we presume is reinforcing; (c) has a greater likelihood of eliciting nonverbal behavior from the audience, if any; and (d) is secondarily reinforcing. All of this should lead to the greater selection of some sequences over others with this particular "operator" and, because of the semantic correlates probable in the successful utterances, to a semantic correlate of the class. It should be noted here that reference probably enters both in the original vocabulary development (the kinds of things talked about with children) and in the clarification and distillation of the class. One presumes that these dual determinants lead to the first class of this sort being "noun-like," although it is probably too gross to be given even that much of a name.

As utterances increase in length, the class formation process will continue to proceed to develop additional classes and finer and finer distinctions within classes. At this point a fairly complex phenomenon should begin to be manifest. Suppose that we are dealing with three-word utterances. Let us assume that we find a sequence A-B-C and also the sequence A-B-D. We conclude, of course, that C and D are members of the same class. Now we find E-B-C. We conclude that E and A are of the same class and predict the possibility of E-B-D. If we now find F-B-D, we would class it with A and E though in fact it has never appeared in the same specific context as E. If B has several equivalents, it is apparent that we may have many class members which have never appeared in the same context. It is clear, of course, that we are dealing with probabilities here. Not all words in a class will have equal probabilities of occurrence in a particular frame or sequence. We feel that behaviorally at this point we must go slowly. Our experience with laboratory learning leads us to at least two cautions here: first, it is probable that such classes develop quite slowly from the syntax base alone and require very high frequencies of occurrence to become firmly established; second, one must postulate varying degrees of strength of relationship between elements within classes, dependent on the number of contexts which they share and the degree of similarity of those contexts. It is clear that this is a potential source of trouble, because the "degree of similarity of contexts" will in turn depend on the degree of interchangeability of the words in the specific context with the other words in their respective classes. The difficulty here is expected to be great.

Basically the ideas we want to present here are of two sorts: *sequence* and *class*. We know that serial acts performed over and over become smooth, polished, easily performed, and integrated. This scarcely poses a problem for the specific act in question. The puzzling question is how a set of behaviors can become a smooth, polished performance when the entries in the behavior sequences are not the same specific entries from time to time. The appeal must clearly.be made to a hierarchy notion. The sequences are the "same" because the entries are members of the "same" classes even though they may be different entries from time to time. Thus, a given sequence may begin with an *A*. Note that it is not A as a specific thing because A′, A″, A‴, etc. may be used. This is followed by a *B,* again, not B as a specific thing but B′, B″, B‴, etc. In this fashion a sequence may be developed and polished even though it appears to be different every time or nearly every time it is run off. But this creates two new responsibilities: (a) Can it be shown that classes really can be manipulated in this way? (b) How do members of the response community become organized into classes?

The first question is answered by language itself if we consider its entries as classes: "Colorless green ideas sleep furiously" is a sentence in English not because it is true, or sensible, or interpretable by the listener, but because it is a "correct" assembly of classes appropriately modulated, (i.e., they are the right general classes of entries properly modified to take their places in the particular sequence). If it is true, as Chomsky (1957) asserts, that such sequences are more easily spoken, recalled, learned, etc., than nongrammatical assemblies of words, then we have prima facie evidence that particular sequences, not previously experienced, are facilitated (polished, integrated, etc.) by practice of sequences of like classes. The critical question, then, is seen to be that of the organization of the elements into classes. For this question, we have proposed an answer from the point of view of the experimentalist interested in verbal behavior and mediation paradigms by outlining the three basic mediation processes we discussed earlier.

It should be clear, if our analysis is correct, that, in the natural language, class and sequential structure are learend simultaneously and interdependently. While this makes the detailed description of the process difficult and gives it the appearance of uncertainty, it is, nevertheless, our conviction that this is a valid contention.

Given that the child has a set of classes which he can arrange in functional sentences or utterances, all of the processes which led him to this point will similarly lead him to extend his behavior repertoire to other forms of ordering. Similarly, as he learns new sentence forms, he begins almost immediately on the learning of transformation rules. At this level of sophistication, we encounter trouble again. If the child were a complete grammarian, we could let him name the classes and proceed to learn the trans-formation rules by rote, but this is obviously ridiculous. Not only does he not have names for the categories he is supposed to label, but the linguists are still attempting to state explicitly the transformation rules he is supposed to learn.

At this point, at the risk of being regarded as hopelessly muddleheaded, we would like to reintroduce the notion of reference. We applaud and re-spect the efforts of grammarians to create a grammar without reference to meaning, and we feel that such proposals call attention to the syntactic contribution to the formation of classes which we feel is highly significant. We must, however, remember that there are semantic correlates of the major classses and that the main business of language is wrapped up in function and reference. From a psychological point of view it seems to us highly unlikely that transformations are generated without semantic sup-port. We can facilitate the application of our mediation models by providing that the new forms (which are to be the transforms) are first learned instance by instance as independent constructions, and that the equivalences between such forms and the basic or kernel forms are identified and medi-ated semantically. It is our argument that the "thingness" of nouns is recog-nized and responded to as the implicit characteristic of the class; the "active-ness" of verbs is similarly important, and the noun phrase, verb phrase, and even the sentence have semantic properties recognized, even though un-verbalized, by the fledgling speaker of the language.

As the speaker becomes more and more practiced in the language, the precise semantic content may be supposed to recede in importance, and the (by this time) well-learned structural properties take over virtually un-conscious control of the structure of the utterances.

In summary, we are suggesting that children's language begins with a form of imitation followed by the acquisition of a number of simple S-R connections between verbal labels and salient features of the environment to which they become attached. With a core of labels available, the child attaches words with other words in sequences, and the ordering or struc-turing begins. Particular structuring occurs more and more frequently because of the greater utility of some orders over others. With the develop-ment of particular structures, some words form classes in the sense that they take a particular position in an utterance which is different from the position which other words may take. Through the stimulus and response equiv-alence mechanisms, these classes of words become substitutable for each other in particular structural frames. Thus, new utterances may occur with-out prior training by the substitution of previously acquired equivalences. Transformations, initially learned independently, are facilitated by semantic mediation. Eventually the semantic basis of structure recedes, once the basic adult classes of structure have been acquired (more specific equivalences), and then structure is adhered to (within larger units) without conscious effort.

At the present time the evidence for the approach offered here is fragmentary and only suggestive; but we believe that it forms a pattern.

Werner and Kaplan (1950) imbedded nonsense words in sentences and invited children to give them meaning as in " A wet *corplum* will not burn." Young children gave contextual associations (i.e., sequences); older children gave potential substitutions (i.e., members of the implicit class). Werner and Kaplan report:

> . . . we should like to mention briefly that there are aspects of language development other than semantic, discussed in this paper, which showed similar abrupt changes at the same age levels. This is particularly true with respect to grammatical structure. The data indicate that there is a growing comprehension of the test sentence as a stable grammatical structure.
>
> The close correspondence of the developmental curves . . . between two seemingly independent aspects of language lends support to those theories that assume a genetic interdependence of meaning and structure (pp. 256-257).

In the gross sense we see this as supporting our general position that the items must first be learned in sequences (the sequences being reported as the "meaning" by the younger children), and after much sequence learning the emergence of classes and the identification of substitution with meaning occurs. This is also some evidence, we think, for the relatively slow development of complete systems.

In 1957, Brown reported evidence demonstrating that in children's speech the nouns are quite likely to be names of things and the verbs quite likely to be names of actions; furthermore, it was shown that children reliably respond to the semantic cues furnished by the parts of speech when nonsense entries are used for mass nouns, count nouns, and verb forms. This experiment indicates that the learning of structure and class membership may well be facilitated by semantic relations, as we suggested above, and that, once established, this relation may play a dual role: new entries may be classified semantically on the basis of syntactic cues, and new structures may be understood and related to old structures on the basis of semantic content.

Berko (1958) showed that the development of control over classes and their use is a continuous process with age. Extension to new cases of the "automatic" responses (such as pluralization) may be relatively late, with even the first graders having severe difficulty with some of the nonsense materials, though they were well able to handle most of the familiar material.

In addition, Brown and Berko (1960) have shown that, as the child grows older, the change in the form of word association responses is progressive toward "same class as the stimulus" responses (as Ervin, 1957, has also demonstrated) and that the change in word association is accompanied by the ability to make grammatical use of new words.

These findings give active support to the point of view we have endorsed concerning the shift from sequence to classes. It was a consideration of word association data, in fact, which led one of the writers of this paper to the exploration of the mediational models given above (see Jenkins, 1959). Saporta (1959) presented a paper containing material illustrating that subjects will often substitute an associate for a word in a sentence, if requested to strike out a single word and replace it. In a set of studies at Minnesota we have extended these findings with college students in the following respects: (a) On grammatically diverse sets of stimulus words, we have found that the part of speech of the stimulus word is most frequently matched by the popular response words. (b) We have found that, when one "sets" the subjects to give a response in the same class as the stimulus by giving a phrase stem for completion (e.g., table and ——, light or ——), one elicits most of the normal popular associates of the words. When one uses a sequential fragment (e.g., table is ——, or —— is heavy), one elicits the less frequent associative responses. (c) We have directed subjects to write sentences using selected stimuli, then directed them to strike out the key word and substitute another one. The substitute (as Saporta, 1959, suggested) is likely to be a high frequency associate. As an additional check on this line of thought, one more associative study has recently been performed. It was argued that in all probability a word must appear in several frames before it could gain effective class membership. An attack was made on this question by randomly choosing rare adjectives from the Thorndike Lorge list (1944) for use as associative stimuli. As was predicted, the associates to the rare adjectives turned out predominantly to be nouns. Apparently, such words do not appear in enough different sequences to attain strong relations to any other words of the same class. This suggests that the progressions observed by Brown, Berko, and Ervin are still proceeding (though at a very advanced level) with adult subjects.

A final piece of research with adults has greatly impressed us also with respect to the role of reference, as well as sequence, in the acquisition of language-like behaviors. Johnson, in his Ph.D. thesis at Minnesota (1961), attempted to teach a group of subjects a formal word ending for nouns and for adjectives in simple sentences of the form:

Article (adjective) (noun) verb.

Either the adjective or the noun was replaced by a nonsense form in a particular sentence. If the noun was replaced, the nonsense form appeared in the third position and ended in the syllable "pod"; if the adjective was replaced, the nonsense form appeared in the second position and ended in the syllable "lef." Sentences were then like the following:

> The green dupod rolled.
> The nolef ball bounced.

After intense training with many instances of this sort (which included, in some experiments, anticipation training so that the subject was forced to learn the nonsense syllable for each of several sentences), it was possible to obtain generalization to the extent that, given an "old" sentence (one used in the learning procedure), the subjects could pick out a correct filler from a choice of two new words (one a *pod* word and one a *lef* word). Similarly, given a pair of "old" words (words used in training), the subject could correctly pick the appropriate one for a new sentence requiring either an adjective or a noun. However, given both new words and a new sentence, the subjects did no better than chance.

This somewhat unbelievable finding was replicated on both general population adults and college students in several conditions. In addition, it was established that grammatical naiveté was enormous. Given an example of each kind of sentence and asked to sort a set of sentences into those of the same kinds, eight out of 10 subjects could correctly perform the task. Asked what characterized the two sets of sentences, only one out of these eight was able to give a specific reason for the separation.

Complete generalization was achieved (new words correctly chosen for new sentences) *only* when, prior to the training trials, the subjects were shown pictures of objects which were identified as being examples of particular "pod" words and squares of color identified as being "lef" words. Under these circumstances generalization was complete. As a control procedure the reference identification was given without the sentence training procedure. These subjects showed no generalization of the experimental words to appropriate sentences. At present it appears that, at least with an artificial and non-English procedure such as this, *both* semantic and syntactic cues are necessary to assign grammatical class to new instances of terms identified by formal characteristics.

SUMMARY

This paper points out that the problems of grammar have rarely been made the subject of psychological analysis, although many psychologists have recognized the importance of such problems. Three general forms of mediational paradigms were advanced to be used as a basis for the explication of grammatical phenomena. These paradigms were applied in detail in explaining the behavior of subjects in two artificial language experiments.

General extension of this line of analysis to the question of the acquisition of grammar of natural first-language learning was attempted. Some experimental findings which seemed to be consistent with the approach offered here were briefly mentioned.

FORMAL DISCUSSION

JEROME KAGAN
Fels Research Institute

It is a happy privilege to assume the role of discussant for this thoughtful and provocative essay. Since our major concern here is with early language learning, I will restrict my remarks to the authors' theoretical suggestions for explaining how the child learns to produce grammatically correct utterances. The authors have dealt not only with this problem, but also with issues pertaining to why the child speaks at all. They assume, for example, that the initial imitation of speech is universal and perhaps unlearned and that this tendency is supported by socially derived secondary reinforcements. However, I want to set these assumptions aside and attend specifically to the central concern of the paper, that is, the arguments advanced to account for the child's increasing degree of syntactic maturity.

The authors make three critical assumptions:

1. Words have both meaning and structural properties.

2. Learning about meaning and syntax proceeds simultaneously and interdependently.

3. Mediation theory (that is, simple mediation as well as response and stimulus equivalence) can explain the child's gradual acquisition of adult grammar.

There should be little argument with the first two assumptions. The degree of accord with the third, however, depends upon the proposed bases of similarity that give life to the mediational principles. Let us turn to this assumption, for it forms a pivotal part of the essay. The remarks that follow should be viewed as complementary to the hypotheses of Jenkins and Palermo, for I do not disagree with their basic theme, only with where they choose to place the accents.

Jenkins and Palermo propose that simple mediation and stimulus and response equivalences carry a large burden of explaining syntactic learning. This position is reasonable and intuitively persuasive. However, a precise account of how this learning proceeds requires an understanding of the nature of the similarities upon which words are grouped into syntactic classes. The authors stress the qualities of semantic reference and sequential position as fundamental for these mediational equivalences. However, they fail to emphasize the fact that words and phrases also have different loudness contours, situational contexts, and communication functions. For the child, these three attributes may be as salient as sequential position. Requests, questions, or commands have verbs in the initial position in the utterances; declarative sentences give nouns the privilege of first place; answers to questions often place adverbs and adjectives in the lead position. Thus, the communication function of a sentence is an important clue to syntax.

Further, we have not paid sufficient attention to possible differences in sentence structure when the child is in varied social or emotional situations (e.g., talking to a peer or to an adult; when emotionally upset or calm; when in his own home or in a strange environment). Finally, regularities in inflection may furnish the child with important foundations for learning equivalent word classes. In this regard it would be of interest to perform the following naturalistic experiment: Locate groups of parents who differ in the classes of words to which they give vocal emphasis and assess whether such systematic emphasis in the parents' vocalizations influences the syntax of the young child's speech.

Current developmental hypotheses suggest that perceptually salient cues are more important in directing the classifications of the preschool child than conceptual considerations. Inflection and situational contexts seem to have more, or at least as much, perceptual salience as the characteristic of sequential position.

For the remainder of this discussion I would like to examine the authors' specific suggestion that (a) word position and (b) the "thingness" of nouns and "activeness" of verbs form major classes of similarity and catalyze the learning of equivalences. Although it is reasonable that position, thingness, and activeness seed the crystallization of word classes, the data in the protocols presented by Brown and Fraser pose some difficulties for this hypothesis. According to Jenkins and Palermo, the child gradually comes to learn that words in the first position in an utterance have an equivalence and, therefore, are interchangeable. Abel's protocols, however, contain instances in which verbs, nouns, and articles all appear in the first position. Similarly, nouns, verbs, qualifiers, and locatives all appear in the second position in Abel's two-word utterances. In these two-word utterances all the major parts of speech occur in both the first and second position. Similarly, the protocol of Adam (28½ months old) contains instances in which the word *here* occurs in both the first and last position in three word utterances; the word *block* in both second and third position. All these sentences, however, are correct grammatically. In preparation for this meeting I sampled the speech of my 7-year-old daughter and discovered that in less than 10 minutes she had used a noun, a verb, and an adverb as the initial word in complex utterances. Thus, similarity in position, per se, would appear to be neither sufficient nor primary in the emergence of syntactic equivalences. It is well established that nouns, verbs, and adjectives bear the burden of communication in a school age child's speech. Yet nouns or verbs can occur in the middle, beginning, or end of sentences as in utterances like "The dogs are here," "Watch the dogs run home," "Look at those dogs," or "Come here," "We'll come tomorrow," "The dog came." Surely position alone does not unambiguously define a grammatical class.

The authors suggest that mediational principles transform pairs of words that have similar sequential characteristics into similar syntactic classes. For example, in phrases like "The boy," and "The dog," both *boy* and *dog* follow the word *The*. It is assumed, with the help of the response equivalence, that *boy* and *dog* become members of the same class. It is too easy, however, to find instances in which the principle of response equivalence predicts occurrences that one rarely finds in the speech of children or adults. Let us consider some examples of such predictions that are derived from the principles of response and stimulus equivalence.

The paradigm for the *response equivalence* category is: if AB and AC, then B and C become equivalent. For example, "The dog" and "The mother" imply that *dog* and *mother* elicit each other and become members of the same class. Or "Come here" and "Come quickly" suggest that *here* and *quickly* become members of the same class. In our investigations of the word associations of children, ages 6 through 12, in which both *dog* and *mother* appeared as stimulus words, we never obtained the sequence *dog-mother* or its reverse. The popular association to *dog* is either a phrase completion, or, if it is a noun, it is a semantically related noun such as *bone* or *cat*. The dominant associations to other nouns all had some degree of similarity in meaning.

The model in the case of *stimulus equivalence* is: A-B, C-B, A-D; then, C and D become equivalent. An example of this theoretical sequence would be: "This car," "Little car," "This is," implying that *little* and *is* have gained communality. Similarly, the trio "Throw ball," "Red ball," and "Throw away," implies that the words *red* and *away* should be regarded as equivalents. These are only a few quickly composed examples of the non-occurring predictions that emerge from a view that regards sequential position alone as a major basis for equivalence. Jenkins and Palermo, of course, do not take such an extreme view. I have taken the time to present the problems associated with an extreme sequential hypothesis because I believe it is valuable to point out that sequential attributes are not able to bear the burden of explaining how equivalent classes are formed without at least taking semantic meaning into account.

If one studies the changing word associations of children between 6 and 10 years of age, one notes that the gradual substitution of nouns for verbs to noun stimuli is not random but typically based on similarities in meaning.

Thus, *dog-cat* replaces *dog-bark* rather than *dog-star*, *dog-baby*, or *dog-table*. I would emphasize the authors' suggestion that reference and syntax are completely interdependent.

Let us consider a second basis for equivalence offered by the authors. They tentatively suggest that the young child recognizes the "thingness" of nouns and the "activeness" of verbs and that this recognition acts as an important basis for similarity. Once again, study of the protocols in the Brown and Fraser paper is enlightening. Of the nine transitive verbs uttered by Abel, five were *get, need, want, see,* and *find*. These verbs have minimal activity attributes, and it is difficult to believe that the potential activeness of these words somehow endows them with similarity. Indeed, the verbs *want* and *need* are psychological states that do not refer to overt actions. In the same vein, the nouns uttered by Abel include *tiger, eye,* and *cake,* and my intuition rebels somewhat at the assumption that the "thingness" of these objects is a basic source of communality among them.

I apologize for not being more constructive. It is easier to point to minor defects in another's theory than to construct a more elegant one. It would be nice to be able to pull off a tour de force and outline the rules that direct the child's language learning and allow him to proliferate novel, yet, correct utterances. As I listen to the interchange between 3- and 4-year-olds and study the Brown and Fraser protocols, the following conclusions, some of which have been detailed by Jenkins and Palermo, seem to be good working hypotheses.

The child's early sentences are imitations of those parts of the adult utterances that are semantically meaningful and perceptually salient. Perceptual salience, I suggest, is based primarily upon inflection and loudness and secondarily upon sequential position. The next step in this process may be a matching of utterances to the adult model through discrimination and differentiation and utilization of different sentence frames depending on the function of the communication. The fact that the sentences of the 5-year-old are relatively accurate may arise initially from an intimate inter-action between similarities in meaning and inflection and only later from similarities in word sequence. This suggestion would agree with the data presented by Brown and Fraser. I heartily endorse the authors' suggestion that S-R contingencies are developed where the fundamental structure is of the acquired distinctiveness sort, but would place more emphasis upon meaning and inflection than on position in determining the distinctiveness of the stimulus. Current research by students of development indicates that the child's attention is captured by perceptually salient dimensions, and I suggest that whether a word is second, third, or fourth in an utterance does not have the degree of salience necessary to lead to early class formation on this dimension without major support from other speech characteristics.

Jenkins and Palermo have written a stimulating and insightful essay that has several testable hypotheses. Both their paper and this discussion give semantic meaning an enormously influential role in the acquisition of grammar. The investigator who is able to assess the effect of meaning in the mastery of this developmental task will have achieved no small goal.

Moreover, it is not unreasonable to expect that explanation of the learning of syntax may well provide psychology with an important general insight into the nature of human learning. For the implicit and all-or-none character of language learning resembles in many ways the major response classes humans acquire during the first two decades of their lives.

OPEN DISCUSSION

Almost all of the discussion at this meeting came from the psychologists. A great deal of it was in direct response to issues formulated by Kagan.

1. Most of the data cited in the papers of Brown and Fraser and also in the paper of Miller and Ervin are two-word utterances. Now, in addition, Jenkins and Palermo had offered pair-wise learning paradigms. This concentration on the two-word sequences was somewhat unlucky because such sequences are imperfectly representative of linguistic syntax. In verbal pairs context can only occur on one side of a word: after the initial form and before the final form. The more usual linguistic case is that in which a form is surrounded by context. In addition, the verbal pair readily suggests that syntactic positions or privileges of occurrence can be identified with an absolute ordinal position in a sequence. This is not the case. Since the papers had seemed to suggest that it is the case, some clarification was needed.

Even in the two-word utterances of very young children the same word may occur in both first and second positions; for example, this might happen with the words *here* and *come*. That would not necessarily mean that these words are employed in a random unstructured way. It might be the case that *here* initially is generally followed by a noun, as an ellipsis of such adult sentences as *"Here* is your *ball,"* and *"Here* is the *doggie."* In second position *here* might generally be preceded by the verb *Come*. The word *Come* in initial position would generally be followed by *here* and not by such nouns as *ball* and *doggie*. The word *come* in final position might generally be preceded by such nouns as *Ball* and *Doggie*.

In the above hypothetic instance it is not the case that *here* and *come* occur in all possible positions, because a position is not an ordinal slot, but is rather a slot defined with reference to the words in other slots. It is not the case that *here* and *come* have identical privileges of occurrence and so must be assigned to the same syntactic class, because privileges of occurrence are not ordinal positions but are positions defined with reference to other words. The hypothetical distributions of *here* and *come* are completely nonoverlapping. Where the one word occurs, the other does not. They would be assigned to different syntactic classes on the basis of these data. The fundamental point is that syntactic positions are not to be understood as Position One and Position Two, though the papers presented had unintentionally suggested that interpretation.

2. The pair-wise paradigm does, easily, suggest that, since *dog* and *mother* can both be preceded by *the*, the two nouns are close syntactic equivalents and so ought to elicit one another in word associations. A fuller examination of adult linguistic contexts, however, would show that *mother* is more closely matched with *father*, and *dog* with *cat*. One way of demonstrating this is to have subjects write sentences utilizing the word *mother* and then ask them to say in how many of these cases would *father* be an acceptable substitute, and in how many case would *dog* be an acceptable substitute. (Ervin, 1957, Jenkins, 1959, and Saporta, 1959, have all done this kind of thing.) The point is that syntactic similarity is a matter of degree, and equivalence of two words in one simple context ("The ———") does not necessarily indicate a more general equivalence.

3. The nearer syntactic equivalence of *mother* and *father* than of *mother* and *dog* goes with a greater semantic similarity, and that is generally the case. Such syntactic classes as "mass nouns" and "animate nouns" are in fact named in semantic terms. Even for a grammarian the semantic similarity of referents may be a good guide to syntactic classes. It follows, therefore, that semantic similarity could help a child to learn how to group words into syntactic classes and could tell him which words should be listed together.

It is essential to notice, however, that semantic similarity cannot alone teach a child how to use words in novel constructions. There is more to syntax than classes of equivalents. One must know what the equivalence amounts to in terms of privileges of occurrence. Suppose the "thingness" of a child's nouns and the "activeness" of his verbs teaches him to put nouns together and verbs together. Then what? In order to go on to make correct but novel use of nouns and verbs he must know how they can be combined with other words; he must know syntax. Semantics can support syntax, and the findings reported by Jenkins and Palermo suggest that the support is important, that pure syntax is hard to learn. But semantics can only be a support, it cannot replace syntax. For a deck of cards the colors and designs and numbers can show us which cards are equivalent, but we cannot play a game unless we know how the cards are utilized.

4. Kagan noted that some of the verbs that occurred frequently in Abel's record are not names of motor activities; they are *get, want, need, see,* and *find*. That is an interesting observation. There may actually be a semantic common denominator for some of these. Kagan, for example, identified

want and *need* as psychological states; one might say motivational states. It is not necessary to the thesis that semantics supports syntax for the semantic similarity in particular subclasses of verbs to be gross motor activities. Still it is somewhat surprising that these early verbs should be ones whose semantic quality is rather obscure. It may be that they come to be used early because they serve to distinguish a child's "mands" (when he is asking for something) from his "tacts" (when he is simply naming something).

5. There may be a complication in the *mother-dog* case other than the complication that has been mentioned. Very young children do not have long sentences, and it is conceivable that in their speech these two nouns are indeed syntactic equivalents. After all it is much older children and adults who produce *father* as a response to *mother* and who do not produce *dog*. One should consider the possibility that the child's early syntactic classes are not the same as adult classes. Perhaps the child for whom *mother* and *dog* have similar privileges of occurrence would, in a word association test, produce one in response to the other.

The example is a little grotesque as it is unlikely that *mother* and *dog* are ever syntactic equivalents. However, the principle is important: one ought not to impose on a young child the syntactic categories of adult speech. To do so is to eliminate much of the problem of speech acquisition. Could one use the word association test with very young children to validate inferences about their syntactic organization?

The current view is that young children respond in accordance with sequential probabilities rather than syntax; *to send* elicits *a letter* rather than *to receive*. It is likely that since the very young child does not have experience of a great variety of contexts he is in the position of the older subjects of Jenkins and Palermo who respond to the word *intercontinental* with *missile*. The word-association experiment is very difficult to do with young children; for one thing, they often respond to a stimulus word with a phrase rather than a single word.

VII

COMMENTS AND CONCLUSIONS

JAMES DEESE

Johns Hopkins University

I have been asked to comment on the proceedings of this conference as a representative from the field of learning and from the point of view of contemporary learning theory. This assignment is difficult for me because I had the conviction before the conference—and little has occurred to change that conviction—that contemporary learning theory has little to contribute to the problem of the analysis of language acquisition. There are, of course, some important exceptions to the extraordinary lack of concern with grammar and its acquisition, and I would like to mention at least one of these exceptions. I should also hasten to add that the lack of contribution from learning theory is not because of inherent weakness of current learning theory. It is, primarily, because the problems raised by the Ervin and Miller and the Brown, Fraser, and Bellugi papers have not been tackled by learning theorists.

There is a strong tradition in learning theory that language is somehow just like any other behavior. The classical attitude of many learning theorists towards the problem of language is that language learning is simply a matter of individual adjustment on the part of the organism. This belief provides the basis of most textbook accounts of language learning. The rules of the acquisition of linguistic responses are supposed to be not different from the rules of acquisition of any other kind of responses. From the 1920's on, there has been the feeling that one can deal with the acquisition of the individual elements of language by the principles of classical and/or instrumental conditioning. Such a view implies that one modifies and applies the apparatus of contemporary learning theory—stimulus generalization and the like—to the acquisition of language in general and grammar in particular.

However, the papers presented at this conference, particularly the two papers on grammar and the Jenkins and Palermo analysis of the Esper experiments, make it clear that we are dealing with systematic intraindividual organizations which require a different conceptual apparatus from that provided by traditional learning theory. The two papers on the development of grammar in children present for learning theorists a clarification of

177

the nature of the problem to which learning theory should address itself. This result may be one of the most important consequences of those papers. It may be indeed, as the linguists seem to assert, a virtually impossible task to write a grammar from the kinds of protocols or data presented in these papers; but the data presented there do provide the kinds of raw materials for inferences about the process of acquisition of learning of the kinds of structures apparent in the emitted verbal behavior of the child. These are the data to which one should address a theory, and the function of a theory so oriented is to recover the process—that is, to predict the sequences and the orders of emissions in the behavior under study.

Learning theorists, with a few exceptions, no longer regard the human organism as an indifferent, undifferentiated representative of all vertebrates so far as learning and conditioning are concerned. The notion of species-specific behavior has permeated modern learning theory. There are some species characteristics which have to do with the patterning of stimuli that impinge on the central nervous system, the organization of the central nervous system, maturational effects, and other special properties. Such a view, however, has not gone far enough in considering the special problems introduced by human language and particularly the grammar of human language.

One way in which an extension of modern learning theory has tried to deal with grammar is by mediation theory. Such a use of mediation theory is implicit in the classical treatment by Cofer and Foley (1942), and Jenkins and Palermo, in their paper presented here, make such a treatment quite explicit. The concept of mediation is built on the idea of stimulus-response units or contingencies between responses and events which precede them and which control their emission. Jenkins and Palermo make the assumption that these stimulus-response units can be chained together to form the flow of ordinary discourse, and they reduce the rules of such discourse to the stimulus equivalence and response equivalence paradigms of mediation theory.

The mediation model provides a very powerful tool of analysis, and it is a good beginning for the description of the emission of verbal behavior. It does come from learning theory and, so far as I know, is the most thorough contribution stemming from learning theory to the analysis of the acquisition of language. For this reason, if for no other, it deserves special attention.

The objection has been raised that the mediation model implies a left-to-right chaining of linguistic behavior. There are really two problems, however, in the implication of left-to-right chaining. One is simply the description of the order in which behavior occurs, and it is hard for me to imagine linguistic events in anything but a successive time order. The other problem, however, is more sophisticated, and it is the problem of how the rules constraining successive elements in an utterance are generated. Here we are dealing with such things as the possible nested properties of sentences. Yet, it seems to me, the question of a linguistic analysis of an utterance as a structural left-to-right unfolding, or as nested dependencies, may be irrelevant to the usefulness of the mediation model as a predictive device in describing the verbal behavior of children.

For one thing, we know that people can store words in their heads for short periods of time and react to these stored words as intraorganic events. Jenkins and Palermo give an example of a set of nested dependencies: "The boy . . . who lives in the big white house across the street from the curious looking bank. . . ." One can imagine such an utterance being generated in a time ordered way, but the order of generation is not necessarily the order of emission. "The boy" may be generated, and this set of elements in turn may generate the ultimate predicate phrase and then generate several dependent clauses. The predicate phrase is held in storage, however, until the long sequence in the middle is emitted. In fact, if it is held too long, it may be lost; such effects may be responsible for the evident disorganization of emitted speech seen in a literal transcription. There can be fairly complicated patterns built on temporary storage of material which has been generated but not emitted until some later time. Of course, what is stored may be altered by what is emitted in the meantime, which makes the problem of analysis of the emitted sequence even more difficult.

The mediation model, in the present context, can be taken as a notion as to how words become members of formal classes. It is also a model for the emission of verbal behavior, and because of its dual function it covers more ground than any comparable theory coming from the study of learning. Jenkins and Palermo are obviously interested in both aspects of mediation theory; though, in the present context, they are more concerned to show how the model describes the formation of verbal classes. It should be noted that the theory is built entirely upon the contingency rule. Classes or categories are derived from contingencies in perception and responding; the organism takes a kind of semirandom nature and organizes it into a highly structured intellectual system by a stimulus equivalence rule. Because of its dependence upon the contingency rule (contiguity), mediation theory ignores the possibility of innate intraindividual organizations. Gestalt psychologists, of course, have considered such organizations in a description of the perceptual world, but very little has been said about similar rules of organization in linguistic behavior. Despite the dependence of the Jenkins and Palermo mediation model upon stimulus-response contingencies, I do not think there is anything in the model which would preclude or deny innate organizations. Indeed, classical learning theory has one such innate organization in the form of stimulus generalization. Mediation may be viewed as an alternative to stimulus generalization, but it may also be viewed as something above and beyond primary stimulus generalization (such was the view of Cofer and Foley, 1942).

Mediation theory, at any rate, is one inheritance of learning theory in the study of language acquisition that is of potential importance. It may provide an extremely powerful tool for extending the experimental data on the acquisition of verbal behavior to the kinds of data observed by Ervin and Miller and Brown, Fraser, and Bellugi.

There is another side of modern learning theory that has received much attention lately in the study of verbal behavior, and a word should be said about it. This aspect of learning theory is not so concerned with description of the structure of verbal behavior (I view mediation theory as being so concerned) as with the incentive and motive conditions which control the production or emission of behavior. I am talking about the behaviorism of Skinner (1957). The essence of the Skinnerian analysis is concerned with incentive conditions. Skinnerian behaviorism is hardly at all concerned with learning—learning is early and easily dismissed. The Skinnerian, however, is concerned with describing the way in which environmental reinforcement contingencies and the like control the emission of behavior. The result of such an analysis is that one can write an historical account of how sequences of reinforcement contingencies produce particular outcomes in behavior.

Of recent years, this analysis has been applied to the emission of words, both in Skinner's own discursive treatment of verbal behavior and in a large number of experiments on the effects of reinforcement schedules on classes of verbal elements. The whole point of the application to verbal behavior is to show—and I am exaggerating only slightly—that verbal behavior is not different from any other class of operant or emitted behavior.

The Skinnerian analysis of the conditions controlling the emission of behavior is a very powerful one, and it is easy to be convinced that verbal behavior, along with other kinds of behavior, is under the control of reinforcement contingencies. Nevertheless, it is language which is central to a lot of the human being's specific characteristics, and we define language in such a way as to say precisely that it is not entirely under the control of reinforcement contingencies. It is, to a considerable measure, internally controlled by its own structural relations. That seems to be the point of a great deal of linguistic analysis. The human being is able to transcend the effects of a reinforcement schedule through his ability to store and internalize environment behavior and intrabehavioral relations through the mediation of language. Therefore, it is that aspect of language which makes it different from elements of behavior simply and entirely under the control of reinforcement contingencies, which makes language unique and worth studying in its own right.

All this has relevance to the study of language acquisition in children, for we must suppose that, as children acquire and use language, they divorce themselves in considerable measure from direct control through reinforcement contingencies. The internal events that can go on through the mediation of language take away some of the power of the environmental contingencies to control in a simple and direct way. Language must modify control exerted by external reinforcement. Thus, if we are to understand thoroughly the control exerted by reinforcement on the behavior of linguistically behaving children, we must find some way of externalizing (finding out about) the operations which the child performs upon his own behavior linguistically before we can make any real sense about the control of the behavior of children by reinforcement.

If we really want to have some leverage on the problem of the control of the emission of behavior in the young child, we must make usable some of the conceptual apparatus that is implied by the term "expectancy" and the like. We have little or no conceptual apparatus for dealing with such problems, but, if we are to appreciate the control exerted over the linguistically active child by his environment, we need some useful ideas about what goes on intraorganically, and specifically intralinguistically. Therefore, rather than using the data on reinforcement schedules to "explain" the acquisition of language, we need information about the acquisition of language in order to understand the effect of reinforcements upon the young child.

In this sense as well as others, the study of the nature or structure of language in children may well provide an important part of the information needed to control and predict the behavior of children. The structural study of children's language, then, may make as much of a contribution to the uses of learning theory as learning theory can make to an understanding of how those structures are acquired.

COMMENTS AND CONCLUSIONS

Omar K. Moore
Yale University

Deese's remarks will serve as a convenient starting point for my comments. First of all, I am less hopeful than he is about the possibility of successfully applying any of the current theories of learning to the acquisition of a first language; as a matter of fact, I do not think that they are adequate to explain the learning of anything very complex. There are many reasons why I am dissatisfied with contemporary learning theories: they tend to confound *learning* and *performance;* they tend to neglect the cue value of reinforcing agents; and they make the assumption that reinforcement is essential for learning, whereas I do not think that reinforcement is either necessary or sufficient for learning.

Today, however, I would like to draw your attention to the fact that learning theories fail to satisfy what is sometimes called the "sufficiency criterion." What do I mean by the "sufficiency criterion?" Imagine that we wish to evaluate some theory of learning; let us disregard the problem of whether human beings actually behave as the theory stipulates. Instead, let us ask whether *any* entity, which behaves as the theory prescribes, could learn the things which we know human beings do learn. If we find that no entity which behaves in strict accordance with the candidate theory of learning could learn what human beings obviously do learn, then the theory fails the sufficiency criterion. One practical way to test a theory for sufficiency is to construct a working model of the theory—give the working model appropriate inputs and see whether or not it does in fact learn. It is unnecessary to build a working model of most learning theories because it is obvious at first glance that these theories have almost nothing to say about what a working model should do with input data. A few researchers have made models of their own intuitive guesses about learning processes: for example, Newell, Shaw, and Simon (1958) have done this with the help of computers. And their research, unlike the work of most learning theorists, is at least relevant to the problem of constructing a theory of learning which would pass the sufficiency test.

My remarks up to this point may have been too general to convey clearly what I have in mind, so let me be more specific. We know that human beings frequently solve problems which have the following characteristics: (a) the likelihood of obtaining solutions by random, or quasi-random, trial and error is virtually zero; and (b) no practical algorithms exist for obtaining solutions (an algorithm is a method which guarantees a solution if one exists, or, in the case of a problem with no solution, will indicate that there is none). As I mentioned before, human beings frequently solve such problems, and, by definition, the learning process can neither be a purely random one nor a purely mechanical one. The question is, "How do human beings learn to solve such problems?" The most suggestive material that I have encountered for unraveling this mystery is contained in the writings of logicians on the topic of "natural deduction" (see, for example, Fitch, 1952). The various nonalgorithmic problem-solving schemata which logicians have developed in recent years as heuristic devices for approaching such problems—and which are very helpful, as a matter of fact—have certain features to which I would like to call attention. For the purposes of this discussion I will use Fitch's method of subordinate proof as an illustrative case.

Probably the most striking feature of Fitch's method is that the problem solver's attention is first directed to the goal, here, the theorem to be deduced. In brief, the learner is invited to behave in a goal-directed way. The first task of the learner is to work backward from the goal toward the initially given data. This process of working backward ordinarily requires the setting up of subgoals and of subsubgoals. From each subgoal the learner is enjoined to continue this backward working process. Of course, each subgoal must stand in some plausible relation to both superordinate and subordinate goals. Also, Fitch's method specifies ways of interrelating this hierarchy of proof sequences, and it also makes explicit provision for moving forward from the initial starting point to subgoal sequences. In sum, Fitch's method makes explicit provisions for working backward from a goal and working forward from some starting point, and also for the elaboration of an interlocking network of subgoals which are tied to both the goal and the starting position. Now the trouble with most learning theories is that they simply do not make provision within the structure of the theories themselves for any such system of goal-directed activity. I do not suggest that Fitch's system, or any other system of natural deduction, should be thought of as a learning theory, but I do say that learning theories should be at least as rich as the methods of natural deduction in specifying the procedures whereby learning could take place. And, since they are not adequate in this regard, I think it is obvious that they fail the sufficiency criterion.

From my point of view it is clear that the standard learning theories are not going to be of much help in understanding the acquisition of a natural language. After all, natural languages are much more complex than the simple, straightforward symbolic systems for which natural deduction is a useful tool. It is distressing to think that learning theories may well have to be recast at this late date, but perhaps we can begin in a more sophisticated way.

In our next attempts to construct theories of learning I think it would pay us to attend more closely to the formal disciplines, namely, mathematics and mathematical logic. For instance, it would seem wise to take into account the work of Church (1936). Prior to, say, 1930, I think that most researchers, certainly most logicians, would have thought it possible, in principle, to write a program which would constitute an effective method for solving any arbitrarily selected problem in any well specified class of problems. However, it is now clear that there are intrinsic limitations on the development of effective procedures; namely, in certain cases at least, the goals of achieving completeness and consistency are antithetical. From time to time during this conference we have talked about the possibility that there is a language generator within human beings which, granted certain inputs, would be capable of generating well-formed expressions in a natural language. It may be that such a language generator is impossible in principle. Perhaps there are formal arguments of the kind Church (1936) and Gödel (1931) have used which would make clear what some of the boundary conditions are for the development of adequate theories of learning. In any case, it would be worthwhile to give a great deal of thought to the problem of specifying what characteristics we might want in the way of a heuristic language generator.

Thus far I have talked almost exclusively about the inadequacies of learning theories. I would like now to make a few comments about the linguistic side of the problem of understanding language acquisition. We all recognize that linguists have made considerable headway in analyzing the structure of natural languages. The work on generative grammars is particularly clarifying. In my opinion, many of the empirical studies reported at this conference do not take account of the best that is known in linguistics. In particular, linguists are making it more and more evident that the structure of a language is best treated as a system—a system in which what were formerly thought of as more or less autonomous parts can now be seen to be only contingently autonomous. For example, it may be very misleading to think of language as consisting of a complex structure made up of elementary units, for example, built up out of phonemic classes— the status of a phoneme qua phoneme may well be dependent upon its relation to a complex set of formation and transformation rules. Now it seems to me that it would be most unfortunate if psychological research on language acquisition were to be carried out on the assumption that a language consists of a hierarchy of complex elements constructed out of elementary building blocks. If the "new look" in linguistics—by the "new look" I mean the work of Chomsky and his colleagues—is at all viable, it would be a serious mistake to conduct empirical studies of first language acquisition on the assumption that to master a language is to learn to handle the kind of linguistic entity posited by linguists in the 1930's and 1940's.

FINAL DISCUSSION

The final discussion was not the best. There was a long argument about algorithms and heuristics that stimulated people to check and see whether they might not catch an earlier plane. But several points that had been separately developed on different days were discovered to be related and were put together.

1. The distinction between linguistic competence and linguistic performance is tied to the call for research on grammar comprehension, and also to the position that there must be more required of a grammar than the generation of properly formed sentences. Lenneberg's case study of a child who understood a great deal but spoke not at all is a central datum. Here is one case, at least, where the naturalistic study of speech in the manner of Brown

and Ervin and their associates would have captured nothing of the actual linguistic competence. To learn about competence it will be necessary to do active experimentation in addition to naturalistic observation; to elicit speech, to force linguistic performances that would not otherwise have been obtained. In addition, it will be necessary to find ways of studying the comprehension of grammar; Lenneberg's methods are suggestive on this point. Finally, in order to find clear grounds for preferring one grammar to another, it will be necessary to get evidence of the constituent structure of a child's sentences and also perhaps judgments of degree of grammaticality.

The above position was the position of the generative grammarians—the M.I.T. school of linguistics. It is essentially a call for a change of method of investigation, from naturalistic observation to experimental intervention in the process of language acquisition. In view of the fact that no complete generative description has yet been written for the adult version of any natural language, those who would study the speech of children from the generative point of view are indeed on a remote frontier.

2. There were some unplanned but very satisfying convergences among the papers. Brown, Fraser, and Bellugi in Cambridge and Miller and Ervin in Berkeley had been studying the speech of children of the same age and using very similar naturalistic methods. Furthermore, their descriptions were strikingly similar—the same constructions and even very similar vocabularies. The principal novelty in these descriptions, by comparison with prior work on child speech, is the suggestion that utterances are generated by a program involving selections from syntactic classes in a particular sequence. In the opinion of several of the linguists, the work done thus far rather convincingly demonstrates that the earliest sentences, at least, can be understood in this way.

The principal kind of learning that these descriptions attribute to the child is the formation of syntactic classes, classes of words having similar privileges of occurrence. There was a striking convergence here with the paper by Jenkins and Palermo. That paper describes learning paradigms (in terms of mediation) for the very structure that is the focus of the work with children—the syntactic class. In addition, Jenkins and Palermo reported an experiment done by Johnson (1961) suggesting that semantics might be an important factor in the acquisition of such classes.

3. On some things there was agreement. The facts about child speech, and even more, a generative description of adult speech, pose problems that probably cannot be handled by present learning theory. Some thought these theories might be redeemed; others thought them hopelessly inadequate even for problems very much simpler than the acquisition of language.

The child's acquisition of a phonemic system is an almost untouched problem, and it is very much to be hoped that the work of Bullowa, Jones, and Bever will illuminate it. They have devised ingenious ways of collecting more complete data on early vocalizations than has heretofore been collected.

It was suggested that a good point where the fields of linguistics and psychology can cross is in the kind of research that was suggested in a paper by Sapir called "The psychological reality of phonemes" (1949). In this paper, a linguist is making certain claims about the structure of the language, and the psychologist could, by experimental procedures, test these intuitive observations. This, for example, is an open and extremely important area for investigation.

Language compels us to ask the following question: What kinds of structures can the human brain learn from a relatively small sample of data? It compels us also to ask: How does the brain operate in learning such structures? Every sort of information on the higher cognitive processes is relevant to these great questions. The study of the acquisition of natural languages is one of the many studies that must be undertaken.

REFERENCES

ABORN, M., & RUBENSTEIN, H. Word-class distribution in sentences of fixed length. *Language,* 1956, 32, 666-674.

ADRIAN, E. D., & BUYTENDIJK, F. J. Potential changes in the isolated brain stem of the goldfish. *J. Physiol.,* 1931, 71, 121-135.

BARKER, R. G., & WRIGHT, H. F. *Midwest and its children.* Row, Peterson, 1954.

BATESON, G., JACKSON, D. D., HALEY, J., & WEEKLAND, J. Toward a theory of schizophrenia. *Behav. Sci.,* 1956, 1, 251-264.

BERKO, J. The child's learning of English morphology. *Word,* 1958, 14, 150-177.

BERNSTEIN, B. Aspects of language and learning in the genesis of the social process. *J. Child Psychol. Psychiat.,* 1961, 1, 313-324.

BIRGE, J. S. The role of verbal responses in transfer. Unpublished doctoral dissertation, Yale Univer., 1941.

BLANKENSHIP, A. B. Memory span: a review of the literature. *Psychol. Bull.,* 1938, 35, 1-25.

BOUSFIELD, W. A. The problem of meaning in verbal learning. In C. N. Cofer (Ed.), *Learning and verbal behavior.* McGraw-Hill, 1961.

BROWN, R. W. Linguistic determinism and the part of speech. *J. abnorm. soc. Psychol.,* 1957, 55, 1-5.

BROWN, R. W. How shall a thing be called? *Psychol. Rev.,* 1958, 65, 14-21. (a)

BROWN, R. W. *Words and things.* Free Press, 1958. (b)

BROWN, R. W., & BERKO, J. Word association and the acquisition of grammar. *Child Develpm.,* 1960, 31, 1-14.

BRUNER, J. S. Review of K. W. Spence, *Behavior theory and conditioning. Contemp. Psychol.,* 1957, 2, 155-157.

CANTOR, C. N. Effects of three types of pretraining on discrimination learning in preschool children. *J. exp. Psychol.,* 1955, 49, 339-342.

CARROLL, J. B. *The study of language.* Harvard Univer. Press, 1953.

CHOMSKY, N. *Syntactic structures.* The Hague: Mouton, 1957.

CHOMSKY, N. Review of B. F. Skinner, *Verbal behavior. Language,* 1959, 35, 26-58.

CHURCH, A. A note on the Entscheidungsproblem. *J. symbolic Logic,* 1936, 1, 40-41.

COFER, C. N., & FOLEY, J. P., JR. Mediated generalization and the interpretation of verbal behavior: I. Prolegomena. *Psychol. Rev.,* 1942, 49, 513-540.

CUNNINGHAM, J. W., NEWMAN, S. E., & GRAY, C. W. Stimulus-term and response-term recall as functions of number of paired-associate training trials. Paper presented at Midwest. Psychol. Ass., May, 1961.

DEGROOT, A. W. Structural linguistics and syntactic laws. *Word,* 1949, 5, 1-12.

DOLLARD, J., & MILLER, N. E. *Personality and psychotherapy.* McGraw-Hill, 1950.

DRILLIS, R. Objective recording and biomechanics of pathological gait. *Ann., N.Y. Acad. Sci.,* 1958, 74, 86-109.

ERVIN, S. M. Grammar and classification. Paper read at Amer. Psychol. Ass., 1957.

ESPER, E. A. A technique for the experimental investigation of associative interference in artificial linguistic material. *Language Monogr.,* 1925, No. 1.

ESPER, E. A. Studies in linguistic behavior organization: I. Characteristics of unstable verbal reactions. *J. genet. Psychol.,* 1933, 8, 346-379.

FITCH, F. B. *Symbolic logic.* Ronald, 1952.

FORD, F. R. *Diseases of the nervous system in infancy and childhood.* (4th ed.) Thomas, 1960.

FRANCIS, W. N. *The structure of American English.* Ronald, 1958.

FREUD, S. On narcissism: an introduction. In *Collected papers,* Vol. IV. London: Hogarth Press, 1914. Pp. 30-59.

FRIES, C. C. *The structure of English.* Harcourt, Brace, 1952.

GESELL, A., *et al. The first five years of life: a guide to the study of the preschool child.* Harper, 1940.

GLEASON, H. A. *An introduction to descriptive linguistics.* (2nd ed.) Holt, Rinehart & Winston, 1961.

GÖDEL, K. Über formal unentscheidbare Sätze der Principia Mathematica und verwandter Systeme I. *Monantshefte für Mathematik und Physik,* 1931, 37, 349-360.

GOUGH, P. B. The study of mediation in animals. Unpublished doctoral dissertation, Univer. of Minnesota, 1961.

GRAY, J., & LISSMAN, H. W. The coordination of limb movements in the amphibia. *J. exp. Biol.,* 1946-47, 22-23, 133-142.

GREENBERG, J. Some universals of grammar with particular reference to the order of meaningful elements. Paper for SSRC Conference on Language Universals, 1961.

GRÉGOIRE, A. *L'apprentissage du langage: les deux premières années.* Paris: Droz, 1937.

GROSSMAN, J. B. Trembling of the chin. *Pediatrics,* 1957, 19, 453.

GUILLAUME, P. Le développement des elements formels dans le langage de l'enfant. *J. Psychol. norm. path.,* 1927, 24, 203-229.

HARRIS, Z. S. *Methods in structural linguistics.* Univer. of Chicago Press, 1951.

HEBB, D. O. *The organization of behavior.* Wiley, 1949.

HEBB, D. O. *A textbook of psychology.* Saunders, 1958.

HELD, R. Exposure-history as a factor in maintaining stability of perception and co-ordination. *J. nerv. ment. Dis.,* 1961, 132, 26-32.

HILL, A. Grammaticality. *Word,* 1961, 17, 1-10.

HOCKETT, C. F. *A course in modern linguistics.* Macmillan, 1958.

HORTON, D. L., & KJELDERGAARD, P. M. An experimental analysis of associative factors in mediated generalizations. *Psychol. Monogr.,* 1961, 75, No. 11.

HULL, C. L. The problem of stimulus equivalence in behavior theory. *Psychol. Rev.,* 1939, 46, 9-30.

HYMES, D. H. Functions of speech: an evolutionary approach. In F. C. Gruber (Ed.), *Anthropology and education.* Univer. of Pennsylvania Press, 1961. Pp. 55-83. (a)

HYMES, D. H. Linguistic aspects of studying personality cross-culturally. In B. Kaplan (Ed.), *Studying personality cross-culturally.* Row, Peterson, 1961. Pp. 313-360. (b)

HYMES, D. H. The ethnography of speaking. In T. Gladwin & W. C. Sturtevant (Eds.), *Anthropology and human behavior.* Washington, D.C.: Anthropol. Soc., 1962. Pp. 13-53.

JAKOBSON, R. *Kindersprache, Aphasie, und allgemeine Lautgesetze.* Uppsala: Almqvist & Wiksell, 1941.

JAKOBSON, R. Linguistics and poetics. In T. A. Sebeok (Ed.), *Style in language.* Technology Press & Wiley, 1960. Pp. 350-377.

JEFFREY, W. E. The effects of verbal and nonverbal responses in mediating an instrumental act. *J. exp. Psychol.,* 1953, 45, 327-333.

JENKINS, J. J. A study of mediated association. Report No. 2. Studies in verbal behavior. N.S.F. Grant, Univer. of Minnesota, 1959.

JENKINS, J. J. Mediated associations: paradigms and situations. In C. N. Cofer & B. S. Musgrave (Eds.), *Verbal behavior and learning.* McGraw-Hill, 1963. Pp. 210-245. (a)

JENKINS, J. J. Stimulus "fractionation" in paired-associate learning. *Psychol. Rep.,* 1963, 13, 409-410. (b)

JENKINS, J. J., & BAILEY, V. B. Cue selection and mediated transfer in paired-associate learning. *J. exp. Psychol.,* 1964, 67, 101-102.

JESPERSEN, O. *Growth and structure of the English language.* (9th ed.). Doubleday, 1938.

JOHNSON, N. F. The cue value of sentence frames for the acquisition of speech categories. Unpublished doctoral dissertation, Univer. of Minnesota, 1961.

KAHANE, H., KAHANE, R., & SAPORTA, S. Development of verbal categories in child language. *Int. J. Amer. Linguistics,* 1958.

KANTOR, J. R. *An objective psychology of grammar.* Principia Press, 1936.

KIMBLE, G. A. *Hilgard and Marquis' conditioning and learning.* Appleton-Century-Crofts, 1961.

KLÜVER, H. *Behavior mechanisms in monkeys.* Univer. of Chicago Press, 1933.

KÖHLER, W. Aus der Anthropoidenstation auf Teneriffa: IV. Nachweis einfacher Strukturfunktionen beim Schimpansen und beim Haushuhn. *Abh. preuss. Akad. Wiss., phys.-math. Kl.,* 1918, 2, 3-101.

KUENNE, M. R. Experimental investigation of the relation of language to transposition behavior in young children. *J. exp. Psychol.,* 1946, 36, 471-490.

LASHLEY, K. S. The problem of serial order in behavior. In L. A. Jeffress (Ed.), *Cerebral mechanisms in behavior: the Hixon symposium.* Wiley, 1951. Pp. 112-136.

LEES, R. B. The grammar of English nominalizations. *Int. J. Amer. Linguistics,* 1960, 26, No. 3.

LENNEBERG, E. H. A laboratory for speech research at Children's Hospital Medical Center. *N.E.J. Med.,* 1962, 266, 385-392.

LENNEBERG, E. H. Understanding language without ability to speak: a case study. *J. abnorm. soc. Psychol.,* 1962, 65, 419-425.

LIBERMAN, A. Some results of research on speech perception. *J. acoust. Soc. Amer.,* 1957, 29, 117-123.

LURIA, A. R. The directive function of speech (I and II). *Word,* 1959, 15, 341-352 and 453-464.

McCARTHY, D. Language development in children. In L. Carmichael (Ed.), *Manual of child psychology.* (2nd ed.) Wiley, 1954. Pp. 492-630.

McGEOCH, J. A., & IRION, A. L. *The psychology of human learning.* Longmans, Green, 1952.

MACKAY, D. M. Towards an information-flow model of human behaviour. *Brit. J. Psychol.,* 1956, 47, 30-43.

MACLAY, H., & SLEATOR, M. Responses to language: judgments of grammaticalness. *Int. J. Amer. Ling.,* 1960, 26, 275-282.

MAGNI, F., MELZACK, R., MORUZZI, G., & SMITH, C. J. Direct pyramidal influences on the dorsal-column nuclei. *Arch. ital. Biol.,* 1959, 97, 357-377.

MARTIN, J. G. Mediated transfer in two verbal learning paradigms. Unpublished doctoral dissertation, Univer. of Minnesota, 1960.

MAY, M. A. Experimentally acquired drives. *J. exp. Psychol.,* 1948, 38, 66-77.

MILLER, G. A. The magical number seven, plus or minus two: some limits on our capacity for processing information. *Psychol. Rev.,* 1956, 63, 81-97.

MILLER, G. A., GALANTER, E., & PRIBRAM, K. H. *Plans and the structure of behavior.* Holt, 1960.

MINK, W. D. Semantic generalization as related to word association. Unpublished doctoral dissertation, Univer. of Minnesota, 1957.

MOTT, F. W., & SHERRINGTON, C. S. Experiments upon the influence of sensory nerves upon movement and nutrition of limbs. *Proc. royal Soc.,* 1895, 57, 481-488.

MUNN, N. L. Learning in children. In L. Carmichael (Ed.), *Manual of child psychology.* (2nd ed.) Wiley, 1954. Pp. 374-458.

NEWELL, A., SHAW, J. C., & SIMON, H. A. Elements of a theory of human problem solving. *Psychol. Rev.,* 1958, 65, 151-166.

NORCROSS, K., & SPIKER, C. C. Effects of mediated associations on transfer in paired-associate learning. *J. exp. Psychol.,* 1958, 55, 129-134.

Osgood, C. E. *Method and theory in experimental psychology.* Oxford Univer. Press, 1953.

Osgood, C. E., & Sebeok, T. A. Psycholinguistics: a survey of theory and research. *J. abnorm. soc. Psychol.,* 1954, 49, Supplement, Part 2.

Osgood, C. E., Suci, G. J., & Tannenbaum, P. *The measurement of meaning.* Univer. of Illinois Press, 1957.

Pike, K. *Language in relation to a unified theory of the structure of human behavior,* Part I. (prelim. ed.) Glendale: Summer Inst. Linguistics, 1954.

Probst, M. Über die anatomischen und physiologischen Folgen der Halbseitendurchschneidung des Mittelhirns. *Jb. Psychiat. Neurol.,* 1903, 24, 219-325.

Reichling, A. J. B. N. Principles and methods of syntax: cryptanalytical formalism. *Lingua,* 1961, 10, 1-17.

Rudel, R. G. Transposition of response by children trained in intermediate-size problems. *J. comp. physiol. Psychol.,* 1957, 50, 292-295.

Rudel, R. G. Transposition of response to size in children. *J. comp. physiol. Psychol.,* 1958, 51, 386-390.

Rudel, R. G. The absolute response in tests of generalization in normal and retarded children. *Amer. J. Psychol.,* 1959, 72, 401-408.

Rudel, R. G. The transposition of intermediate size by brain-damaged and mongoloid children. *J. comp. physiol. Psychol.,* 1960, 53, 89-94.

Sapir, E. Communication. In D. Mandelbaum (Ed.), *Selected writings of Edward Sapir.* Univer. of California Press, 1949. Pp. 104-109.

Sapir, E. The psychological reality of phonemes. In D. Mandelbaum (Ed.), *Selected writings of Edward Sapir.* Univer. of California Press, 1949. Pp. 46-60.

Saporta, S. Linguistic structure as a factor and as a measure in word association. In J. J. Jenkins (Ed.), *Associative processes in verbal behavior: A report of the Minnesota conference,* 1959.

Shepard, W. O. The effect of verbal training on initial generalization tendencies. *Child Develpm.,* 1956, 27, 311-316.

Shepard, W. O., & Schaeffer, M. The effect of concept knowledge on discrimination learning. *Child Develpm.,* 1956, 27, 173-177.

Shipley, W. C. Indirect conditioning. *J. gen. Psychol.,* 1935, 12, 337-357.

Skinner, B. F. *Verbal behavior.* Appleton-Century-Crofts, 1957.

Smart, W. K. *English review grammar.* (4th ed.) Appleton-Century-Crofts, 1957.

Smith, M. E. Grammatical errors in the speech of preschool children. *Child Develpm.,* 1933, 4, 182-190.

Spence, K. W. The differential response in animals to stimuli varying within a single dimension. *Psychol. Rev.,* 1937, 44, 430-444.

Sperry, R. W. Neural basis of the spontaneous optokinetic response produced by visual inversion. *J. comp. physiol. Psychol.,* 1950, 43, 482-489.

Spiker, C. C. Stimulus pretraining and subsequent performance in the delayed reaction experiment. *J. exp. Psychol.,* 1956, 52, 107-111.

Spiker, C. C., Gerjuoy, I. R., & Shepard, W. O. Children's concept knowledge of middle-sizedness and performance on the intermediate size problem. *J. comp. physiol. Psychol.,* 1956, 49, 416-419.

Staats, C. K., & Staats, A. W. Meaning established by classical conditioning. *J. exp. Psychol.,* 1957, 54, 74-80.

Stutsman, R. Performance tests for preschool age. *Genet. Psychol. Monogr.,* 1926, 1, 1-67.

Teuber, H. -L. Perception. In J. Field, H. W. Magoun, & V. E. Hall (Eds.), *Handbook of physiology, Section 1. Neurophysiology,* Vol. 3. Washington, D.C.: Amer. Physiol. Soc., 1960. Pp. 1595-1668.

Teuber, H. -L. Sensory deprivation, sensory suppression and agnosia: notes for a neurologic theory. *J. nerv. ment. Dis.,* 1961, 132, 32-40. (a)

TEUBER, H. -L. Brain and behavior: summation. In M. A. B. Brasier (Ed.), *Brain and behavior*. Washington, D.C.: Amer. Inst. Biol. Sci., 1961. Pp. 393-420. (b)

THORNDIKE, E. L., & LORGE, I. *The teachers' word book of 30,000 words.* Teachers College, Columbia Univer., 1944.

TOWE, A., & JABBUR, S. J. Cortical inhibition of neurons in dorsal column nuclei of a cat. *J. Neurophysiol.*, 1961, 24, 488-498.

UNDERWOOD, B. J. Stimulus selection in verbal learning. In C. N. Cofer & B. S. Musgrave (Eds.), *Verbal behavior and learning.* McGraw-Hill, 1963. Pp. 33-48.

UNDERWOOD, B. J., & SCHULZ, R. W. *Meaningfulness and verbal learning.* Lippincott, 1960.

VON HOLST, E. Die relative Coordination als Phänomen und als Methode zentralnervöser Funktionanalyse. *Ergebn. Physiol.*, 1939, 42, 228-306.

VON HOLST, E., & MITTELSTAEDT, H. Das Reafferenzprinzip (Wechselwirkungen zwischen Zentralnervensystem und Peripherie). *Naturwiss.*, 1950, 37, 464-476.

VON SENDEN, M. *Raum- und Gestaltauffassung bei operierten Blindgeborenen vor und nach der Operation.* Leipzig: Barth, 1932.

WEISS, P. Self-differentiation of the basic patterns of coordination. *Comp. Psychol. Monogr.*, 1941, 17, No. 4 (Whole No. 88).

WERNER, H., & KAPLAN, E. Development of word meaning through verbal context: an experimental study. *J. Psychol.*, 1950, 29, 251-257.

WHORF, B. L. Linguistics as an exact science. Reprinted in J. B. Carroll (Ed.), *Language, thought and reality.* Technology Press & Wiley, 1956. Pp. 220-232.

WICKENS, D. D., & BRIGGS, G. E. Mediated stimulus generalization in sensory preconditioning. *J. exp. Psychol.*, 1951, 42, 197-200.

YNGVE, V. Random generation of English sentences. Mechanical Translation Group, M.I.T., (Memo 1961-4) 1961.